Reading the Qur'an in Century

MW00790895

"Readers seeking to understand the current diversity in ways Muslims read and interpret the Qur'an will find in Abdullah Saeed a sure-footed guide. He demonstrates how a reading that respects context is firmly rooted in the Islamic tradition from the earliest days."

Daniel A. Madigan, *Georgetown University, USA*

Reading the Qur'an in the Twenty-first Century considers the development of Qur'anic interpretation and highlights modern debates around new approaches to interpretation. It explores how Muslims from various theological, legal, socio-political, and philosophical backgrounds think about the meaning and relevance of the Qur'an, and how their ideas apply in the contemporary world. This book:

- reflects on one of the most dominant approaches to interpretation in the pre-modern period, textualism, and the reaction to that in Muslim feminist readings of the Qur'an today.
- emphasises the importance of a contextualist reading of the Qur'an, and covers issues such as identifying the hierarchical nature of Qur'anic values, the criteria for the use of hadith in interpretation, fluidity of meaning, and ways of ensuring a degree of stability in interpretation.
- examines key Qur'anic passages and compares pre-modern and modern interpretations to show the evolving nature of interpretation. Examples discussed include: the "authority" of men over women, the death of Jesus, *shūra* and democracy, and *riba* and interest.

Abdullah Saeed provides a practical guide for interpretation and presents the principal ideas of a contextualist approach, which situates the original message of the Qur'an in its wider social, political, cultural, economic, and intellectual contexts. He advocates a more flexible method of interpretation that gives due recognition to earlier interpretations of the Qur'an while also being aware of changing conditions and the need to approach the Qur'an afresh today.

Abdullah Saeed is Sultan of Oman Professor of Arab and Islamic Studies at the University of Melbourne, Australia. His previous books for Routledge include *Interpreting the Qur'an* (2006), *Islamic Thought: An Introduction* (2006), and *The Qur'an: An Introduction* (2008).

Reading the Qur'an in the Twenty-first Century

A Contextualist Approach

Abdullah Saeed

Routledge
Taylor & Francis Group

LONDON AND NEW YORK

First published in 2014
by Routledge
2 Park Square, Milton Park, Abingdon, Oxon OX14 4RN

and by Routledge
711 Third Avenue, New York, NY 10017

Routledge is an imprint of the Taylor & Francis Group, an informa business

British Library Cataloguing in Publication Data
A catalogue record for this book is available from the British Library

Library of Congress Cataloging in Publication Data
Saeed, Abdullah.
Reading the Qur'an in the twenty-first century : a contextualist approach / Abdullah Saeed.
pages cm
1. Qur'an–Criticism, interpretation, etc. 2. Qur'an–Reading. 3. Qur'an as literature. I. Title.
BP130.4.S32 2013
297.1'226–dc23
2013031219

ISBN: 978-0-415-67749-3 (hbk)
ISBN: 978-0-415-67750-9 (pbk)
ISBN: 978-1-315-87092-2 (ebk)

Typeset in Bembo
by Taylor & Francis Books

Contents

List of figures

Acknowledgements

In writing the book, I have benefitted from the work of many scholars and thinkers, many of whom are referred to in this book. In presenting their views, while I have tried to be as faithful as possible, it is inevitable that some distortions can occur, for which I seek their understanding and forgiveness.

A number of friends and colleagues have assisted me in various aspects of writing the book. Their research assistance, identifying relevant material, documenting them, checking sources, going over translation of texts, reading the drafts and commenting on them have shaped the final look and feel of the book. Without their help and this significant contribution, this would not have been possible. In this regard I am very grateful for the work of my research assistants and colleagues Rowan Gould, Patricia Prentice, Adis Duderija, Redha Ameur, Cara Hinkson, Helen McCue, and Andy Fuller. Of course, any errors and mistakes in the book should be entirely attributed to me. I thank Adam Hulbert for editing of the first draft and Katia Houghton for copyediting of the text.

This would not have been possible without the support of Lesley Riddle who was the Senior Editor at Routledge and encouraged me to complete the book despite a range of personal difficulties that prevented me from completing the book on time. Her wonderful support kept me going. I am also very grateful for the kind support and assistance provided by Katherine Ong and Emma Hudson of Routledge through all stages of the production of the book.

Finally I am grateful for the wonderful support provided by my wife, Rasheeda and son, Isaam who have always demonstrated an unusually high degree of patience with my never-ending projects of writing with little time for them.

Part I

Background and examples of contextualism

Past and present

1 Introduction and modern emphases in Qur'anic interpretation

This book makes the case for a contextualist approach to interpreting the Qur'an. It also provides, broadly speaking, a theoretical and practical guide for undertaking contextualist interpretation. The contextualist approach reads the Qur'an in light of the historical context of its revelation and subsequent interpretation. In doing so, it strives to understand the underlying objectives and spirit of the Qur'an and thereby highlights the ongoing relevance of the Qur'an to our own time. A contextualist interpretation seeks not to reduce but to expand the contemporary significance of Qur'anic teachings.

In making the case for the contextualist approach, this book explores a perspective on Qur'anic interpretation in which there is widespread interest, particularly among Muslims. Many basic ideas associated with this contextualist approach already exist – and the literature is growing. In this book, I bring together many of these ideas, skilfully advanced by other scholars, and place them in a coherent, easily accessible system. In doing so, I also incorporate a wide range of my own ideas, which I hope will enrich the current debate and clarify some of the difficult issues associated with a contextualist approach.

Contextualism provides a critical alternative for contemporary Muslims to textualism, the dominant mode of interpretation of the Qur'an today. Textualism ranges on a continuum from approaches that place an almost exclusive reliance on the literal meaning of the Qur'anic text ("hard textualism") to perspectives that take some contextual elements into account and so provide a degree of interpretive flexibility ("soft textualism"). As I discuss briefly in Chapter 15 (Epilogue), there are a number of political, intellectual, and cultural reasons for the prominence and popularity of a textualist (particularly the "hard textualist") approach to the interpretation of the Qur'an today.

A textualist approach that relies largely on the "literal" meaning of the text, with some consideration given to the complexities of practical application, has been the chief approach within the *tafsīr* (Qur'anic exegesis) tradition, particularly regarding ethico-legal texts, and in the Islamic juristic literature (*fiqh*). But in all its forms, a textualist reading fails to do *full* justice to *certain texts* it interprets. The result is that those texts of the Qur'an are viewed as irrelevant to many of the vexing problems contemporary Muslim societies face, or are applied inappropriately, in ways that distort basic Qur'anic principles. This should be considered a strong justification for embarking on an approach to interpretation that emphasises the continuing relevance of all Qur'anic texts to the twenty-first century.

Contrary to the hard textualists' position that new ideas or approaches to the interpretation of the Qur'an are un-Islamic or even anti-Islamic, I argue throughout the book that a contextualist approach is very Islamic, and is in fact rooted in the tradition. There are many such ideas in the Islamic juristic and Qur'anic exegetical literature which attempt to relate the Qur'anic texts and their teachings to the changing circumstances and contexts, even though there is no systematic contextualist approach as such in that literature. Both jurists and Qur'an commentators attempted to understand the circumstances in which particular Qur'anic texts were revealed as well as the specific people those texts were addressing and the time of the revelation. Even in the first century of Islam, immediately after the death of the Prophet, figures like Umar b. al-Khattab (d. 23/644), the second caliph, interpreted a range of Qur'anic texts in a manner that could be considered "contextualist". Umar understood Qur'anic revelations in terms of their fundamental principles or objectives and, critically, his understanding was highly contextual.

Such ideas remain at the heart of the contextualist approach to the interpretation today as well. But the contextualist approach of today takes this idea of context much further and develops a method of interpretation based on the notion of context both of the time of revelation and of the twenty-first century.

When presenting arguments in favour of a contextualist interpretation of the Qur'an, I do not argue for a wholesale rejection of the authority of pre-modern Muslim scholarship, theology, or law. Instead, this book should be considered a contribution to the evolving scholarship on the Qur'an that assigns greater emphasis to the idea of a contextually relevant reading of the Qur'an. I argue that a contextualist approach provides a valid method of interpreting the Qur'an: one that gives due recognition to earlier approaches to interpretation while also being aware of changing circumstances and social, political, and cultural conditions which need to be considered before any interpretation of the Qur'an may be deemed contemporary and more importantly relevant as well.

Key ideas of a contextualist approach

Contextualists place great hermeneutic value on the historical context in which the Qur'an was revealed – the early seventh century CE – and subsequently interpreted. They argue that scholars should be highly sensitive to the social, political, economic, intellectual, and cultural circumstances of the revelation, as well as the setting in which interpretation occurred in the past and occurs today. Contextualists thus tend to see the Qur'an as a source of practical guidelines. They believe that these guidelines should be implemented in new ways whenever changing circumstances warrant them, and so long as these novel implementations do not impinge on the "fundamentals" of Islam.[1]

Central to the contextualist approach is the idea of context. Context is a broad concept which may include, for instance, the linguistic context, and also what I call the "macro-context". The linguistic context is related to the way a particular phrase, sentence, or short text is situated within a larger text. Usually, this involves situating the text in question within the texts that immediately precede or follow it. This type of context, while important for getting a basic understanding of what the text is conveying, is not the primary focus of the contextualist. Instead, more interesting and useful for a contextualist is what I call the "macro context". This refers to the social, political, economic, cultural, and intellectual settings of the Qur'anic text under consideration. The macro context considers also the place in which the revelation occurred and the people to whom it was addressed. In addition it includes the ideas, assumptions, values, beliefs, religious customs, and cultural norms that existed at the time. An understanding of these elements is important to the process of interpretation, as the Qur'an responded to, interacted with, and praised or rejected these contextual connections.

The purpose of studying the macro context is to obtain a reasonably good sense of the overall setting in which the particular Qur'anic text was given and to understand how the "meaning" of the text was related to that setting. We can term this context of revelation as "macro context 1". Equally important is the macro context of the present period, that is, the context in which the act of interpretation is occurring today. We can term this "macro context 2". This context also has various elements, which include: the period in which the interpreter is living; the physical places in which society functions; contemporary cultural and religious norms; political ideas; economic institutions and ideas; and other systems, values, and norms. This context also includes the kinds of educational, economic, and political opportunities that are available, and the protection of the various rights that are afforded in modern societies.

For the contextualist, it is important to compare the two macro contexts as thoroughly as possible, in order to "translate" the meaning of the Qur'anic text from macro context 1 to macro context 2 without bypassing the context of the intervening periods. This involves drawing a close connection between the Qur'anic text at the time of the revelation and the context of the time of interpretation, without divorcing either context from the other. The connecting elements for these are the intervening historical periods. These can be understood in terms of the ideas, scholarship, and interpretations that have continuously adapted the Qur'an to emerging contexts. I term this the "connector context". Without the connector context, it would not be possible to link macro context 1 and macro context 2. The intermediary role of the connector context demonstrates how successive generations of Muslims have applied the Qur'anic text and its norms to their lives. In a sense, the accumulated tradition, experience, and practice are always there to help the interpreter to connect with the context of the Qur'an at the time of revelation. With this framework, it is possible to read the Qur'an in a way that emphasises its ongoing relevance to society in the present and to the generations that will follow.

It is worth noting that many parts of the Qur'an do not require a con-textualist reading, as they are immediately relevant to different contexts. Thus, only certain texts need to be read contextually. The historically oriented texts that occupy such a large portion of the Qur'an, for example, do not usually require a contextualist reading. These historically oriented texts could reason-ably be expected to contain many specific details in order to make sense of the events, figures, and concerns to which the Qur'an is making reference. How-ever, the Qur'an on the whole does not provide such specific details about places, people, or events. Nor is it concerned with presenting the life story of the prophets or even of the Prophet Muhammad. The historical references in the Qur'an, almost always, do not refer to dates or place names. The Qur'an has a tendency to avoid those specifics and often uses such narratives to expound universal ideas and values. For instance, the story of the creation of the universe and of Adam is concerned with God's creative power, which can be understood as such in any context. Similarly, the story of Moses and Phar-aoh highlights the idea that ultimately good overcomes evil. Such broad ideas and lessons can be readily understood from the text, and applied within a wide range of contexts, cultures, times, and places, as they tend to be universal in nature. These may be considered as the trans-historical or universal aspects of the Qur'anic text.

Other text types, such as those related to theological concerns related to God or those that relate to the afterlife are also not context-dependent or culturally specific. Most such texts can be immediately read, understood, and applied within a whole range of different contexts in different times, places, and cir-cumstances. Believers can easily relate to them regardless of their specific con-texts. For instance, the Qur'an has a number of texts that discuss God's names and attributes and show how God relates to creation. The Qur'an discusses life after death and accountability. It talks about universal ethical and moral values such as honesty. The Qur'an also contains a range of texts about "Unseen" (*ghayb*) which refer to a world that exists beyond human experience. Although some difficulties have arisen in the modern period in relation to a number of these texts, perhaps because of our contemporary understanding of the com-munities or figures that are alluded to in the Qur'an or our scientific take on the nature of the universe and life on earth, these texts by their very nature do not seem to attract many problems or challenges when interpreted and applied to our modern context. This does not mean that we do not, for instance, require other theological interpretations of at least some of the Qur'anic teachings.

However, certain texts in the Qur'an seem to be addressing specific situations and concerns that were strictly pertinent to the time of the revelation or, in other words, that relate to certain aspects of macro context 1 primarily. These texts are within the broad category of what I call "ethico-legal" texts, that are more about ethical, moral, social, or legal matters. Examples of such texts include those that relate to legal matters such as marriage and divorce or inheritance as well as those that refer to the roles of men and women in society, or slaves and slavery, or the status of non-Muslims in Muslim societies. These kinds of texts would have been directly relevant to and meaningful in the context in which they were revealed; however, the relevance of these texts is reduced if they are interpreted literally in contemporary times due to the significant differences between macro context 1 and macro context 2. Essentially, then, the contextualist approach to interpretation is needed largely for those ethico-legal texts in the Qur'an that, by their very nature, are closely connected to the Arabian society of the early seventh century CE. For some of these specific texts, most forms of traditional interpretation dominated by a textualist approach, even the most flexible of them, tend to be problematic in both process and results. A contextualist approach emphasises the organic and symbiotic relationship between the original commandments, instructions, and advice and their context in the seventh century. If this approach is adopted, these texts could be appropriately contextualised by examining the radical difference and continuities between the original context and that of today. This process would then allow for a useful new set of meanings to emerge that remain true to the original teachings of the Qur'an.

An example of this approach can be applied to the institution of *zakāt*, which is one of the fundamental institutions of Islam. *Zakāt* is understood as the giving of a certain percentage of one's income, savings, or earnings from business to certain categories of people who have been explicitly mentioned in the Qur'an. The Qur'an repeatedly emphasises that Muslims must give *zakāt* to the community, the poor, and the needy. Yet the Qur'an does not provide sufficient details about how *zakāt* should be managed. The Prophet, however, has provided plentiful advice and instruction about this issue, and interpreters of today therefore have a reasonably clear understanding of how *zakāt* was practised in the early period of Islam. The system that was introduced in Mecca and Medina as a result of the Qur'anic command to pay *zakāt* was appropriate to those circumstances and to that context. The items that the Prophet spoke about as appropriate for attracting *zakāt* were also very specific to the context, such as sheep, cows, camels, gold, and silver. Although the Qur'an does not specify a percentage of, for example, one's savings to be given as *zakāt*, the Prophet introduced a percentage – 2.5 per cent – that appears to be specific to the context. At that time, there was no formal system of taxation, and the Prophet and the Qur'an were introducing a new tax system in a society where people did not have stable or regular jobs or income, and most people functioned at a subsistence level. Although some individuals were involved in business, these were a minority in that society. The Prophet therefore introduced a tax system that was based on the guidelines set by the Qur'an and also in line with the specific economic, social, and cultural conditions of the time.

Islamic juristic literature (*fiqh*) reveals how the jurists managed the interpretation of *zakāt*-related texts. Although some discussions in the *fiqh* literature seem to take the context of the seventh century into account (for instance, when extending the scope of goods susceptible to *zakāt*), there is still a high degree of rigidity when it comes to the key issues. For instance, the rule that

2.5 per cent of a person's annual savings are subject to *zakāt* seems to have been inflexible, as no consideration was given to the idea that this percentage may have been relevant to the context and therefore could be susceptible to change. In fact, much of the discussion about *zakāt* in the *fiqh* literature is concerned with the specific types of goods that attract *zakāt* and whether the list of these could be extended beyond those specified by the Prophet. However, the analysis does not extend much beyond this.

Although post-prophetic Muslim states have introduced a range of new taxes, *zakāt* has remained sacrosanct, with minimal or no change, into the modern period. Thus the methodology that was adopted by the early jurists in relation to *zakāt* (including the system, framework, key ideas, categories of goods, and percentages) has been retained in a similar form to that of the earliest period of Islam. A common argument for preserving *zakāt* in this form is that it is a religious institution that Muslims have no authority to change.

What is noticeable here is that instead of taking the context, ethos, and spirit of the time into account when interpreting the instructions provided in the Qur'an and by the Prophet, both early and modern commentators of the Qur'an and the jurists adopted a rather literalist and textualist approach to the interpretation of *zakāt*. If they had in fact taken the context of the time into account, then the commentators and jurists would have been able to ask a range of questions about key aspects of *zakāt*. Why only 2.5 per cent and not a progressive tax? Why only focus on the goods that existed at the time of the Prophet with only limited recognition that this list could be expanded, rather than considering *zakāt* as an Islamic taxation system that could respond to changes in society? These and similar questions were not often asked. It is evident that there could be room for rethinking many aspects of *zakāt*, while still retaining the basic idea of *zakāt* and the underlying values it embodies as one of the most fundamental pillars of Islam. In areas such as these, a contextualist reading of the text will produce remarkably different results in new contexts.

Managing communities in our time has become a complex task, and the state is expected to provide a whole range of new services to its citizens. States must continuously work on developing, adjusting, and improving the infrastructure of the community, providing everything from health and education to security services. Given the vast difference between ways of organising societies now and during the time of the Prophet, arguably, a new way of thinking about *zakāt* is required if this institution is to remain relevant to our own context. These new meanings and ideas cannot be generated by an approach that is totally committed to the letter of the law, because the methodology it uses gives minimal or no consideration to contextual factors. In relation to *zakāt*, a contextualist approach to the texts could reveal a dynamic system of Islamic taxation. The emphasis and importance given to *zakāt* at the time of revelation and the values it stands for in the Qur'an will always remain, and the contextualist approach will significantly expand the scope and the purpose of *zakāt* from the discussion on goods and items that were subject to *zakāt* in the early seventh century to a whole new set of items and goods that could be subject to *zakāt* in the modern period. Such interpretations could also address the question of the percentage in order to ensure that it is commensurate with the needs of the community today.

Equally problematic are the interpretations of those Qur'anic texts that discuss the role and status of men and women. This includes the relative status and power of men vis-à-vis women at the time of revelation, the dependence of women economically and socially on men, and the lack of opportunities for women at the time compared with that of the modern period. The Qur'an provided a range of instructions regarding women in the areas of marriage, divorce, inheritance, and child custody, just as it provided instructions in many other areas. Although the bulk of these texts do not disadvantage women, there are a few texts that could be read as doing so if interpreted literally without due consideration given to the context. It is crucial to remember that the Qur'an provided these texts at a time when the conditions of society were very different from those of our own. A textualist approach interprets these instructions in a way that gives a kind of permanence to the way things were in the early seventh century regarding women. Here, a contextualist approach will provide a better understanding of the intentions and underlying objectives of these texts, again by taking into account the context of the time, place, and circumstances, perhaps more so than even the soft textualist approaches adopted by many in Qur'anic interpretation and Islamic jurisprudence.

Muslims hold the view that the Qur'an is a text for all times and places. Contextualist interpretation will help to realise that ideal by providing a systematic methodology of Qur'anic interpretation that will at times depart from the literal meaning of some of the Qur'anic injunctions, while retaining the underlying objective and spirit of these injunctions. When interpreting Qur'anic texts that appear to be applicable in a range of different contexts, a mere literal reading can become an obstruction to realising the higher objectives embedded in Qur'anic values. This is potentially harmful to both Muslim individuals and societies. Following a textualist reading for these texts only increases the gap between what the Qur'an seems to be saying on a particular issue and what Muslims, in their everyday lives, see as relevant, important, and necessary. The two examples above demonstrate a need for a contextualist approach, which will yield significantly better results than a textualist reading as we deal with such contemporary challenges facing Muslims today.

Structure of this book

This book comprises four parts. In Part 1, I outline the development of Qur'anic interpretation up to the modern period. This provides the context in which modern debates on interpretation are taking place and some of the key ideas associated with those debates. I examine some of the concepts and tools that existed in the pre-modern interpretation of the Qur'an, and show how a textualist mode of reading the Qur'an developed in the exegetical tradition. In this first part, I examine a historical example of a quasi-contextualist interpretation of Qur'anic texts: namely, that of Umar b. al-Khattab, the second caliph and a close adviser to Prophet Muhammad. This example is significant, as he was one of the earliest and most important figures in Islam. In general, this shows that the contextualist approach to the Qur'an is not entirely new, and that its roots go back to the earliest period of Islam.

Keeping Umar's precedent in the background, I explore then how the dominance of textualism in the interpretation of women-related Qur'anic texts led to the emergence of a counter position and, in fact, a contextualist approach to interpreting Qur'anic texts in the modern period. I present alternative readings of the relevant Qur'anic texts by female and male Muslim scholars who have questioned key aspects of traditional interpretations in this area and have argued for new interpretations that are more appropriate for today.

In Part II of the book, which forms the most important part, I present the key ideas and principles associated with contextualist interpretation: how revelation was related to its context; the hierarchical nature of the Qur'anic values and how such values can be used in a contextualist framework; the use of parallel texts and the challenges associated with using hadith in contextualist interpretation as well as the criteria for using hadith; the variety of ways in which one can think about the issue of meaning; and the need to maintain the immutable aspects of Qur'anic teaching and the fundamentals of the religion in contextualist interpretation. The final chapter in this part is, in a sense, a summary of the key ideas regarding contextualist interpretation, and is presented as a practical guide for such interpretation.

In Part III of the book, I provide four examples of Qur'anic interpretation that highlight the idea that different interpretations of specific texts emerge in different contexts: a social issue (the authority of men over women), a theological issue (the crucifixion and death of Jesus), a political issue (consultation and democracy), and an economic issue (*riba* and interest). These examples compare the pre-modern and present day approaches to interpretation that Muslim scholars have adopted.

These examples do not examine the pre-modern or modern interpretations in a comprehensive manner. Instead, I have chosen a small number of commentators to give a sense of how various commentators approached the text and to highlight the degree of diversity among them. The pre-modern commentators selected include Tabari, Zamakhshari, Razi, Qurtubi, and Ibn Kathir. Commentators from the Shi'a tradition are also included. The ideas of these scholars reflect how these very important issues, which Muslims are debating in our time, were explored in traditional Qur'anic scholarship. For the modern period, scholars such as Abul Ala Maududi, Tabataba'i, and Sayyid Qutb – names that will be very familiar to students of Islamic thought – are presented. These scholars have, on occasions, emphasised different issues to scholars of the past, as they have responded to the issues that have arisen in the modern era and context.

My purpose in this exploration is to highlight the evolving nature of Muslim thinking on the issue of Qur'anic interpretation, with particular reference to the issues that have become important to modern debates. Each of these four chapters presents various interpretations of a verse (or a part of a verse) that deals with a specific issue. Given the limited space that is available in this book, detailed commentaries are not given for any of the texts. Rather, I summarise the views that each scholar presents on the issue, in order to give a sense of the kind of thinking that may have existed in relation to the interpretation of the verse or phrase in question.

The first example is the first part of Qur'an 4:34. This text of the Qur'an has given rise to debates on issues that are related to gender. Traditional scholarship has tended to emphasise the dominance of men over women's affairs, with some scholars even suggesting that women are inferior to men, based on biological or nature-based arguments. In the modern period, such arguments are largely being sidelined, with new interpretations emphasising gender equality or, at least, complementarity.

The second example examines accounts of the crucifixion and death of Jesus. Pre-modern interpretations of the relevant verses of the Qur'an are uniform in their rejection of the crucifixion and death of Jesus, and usually suggest that someone else was crucified in his place. Although these ideas still dominate in the modern period, a range of perspectives are emerging that are not entirely comfortable with the pre-modern treatment of this issue. A more contextualist approach appears to be gaining ground, even in this controversial area.

The third example shows that pre-modern Qur'anic scholarship had, by and large, a very different focus in its understanding of *shūra* (consultation), and examines how *shūra* was conceptualised in comparison to the modern period. Today, Muslims have moved significantly away from pre-modern understandings and now expand its meaning to cover contemporary ideas about democracy and governance.

The fourth example is the interpretation of *riba* (usury or interest). The emphasis has shifted in the modern period from the approaches of early commentators to the issue as a result of the changed context. Although a large number of Muslims still consider *riba* to be equivalent to *any* form of interest, a range of views now emphasise the ethical and moral nature of the prohibition of *riba*, and the importance of identifying specific transactions and forms of interest that may or may not be acceptable from a Qur'anic point of view.

In Part IV (the Epilogue), I offer some concluding remarks. These highlight some of the key contributions of this book.

The contributions of this book

In this book I hope to demonstrate that a contextualist approach to the interpretation of the Qur'an allows for greater scope to interpret the Qur'an and to question some of the rulings of earlier commentators. This approach has growing support. Over the late twentieth and early twenty-first centuries, contextualist ideas and methodologies have been adopted by an increasing number of Muslim scholars and thinkers. Although some may not refer to the term "contextualist" as such, their methods of interpretation show that they are engaging with the Qur'an in new ways that reflect this approach.

For instance, many scholars have attempted to relate the Qur'an to contemporary concerns and needs by developing ideas and principles that are relevant to the modern period. Their focus is developing new theories of interpretation that take the contextual aspects of the Qur'an into account. These endeavours reflect the need to understand the immutable tenets of the Qur'anic teachings from that of the mutable, and continuously to relate the Qur'anic teachings to our context.

The contribution of this book lies in the justification of a contextualist reading of the Qur'an, and its bringing together of a range of principles and strategies – from both Islamic tradition in the past and contemporary practices – that are closely connected to such a reading. This book also demonstrates the ongoing relevance of the Qur'an as the most important text for Muslims.

I do not claim that most of the ideas in the book are new: indeed, many have already been circulating in the literature for a long time. However, I trust that by bringing together a large number of these ideas, and situating them in a coherent framework, I have provided a useful resource for those interested in a contextualist interpretation of the Qur'an. I believe that this volume provides a useful and much needed contribution to Qur'anic hermeneutics.

Transliteration

I have adopted a simplified transliteration method in this book in order to minimise difficulties of my use of Arabic words in the text. I am conscious of the fact that many readers of this book may not be familiar with the Arabic language and burdening them with a complicated transliteration system with all the dots and macrons may suggest the text is more difficult and cumbersome than it is. I have dropped the "h" to represent the *tā' marbūta* in words like Sunna. The only macrons I use are those that show the long vowels, and only if I am using an Arabic word in the main text. I have avoided using those macrons with any names of people, places, or even bibliographical information to keep the simplified look of the text.

Note

1 See Chapter 9 dealing with this matter.

2   Traditional interpretation, textualism, and the emergence of contextualism

The Qur'an is a text, and like all texts, it requires interpretation. The simple act of reading is itself an act of interpretation. Every time a person reads a text or hears someone speaking, they are interpreting those words. Each individual has learned to process information in certain ways in order to "construct" meaning from texts, even though they are usually unaware of this process. The reader of the Qur'an does not merely remain a neutral, objective observer, but becomes its interpreter, bringing his or her own biases and insights to the interpretation of the text. Due to different life experiences, presuppositions, values, and socio-cultural environments, each individual will "construct" meaning in a different way to reach their understanding of the text. However, this subjectivity of interpretation does not mean that every reading is of equal validity.

Muslim scholars have found the Qur'an to be a complex text. In attempting to discern its meanings, they have made an enormous contribution to the body of literature on interpretation of the Qur'an over the past fourteen hundred years. In the modern period, Muslim scholars continue to expend a great deal of effort to understand and interpret the Qur'an as a whole, and to determine the relevance of particular Qur'anic texts. While doing so, many such scholars have also developed theories about the nature of language and meaning that have offered new ways to better understand the Qur'an.

Approaches to interpretation from the time of the Prophet

The tradition of Qur'anic interpretation began during the time of Prophet Muhammad (d. 11/632). Understanding of the Qur'an was more straightforward during his time, for several reasons. The Qur'an was revealed in Arabic, a language shared by the Prophet and the first recipient community (the "Companions of the Prophet"). Furthermore, these first recipients of the Qur'an shared an immediate personal and social context with the Prophet. The Prophet was also present to elucidate if the need arose. More importantly, the Qur'an was embedded in a much larger context with which it was in a dialogical relationship. The elements of this context included the time of the revelation (610–32 CE), the place where this revelation occurred (Hijaz, in Arabia), and the customs and society in which the revelation occurred. The fusion of the

Word of God with this context, assisted by the presence of the Prophet as the chief exponent of God's Word, provided the foundation for the understanding of the Qur'an among the first generation of Muslims.

However, little of the Prophet's own interpretation of the Qur'an is recorded, and much of what exists at present is in the form of practical exegesis (that is, practical application of Qur'anic teachings), and does not elaborate on his approach to interpretation or offer principles.

With the death of the Prophet in 11/632, two key elements that had provided the basis for understanding God's Word were no longer there: namely, the presence of the Prophet and the overall context (political, economic, social, cultural, and intellectual) in which the Qur'an was being revealed. After the Prophet's death, the Companions used various sources for understanding and interpreting the Qur'an. Their approaches included the use of parts of the Qur'an to explain other parts, recollection of information received from the Prophet, and even the traditions of the Jews and Christians (known as the "People of the Book" or *ahl al-kitāb*). The latter were particularly useful for understanding the narratives about past prophets, peoples, and events that were contained in the Qur'an. The Companions' shared experience of the context of revelation and their vibrant memory of the Prophet's legacy assisted in their common understanding of the Qur'anic text.

Not long after the death of the Prophet, the Muslims rapidly became a powerful political force, and politically or administratively incorporated new regions, cultures, and peoples into the emerging Muslim caliphate. As the Prophet could no longer be consulted, the leading figures of the first recipient community of the revelation acted as the mediators between the Qur'an (as the Word of God) and the new contexts. They did this by relying on their famil-iarity with the original context of the revelation. However, with the gradual elimination of key elements that had formed the foundation for understanding God's Word in context, and with the passing of the stabilising factor of the Prophet as the authoritative exponent of God's Word, these early Muslims began to contest each other's understandings.

The need for interpretation increased with the second generation of Muslims, known as "Successors" (*tābi'ūn*), who did not have a living memory of the Prophet or direct access to the immediate context of Qur'anic revelation, and many of whom came from rather different cultural, intellectual, and social backgrounds. Later generations had to rely on second-hand texts and oral reports to obtain a sense of the context of revelation at the time of the Prophet: texts that later came to be known as hadith (attributed to the Prophet) and/or *athar* (sayings attributed to the first or second generation Muslims). In this way, the context of God's Word came to be mediated through yet another set of texts and oral reports. Philological disciplines were gradually developed in the first three centuries of Islam to understand the text, and principles that were primarily linguistic were developed to guide interpretation of the text.

In the process, the immediate context of the revelation, which had played such a vital role in helping the Muslims relate to God's Word, became distant (except insofar as can be glimpsed from hadith or *athar*, which often did not – or could not – capture the entire context). Although scholars of the Qur'an remained interested in the occasions of revelation (*asbāb al-nuzūl*) and abrogation (*naskh*), primarily as part of developing law, there were no major discussions on the importance of context in the interpretation of the Qur'an and no significant principles were developed to relate God's Word to its context. Instead, contextually contingent texts of the Qur'an were divorced from their context and applied decontextually, largely based on a linguistic analysis of the Qur'anic text.

Traditions of interpretation

Socio-political schisms among Muslims emerged from the first century of Islam, and these later gave rise to different theological and legal schools of thought. These differences had a significant impact on the manner in which the Qur'an was interpreted and on methods and approaches to interpretation.

In general, the tradition of interpretation of the Qur'an developed between four broad approaches:

1　A *linguistically driven approach*: characterised by a faithfully "literal" reading of the text, particularly for interpretation of legal and theological texts.
2　A *reason-based approach*: an exploration of the text that relies, to a significant extent, on a high degree of use of reason, particularly for interpretation of the theological texts.
3　A *mystically driven approach*: a mystically oriented reading of the text that searches for "hidden" meanings of the text.
4　A *tradition-based approach* which relies on hadith and related reports attributed to the earliest Muslims.

Naturally, there were overlaps in these approaches, making it a question of which one of these was more dominant in any particular exegetical (*tafsīr*) work. These approaches are simplified here for analytical purposes only.

Despite these different approaches, there was a remarkable degree of agreement on the importance of a "literal" reading of the legal or quasi-legal texts in the Qur'an among different schools of thought and trends. This approach relied on a philological analysis of the text and the following of the accumulated tradition, in the form of hadith and opinions of prominent scholars from the past. The approach did not place any significant interpretive emphasis on the importance of taking the original macro context[1] of the Qur'an into account, or on identifying how the Qur'an was relevant to that context.

After the first few centuries of Islam, scholars identified specific characteristics that should be possessed by an interpreter of the Qur'an. Interpreters were expected to have an excellent technical knowledge of the Arabic language and the necessary linguistic, literary, and methodological skills to comprehend the text. Importantly, would-be interpreters of the Qur'an were also expected to follow mainstream theological and legal "schools". As Qur'anic interpretation was practised within dominant theological and legal schools, an interpretation was deemed to be proper and valid based on its alignment with a specific theological or legal opinion. Any bias remained unquestioned, as legal schools and theological schools that were established in the first few centuries of Islam were seen to have determined which interpretations of the Qur'an were valid and which were not.

Traditional interpretations and emphases

Traditional interpretation of the Qur'an (*tafsīr* in the pre-modern period) by and large developed a primary focus on philological analysis of the text that was coupled with either a theological, legal, religio-political, or mystical emphasis. Within the *tafsīr* tradition the interpretation of some of the key areas of the Qur'an remained largely uniform, such as the interpretation of legal texts as expressed in the major extant schools of law (Hanafi, Maliki, Shafi'i, Hanbali, and Ja'fari). Qur'anic narratives (*qisas*) were also understood as being literally and historically true, rather than myths or legends. This remarkable degree of uniformity resulted in commentaries that were often very similar in many key respects. A large part of this uniformity can also be attributed to the fact that these commentators borrowed from each other, often quite liberally.

Traditional interpretation of the Qur'an, despite its apparent similarity across theological, religio-political, legal, or mystical trends among Muslims – particularly in the interpretation of legal texts – should not be seen as homogeneous. Neither should it be seen as being entirely focused on a literal reading or a philological analysis of the text. Rather, it is possible to discern layers of analysis: after establishing a grammatical (morphological and syntactic) analysis, individual commentators usually embarked on an interpretation that was faithful to their theological, mystical, or legal position.[2]

Among Sunni scholars, earlier commentators such as Tabari (d. 310/923) were familiar with the concept of multiple layers of understanding of the Qur'an and were able to accommodate a diverse range of views into their exegetical works. Tabari's method of interpretation was to bring together a number of opinions on the meaning of a particular verse or part of a verse. This included the views of the first, second, and third generation of Muslims, and was accomplished without labelling opposing views as heretical or unorthodox. Tabari then gave his preference for one particular view or presented a synthesis of views while still acknowledging the legitimacy of diversity of views. Tabari's approach was common, although not all commentators shared it. In some cases, a commentator would present a range of views on the interpretation; at other times the commentator would simply provide their preferred interpretation.

Within the Shi'a tradition, the idea that the Qur'an has layers of meaning is fundamental. For example, Tabataba'i, a Shi'i scholar of the modern period, describes the meaning of the Qur'an as existing on two levels (esoteric and exoteric), an idea that can be traced to the very beginning of Shi'ism in early Islam:[3]

The Prophet, who is the divinely appointed teacher of the Qur'an, says "the Qur'an has a beautiful exterior and a profound interior." He has also said: "The Qur'an has an inner dimension and that inner dimension has an inner dimension up to seven inner dimensions."[4]

These two levels of meaning do not contradict each other, as Tabataba'i elaborates:

> The interior meaning of the Qur'an does not eradicate or invalidate its outward meaning. Rather, it is like the soul that gives life to the body. Islam, which is a universal and eternal religion and places the greatest emphasis upon the "reformation" of mankind, can never dispense with its external laws which are for the benefit of society.[5]

An implication of the existence of these two interconnected levels of meaning – at least from a Shi'a perspective – is that the Qur'an must be interpreted by an authority who has the ability to decipher its secrets on both the inner and outer levels.[6]

Traditional interpretation of the Qur'an developed a range of concepts that were widely adopted by commentators and that gave the tradition a degree of uniformity despite the existence of diversity. A key issue that is explored among many different interpretations is the need to identify the clarity or ambiguity of the Qur'anic texts. The specific verses of the Qur'an that should be considered clear (*muhkam*) or ambiguous (*mutashābih*) are not agreed upon. Rather, the key issue is which verses are open to debate and interpretation and which are not. The following Qur'anic text is often cited in this context:

> It is He who has sent this Scripture [the Qur'an] down to you [the Prophet]. Some of its verses are definite in meaning – these are the cornerstone of the Scripture – and others are ambiguous. The perverse at heart eagerly pursue the ambiguities in their attempt to make trouble and to pin down a specific meaning of their own: only God knows the true meaning. Those firmly grounded in knowledge say, "We believe in it: it is all from our Lord" – only those with real perception will take heed.
>
> (Qur'an 3:7)

Although there are a number of different understandings of these two concepts, one of the most prevalent views is that that *muhkam* verses are those whose meaning is so clear that they do not need interpretation, while the *mutashābih* verses are those whose meanings are not clear and therefore require interpretation. The latter are often related to theological concerns: for example, in certain passages of the Qur'an, God is described in anthropomorphic terms, as having hands and a face.

A related issue is determining the extent to which there are texts that should be read literally (*haqīqī*) or metaphorically (*majāzī*). In the *tafsīr* tradition, identifying a linguistic (that is, literal) meaning was often considered the starting point in the interpretive task; where a literal reading was not possible the metaphorical meaning of the word or text could be examined. In the case of God's attributes, for example, God's hand can be interpreted metaphorically as God's power. But there has been a significant level of resistance to such metaphorical interpretation as well. Muslim commentators on the Qur'an have long debated the existence of metaphorical language in the Qur'an, with some scholars rejecting the very idea in favour of a literal meaning of the texts.

Historically, many Muslim commentators on the Qur'an have relied heavily on a rather literal reading of the text, examining each word in the text and identifying its literal meaning or, at sentence level, giving the sentence a direct word-for-word interpretation, seeking to remain faithful to the literal meaning of each word and true to the syntactic and semantic features of the language. Ebrahim Moosa notes that this approach to interpretation is based on an assumption that:

> Language is a series of exterior signs representing a pre-existing string of internal thoughts ... it is the absolute signifier, "clear text" (*nass*), and signified, elucidation (*bayān*), that coalesces and transparently constitutes the articulated truth of God as embodied in the eternal language of the Qur'an.[7]

According to Sherman Jackson, traditional approaches to interpretation have had:

> The tendency to stress the essential relationship between the observable features of language (e.g. morphological patterns) and specification of meaning, to strive to preserve a systematic relationship between meaning, textual items and the syntactical structure of sentences.[8]

Jackson argues, however, that this approach to meaning is predicated on the assumption that there is a close relationship between grammar and meaning. This relationship allows the reader access not only to the meaning of words and sentences but also to the actual thoughts in the minds of speakers.[9]

Another set of concepts is associated with the notions of "immediate" meaning and "implied" meaning. For instance, in relation to who is responsible for the expenses of a child, the Qur'an states: "Clothing and maintenance must be borne by the father in a fair manner" (Q. 2:233). The immediate meaning of the verse is that a father is responsible for his child's welfare, and this level of meaning is known as "pronounced" (*mantūq*). Such meanings are understood to be immediately apprehended on hearing the text, without any analysis or reference to other sources.[10] This verse, however, can also be understood to imply that a father should publicly acknowledge his offspring, which is an implied meaning. Such additional meanings may be derived by a process of deduction or induction, through reference to other sources. However, within the tradition immediate meanings have been considered to have more weight than implied meanings, since the former are considered to be less susceptible to errors in reasoning and analysis.[11]

Traditional interpretation of the Qur'an has also differentiated between texts that are general ('*āmm*) and those that are specific (*khāss*).[12] These concepts are particularly useful for legal interpretation of the Qur'anic texts. For example, general texts include terms of address such as "human being", "men", "women", and "Muslims"; whereas specific terms may include "Pharaoh", "Muhammad", or "People of the Book". Specific texts are often assumed to have more clarity than general texts. Typically, when engaging in legal interpretation, some pre-modern scholars gave more importance to specific verses than they did to general verses (that is, a specific text outweighed a general text when dealing with a particular circumstance), although this approach was not taken to be a general rule.

Legal interpretation took the context of a particular text into account – albeit in a very limited way – by upholding the need to explore, where possible, the occasion of the revelation (*asbāb al-nuzūl*). Specifically, in examining several Qur'anic texts on the same legal issue, scholars need to identify which texts came first and which came later. Failure to identify the chronology of the texts can lead to inappropriate interpretation of the texts concerned. For instance, in the case of the consumption of wine, the Qur'an seems to give three different instructions: first, that in the consumption of wine there is some benefit and some sin[13] (thus, consumption of wine remains permissible); second, that if one is intoxicated one should avoid prayer[14] (still no prohibition exists); and third, that a believer must not consume wine at all.[15] If the chronological order is not established, the Qur'anic position on the consumption of wine cannot be clearly identified.

Interpretation and textualism

Despite the richness of the *tafsīr* scholarship and tradition, a high degree of textualism also pervades the tradition, particularly where interpretation of ethico-legal (and even theological) texts is concerned. Textualist approaches emphasise the historically transmitted understandings of the text, which are often based on a literal reading of the text. The emphasis on textualism in interpretation (which I refer to as a "textualist approach") aims to preserve historically transmitted understandings as faithfully as possible and to support these understandings by quoting a range of texts (such as other Qur'anic texts and hadith, as well as the opinions of earliest Muslims, theologians, jurists, and commentators on the Qur'an). For the textualists, the idea that one should take context into account when interpreting Qur'anic texts (be these texts ethico-legal or theological) is irrelevant. In the modern period, textualism is seen as a problem that is specifically associated with contemporary Salafism; however, this approach should be understood to be more widespread, given that much of the traditional thinking about legal and theological interpretation is based on some form of a textualist approach.

Textualist practices exist within a continuum: spanning from *soft textualism* to *hard textualism*. Soft textualism considers the literal meaning to be the basis for the exploration of the meaning of the text, but also allows for some flexibility of interpretation while attempting to preserve the historical meanings. Hard textualism adopts an inflexible understanding of the literal meaning of the words without any regard to the complexities associated with meaning. One problem with hard textualism is that scriptures were not written with a one-to-one correspondence in meaning between the terms and the objects or realities to which they refer. Moreover, the scripture includes ethical, spiritual, and devotional elements, which encompass concepts such as morality, spirituality, and God's transcendence. These are ideas that are deeply abstract, and the language used is often symbolic, figurative, or anthropomorphic. When these are interpreted literally, the specific meaning that is arrived at may conflict with the spirit of the text.

Hard textualists often draw literal meanings from (and find their justification in) dictionaries, which focus on the meanings as understood historically. As a result, the meaning of a word is treated as being static. This approach is based on the idea that these fixed meanings allow the reader to remain faithful to the text and eschew any subjectivity that they may otherwise bring into the interpretation of the text. Thus, meaning is restricted solely to the "observable features of language and any perspectives or presuppositions brought to the text by the interpreter are neutralized or at least limited".[16] However, a dictionary may not fully explain how words are used in each and every context. Furthermore, language and the meaning of words are highly fluid, ahead of the codifying practices of lexicography. A textualist reading of the text invokes claims to orthodoxy and correctness of interpretation, and this allows little room for readers critically to engage with the contextual nature of revelation. Some scholars argue that literalism, by arguing that the text speaks for itself, supresses intentional challenges that have been posed by the text, such as textual ambiguities.[17]

In addition to emphasising the literal meanings of the Qur'anic text, textualist approaches, in general, use other texts to reinforce the historical meanings. These are often hadith, but can also include other texts that are associated with a particular interpretation by a commentator of the Qur'an, a text from a school of law, or a creedal statement. Textualists assume that this form of intertextuality will confer stability and consistency of meaning to the interpretation; however, a large corpus of the available hadith may be unreliable or inauthentic (based on criteria developed by Muslim scholars in hadith scholarship). Furthermore, of those hadith that are considered to be reliable, a large number are solitary hadith (*āhād hadith*), and the validity of their attribution to the Prophet is often uncertain. If the authenticity of the hadith used is uncertain, yet they are used to narrow, limit, or restrict the meaning of the Qur'anic text, this is likely to pose significant problems for the interpretation of the Qur'an.

Textualist readings of Qur'anic texts often fail to consider the broad ethical and moral values and principles that the Qur'an was trying to inculcate in the minds and hearts of believers. Values such as justice, fairness, and equity are important to the interpretation of the texts and should be given sufficient attention. Some textualists[18] have argued that those moral and ethical principles themselves are to be subjected to the textualist reading of the text. One problem with that position, however, is that such a reading may undermine the very ethical-moral foundation of the law. As Hassan Hanafi argues, by focusing on the text and ignoring factors such as context, textualists can often produce partial or contradictory understandings of the Qur'anic text.[19] Although one must acknowledge the existence of *maqāsid* literature (from around the sixth/twelfth century), which focuses on the aims and objectives of the shari'a with a heavy emphasis on ethical and moral values, the influence of this literature on the interpretation of the Qur'an in the pre-modern period is perhaps limited.

Modern concerns and emphases in Qur'anic interpretation

Many Muslim thinkers today are acutely aware of the challenge of relating the Qur'an to the concerns and needs of a modern society. This sometimes requires an interpretation of some texts of the Qur'an – particularly those of an ethico-legal nature – in the light of modern needs. This is based on the Qur'an's authority as the Word of God, and therefore avoids subjecting interpretation *a priori* to the authorities of traditional law, theology, or mysticism. For many Muslims (labelled as "modernist Muslims"), an overarching concern has been how to interpret the Qur'an in the light of modern experiences, ideas, institutions, values, and norms. This perspective, which has been evident since the nineteenth century, differs significantly from traditional Islamic understandings.

From the nineteenth century, under the impact of Western civilisation, early modern Muslim scholars strove to identify compatibility between the Qur'an and modern values and norms. Jamal al-Din al-Afghani (d. 1897) and Muhammad Abduh (d. 1905) were among the first modernist Muslims, as were scholars of the Indian subcontinent, including Sayyid Ahmad Khan (d. 1898) and Muhammad Iqbal (d. 1938). For these scholars, the modern context demanded a reappraisal of the intellectual heritage of Muslims that required giving up the practice of blind imitation (*taqlīd*), which they argued was common among Muslims of their time. These scholars argued that a flexible interpretation of Islam and its sources was necessary in order to develop ideas that were compatible with modern conditions. In this sense, the idea of reform was central to their approach.

In the area of Qur'anic interpretation, modernist scholars generally argued that there was no conflict between revelation and reason. They also tried to revive Islam's rationalist tradition and as such they borrowed heavily from that tradition. Many modernist Muslims identified a need to understand the Qur'an from a scientific worldview perspective, which required a reinterpretation of a number of Qur'anic ideas (such as miracles). They also emphasised the need to avoid the use of much of pre-modern Qur'anic interpretation on the grounds that this contained too much jargon and had made the Qur'anic text more obscure. They felt that the Qur'an should be made accessible to the modern reader, and that pre-modern interpretation was often unhelpful in this regard.

Among these modernists, both Muhammad Abduh and Ahmad Khan each wrote treatises that were entirely devoted to this issue. They were, without doubt, the first modern scholars to introduce methods of interpretation that were not widely used in the Islamic tradition. They both believed that the advances of Western civilisation were due to scientific success and embraced the philosophy of the Enlightenment. Thus, their approach to interpretation was often rationalistic: for them, religion needs to be in line with the pronouncements of the human intellect and the Qur'an should be interpreted in line with reason, where needed. Toward this end, they suggested a need for interpreters to understand the Qur'an as it was understood by the first recipients of the revelation (the Arabs of the seventh century CE) and the metaphorical expressions of the Qur'an need to be reinterpreted – or rather, demythologised – for a contemporary audience.

Abduh, for example, believed that the ultimate aim of the Qur'an was to bestow guidance on humanity (as this is the intention of the author, God) and that interpreters of the Qur'an should guide their audience towards that final divine objective. For him, interpretation should not occupy itself with the task of unravelling mysterious words or extremely obscure grammatical concepts (which were, in all likelihood, unknown to the first recipients). Rather, to understand the sort of guidance that God intends for His audience, it is necessary to understand the Qur'an according to the understanding that had been disclosed to its first recipient community. In his interpretation of the Qur'an, Abduh treated the verses of the Qur'an as having a certain logical unity and dealt with many passages of the Qur'an as if they were single entities, interpreting the words and verses in light of the aims of the passage and its context.

The teachings of Abduh and Khan, and in particular their emphasis on relevance, influenced a number of scholars in the twentieth century. This has led to the emergence and development of a wide range of approaches to the interpretation of the Qur'an: including literary, thematic, scientific, feminist, and later more broadly contextualist interpretation. Scholars associated with these forms of interpretation have put forward methodological ideas and new approaches to interpretation that often depart significantly from the traditional methods. They have also tackled new questions, with the view of making the Qur'anic teachings relevant to the contemporary intellect and the sensibilities of the modern period. These approaches adopt new understandings of the Qur'an as scripture (as text or speech), the nature of revelation, tradition, and interpretation, and new ways of understanding the issue of meaning. They also allow for new ideas in interpretation. One of these approaches, the contextualist approach, is the focus of this book.

Towards a contextualist interpretation

Contextualists are those who believe that the teachings of the Qur'an should be understood both in the way they were understood and applied in the early seventh century CE, and as they might be applied in the modern context.

Contextualists tend to see the Qur'an primarily as a source of practical guide-lines that should be implemented differently when a change in circumstances requires this, so long as the fundamentals of Islam are preserved. Advocates of this approach argue that scholars must be aware of both the social, political, economic, intellectual, and cultural context of the revelation, as well as the setting in which interpretation occurs today.

Over the late twentieth and early twenty-first centuries, contextualist methodologies have been adopted by an increasing number of Muslim thinkers. Although some may not refer to the term as such, their methods of interpretation show that they are engaging with the Qur'an in new ways that reflect this methodology.

During the 1950s, Daud Rahbar, a Pakistani scholar, held that the eternal Word of God was addressed to a particular human situation during a specific time of human history (the Prophet's era). Rahbar argues that no divine message can be sent without reference to actual concrete situations, and that no divine language can be decoded unless it is couched in the linguistic, cultural, and religious values of its first audience. Highlighting the occasions of revelation (*asbāb al-nuzūl*) and issues of abrogation (*naskh*) as a case in point, Rahbar suggests that interpreters should take heed of the fact that the Qur'an, despite its divine origin, had adapted itself to changing historical circumstances even within a relatively short span of time, in accordance with the circumstances.[20]

For Fazlur Rahman, in order to release the eternal message of the Qur'an, as revealed in concrete historical circumstances of Meccan and Medinan society of the Prophet, and to adapt its meaning to today's world, it is necessary to perform a *double movement*:

> (1) One has to understand the import or meaning of a given statement by studying the historical situation or problem to which it was the answer; (2) [one has] "to generalize those specific answers and enunciate them as statements of general moral-social objectives that can be 'distilled' from specific texts in the light of the socio-historical background"; (3) the general has to be embodied in the present concrete socio-historical context.[21]

Nasr Hamid Abu Zayd posits that the Qur'an is primarily a text (*nass*) that can only be understood if its author has composed it in such a fashion that it contains within it signs that could be deciphered by its audience. This audience includes its ideal recipient, the Prophet.[22] Following other scholars of the modern period, Abu Zayd maintains that God must have adapted the revelation to the language, the social situation, and the cultural tradition of the Arabs of Prophet Muhammad's period.[23] Abu Zayd suggests that interpreters of the Qur'an today must strive to gain cognisance of the semiotic world that is associated with the historical context of the Prophet and his direct audience; without knowledge of those linguistic, cultural, and social norms, interpreters will be unable to set apart the mutable and immutable substance of the Qur'an. He joins Rahman in asserting that even though there are valuable insights in the exegetical tradition, the goal of the interpreter resides in translating the message of the Qur'an into a code of language that is contemporary and unique to our situatedness. Unlike Rahman, however, Abu Zayd maintains that the cultural code of the text has been initiated solely by the author (God) and that the Prophet played no role whatsoever in this.[24]

Mohammed Arkoun asserts that speech – rather than text – is the "Qur'anic fact" (the event that all understanding must strive to attain). He suggests that this speech was deployed using a language and symbolic modes that had much to do with a specific historical situation of revelation. Arkoun argues that the text is already impregnated with its theological interpretation. The text there-fore has infinite potential and enjoys an abundance of meaning. Given this, successive interpretive communities have done no more than strive – for better or for worse – to co-opt or appropriate this meaning. According to Arkoun, as long as history continues, new interpretations and new meanings of the Qur'an will be uncovered. Thus a meaningful interpretation is therefore one that is aware of the continuing interaction between the revealed text – *le fait cor-anique* – and history.[25]

As this brief outline shows, much as in the early centuries of Islam, there are today a multiplicity of voices, each claiming authority and legitimacy for their views and putting forward principles and ideas concerning the interpretation of the Qur'an. We are witnessing the emergence of a range of new interpretive communities, each of which shares a common set of ideas and beliefs. Within an interpretive community, individuals may not necessarily agree on all the details, but they share particular assumptions, such as common linguistic practice or a way of talking about text and meaning.[26]

In Islam, historically, there have been many different interpretive communities. Muslim jurists who follow a particular set of principles of jurisprudence may be considered an interpretive community. Muslim theologians who argue that reason should be an important element in thinking about theological matters might be considered to be another. Today's political Islamists, who argue that Muslims should establish an Islamic state or an Islamic socio-political order, are yet another. Those scholars who argue for a stronger emphasis on context in understanding the Qur'anic texts can also be an interpretive community.

Many Muslim women scholars (who are often referred to as "Muslim feminists") have also come together as an interpretive community. They believe that the majority of pre-modern male Muslim interpreters shared a particular set of values and social mores (including the belief that Islam endorses a patriarchal society) and that these men interpreted Islam's sacred texts through this patri-archal lens. They hold that the Qur'an did not specifically endorse patriarchy and patriarchal values, and that it can be interpreted in ways that are liberating to women. This latter interpretive community has adopted a contextualist approach to interpretation of the Qur'an.

The following chapters outline a justification for a contextualist approach. They introduce precedents and contemporary practices as well as the key ideas that are associated with this approach.

Notes

1 "Macro context" refers to the social, political, cultural, economic, intellectual context of the Qur'an in the early seventh century CE in Arabia (Mecca and Medina, in particular).

2 Thus, for example, Zamakhshari (d. 539/1144) provides an excellent linguistic and stylistic analysis of the entire Qur'an, and throughout maintains his Mu'tazili theological emphasis. In his interpretation of God's attributes, for example, he remains strictly within the Mu'tazili framework. Similarly, Tabari's philological analysis is followed by his emphasis on Sunni theological positions, including a cautious approach to interpretation of texts related to the Unseen (*ghayb*). Ibn Kathir, by comparison, emphasises the hadith.

3 Massimo Campanini, *The Qur'an: Modern Muslim Interpretations*, trans. Caroline Higgitt (New York: Routledge, 2011), 21.

4 'Allama Sayyid Muhammad Husayn Tabataba'i, *Shi'ite Islam*, cited in Campanini, *The Qur'an*, 21.

5 Tabataba'i, *Shi'ite Islam*, cited in Campanini, *The Qur'an*, 22.

6 Campanini, *The Qur'an*, 22.

7 Ebrahim Moosa, "The Poetics and Politics of Law After Empire: Reading Women's Rights in the Contestations of Law", *UCLA Journal of Islamic & Near East Law*, 1 (2001–2), 1–28: 8.

8 Sherman Jackson, "From Prophetic Actions to Constitutional Theory: A Novel Chapter in Medieval Muslim Jurisprudence", *International Journal of Middle Eastern Studies*, 25 (1993), 71–90: 78.

9 Sherman Jackson, "Fiction and Formalism: Towards a Functional Analysis of Usul Al-Fiqh", in B. Weiss, *Studies in Islamic Legal Theory* (Leiden: Brill, 2002), 177–201: 182.

10 Kamali, *Principles of Islamic Jurisprudence* (Chicago: Paul & Company Pub Consortium, 2003), 109–56.

11 Kamali, *Principles of Islamic Jurisprudence*, 109–56.

12 Kamali, *Principles of Islamic Jurisprudence*, 109–56.

13 Qur'an 2:219.

14 Qur'an 4:43.

15 Qur'an 5:90–91.

16 Jackson, "Fiction and Formalism", 191.

17 M. Sharify-Funk, "From Dichotomies to Dialogues – Trends in Contemporary Islamic Hermeneutics", in ed. A. Abdul Aziz, M. Abu-Nimer, and M. Sharify-Funk, *Contemporary Islam: Dynamic not Static* (London: Routledge, 2006), 64–80: 67.

18 Yudian Wahyudi, "Hassan Hanafi on Salafism and Secularism", in ed., Ibrahim Abu Rabi', *The Blackwell Companion to Contemporary Islamic Thought* (Malden, MA: Blackwell Publishing, 2006), 257–70: 260.

19 Wahyudi, "Hassan Hanafi on Salafism and Secularism", 260.

20 Muhammad Daud Rahbar, "The Challenge of Muslim Ideas and Social Values to Muslim Society", *The Muslim World*, 48, 4 (1958), 274–85.

21 Fazlur Rahman, *Islam and Modernity: Transformation of an Intellectual Tradition* (Chicago: University of Chicago Press, 1982), 6–7.

22 Nasir Hamid Abu Zayd, *Mafhum al-Nass: Dirasa fi 'Ulum al-Qur'an* (Cairo: al-Hay'a al-Misriyya al-'Ammah lial-Kitab, 1990), 11–12.

23 Abu Zayd, *Mafhum al-Nass*, 25–26.

24 Abu Zayd, *Mafhum al-Nass*, 27–28.

25 Mohammed Arkoun, "The Notion of Revelation: From Ahl al-Kitab to the Societies of the Book", *Die Welt des Islams*, 28 (1988), 62–89.

26 Khaled Abou El Fadl, *Speaking in God's Name* (Oxford: One World, 2001).

3 An early form of contextualism
Umar and interpretation

This chapter examines one of the most influential figures of early Islam, Umar b. al-Khattab (d. 23/644), who was one of the earliest followers of the Prophet Muhammad. Some of his interpretations of key Qur'anic texts are outlined in this chapter as an example of an early form of a contextualist approach to interpretation.

Problems with the sources

I have argued elsewhere in this book (see Chapter 7) that there are significant problems in relying on the use of hadith and other traditions when attempting to understand certain aspects of the Prophet's life or to identify what was happening in the earliest Muslim communities. Given the level of fabrication of hadith that occurred in the first and second centuries of Islam, and the difficulties associated with the biographical material collated by Muslims in relation to the Prophet, the question of authenticity of such material remains an important question in contemporary Islamic scholarship. The opinions and views that are attributed to the first, second, and third generations of Muslims in Qur'anic commentaries are also, in many cases, of questionable authenticity. This means that when dealing with non-Qur'anic material the interpreter is expected to be cautious.

Despite this, when the hadith and the existing biographical, historical, and exegetical material are used with a high degree of caution and care, they can add important insights to some aspects of life in the earliest period of Islam. Although individual hadith reports and traditions may or may not be historically reliable, the overall picture that emerges from a review of this body of material collectively on a particular issue can be used to understand certain issues associated with that in the first century of Islam. Thus, despite the fact that the documentation of hadith and early written biographical works began to occur largely in the second century of Islam, all such material cannot be dismissed as completely unreliable. This has been demonstrated by both Muslim and non-Muslim scholars of early Islam.

For example, when dealing with the opinions or views that are attributed by Islamic tradition to Umar, perhaps not all of the reports that exist in the *tafsīr* tradition or in other sources will be completely accurate. However, it is useful to note that the overall picture that emerges from these texts collectively is that Umar had a significantly different approach to the Qur'anic interpretation than his contemporaries, particularly in relation to some of the more socially challenging texts. So, the purpose of presenting this material in this chapter is not to argue that all the views that are attributed to Umar are historically reliable. Rather, this is to suggest that within the *tafsīr* tradition – and also the legal tradition – ideas that Muslims have, in the past, considered to be acceptable and reliable should, by and large, be taken seriously. The question of historical reliability, although it is an important academic issue, should not prevent us from exploring Muslim tradition and some of the ideas, opinions, and views that are attributed to early figures like Umar.

When new approaches to interpretation of the Qur'an today are discussed, questions are often raised about the legitimacy of the endeavour by many Muslims. This book is situated within this debate, as it emphasises the value of a contextualist approach to the interpretation of the Qur'an. From a Muslim perspective, the ideas, views, and opinions that exist in the Islamic tradition may lend some support for the project of a contextualist reading; while at the same time, any such endeavour should be mindful of the fact that at least some of the supporting opinions and views may not be historically reliable.

Nevertheless, given that these views were circulating among Muslims in the earliest period of Islam prior to being collated in various collections of hadith or Qur'anic exegetical literature, these can safely be assumed to have been the kinds of views that Muslims at the time were comfortable with in attributing to a figure like Umar. Even if some of these opinions were not historically fully reliable, the views expressed in the texts that were seen as acceptable or legitimate in the early Islamic tradition are worthy of exploration in our attempts at justifying a contextualist reading of the Qur'an. Thus, I am presenting some of the views attributed to Umar in the tradition to demonstrate that thinking about Qur'an in context has existed within the Muslim tradition, even in the first century of Islam.

Umar's role and position

Umar played a significant role in the leadership of the Muslim community during both the Meccan and Medinan periods. As a senior Companion of the Prophet, his counsel was often sought on important issues, and his view carried weight with the Prophet. An example of this is the institution of the *adhān* (call to prayer) that was introduced soon after the Muslims' emigration to Medina. The Prophet had initially considered a drum, a bell, or a horn as a means of summoning the believers to perform the daily prayers. However, he decided against these, because they were too similar to the methods used by the Jews and Christians. A hadith indicates that it was Umar who suggested a human voice as the most appropriate method for calling the faithful together.[1]

Umar remained a close adviser to the Prophet until the Prophet's death. This is testified by a number of hadith. For example, one hadith has the Prophet saying: "God has put the truth on Umar's tongue and in his heart." Another hadith, narrated by Uqba b. Amir, attributes to the Prophet the following statement: "If there were to be a prophet after me it would be Umar b. al-Khattab."[2] In a hadith narrated by Abu Hurayra, the Prophet reportedly stated:

> Among the nation of Israel who lived before you, there were men who used to be inspired with guidance though they were not prophets, and if there is any of such persons amongst my followers, it is Umar.[3]

Umar was also the most important adviser to the Prophet's successor, Abu Bakr (d. 13/634), during his short – and socio-politically tumultuous – two-year reign. Indeed, Umar played a central role in having Abu Bakr proclaimed successor to the Prophet, despite the disagreements among some Muslims on this issue immediately after the death of the Prophet in Medina.

Umar was an advocate for many policies, not all of which were adopted by the caliph Abu Bakr. Characteristically, although Umar initially opposed fighting the Bedouin tribes (who had refused to accept Abu Bakr's leadership and to pay taxes to Medina), once the decision had been made, he became Abu Bakr's most important adviser during the campaign.[4] Umar was a key figure in another important development during Abu Bakr's caliphate, the beginning of the conquest of the regions to the north of Arabia and the expansion of the Islamic caliphate. Umar also played an important part in encouraging Abu Bakr to compile the Qur'an as a single book. Umar and others felt that the Qur'an could easily be lost because many people who had memorised it were being killed in battles.[5] At Umar's insistence Abu Bakr appointed a committee, headed by Zayd b. Thabit (d. c. 28/649), whose task was to collect and write down the entire Qur'an using the available materials. These accounts of Umar's role in the early history of Islam highlight how central his involvement was in the development of Islam as a religion and in Muslim society and polity. His interventions at key points have shaped Islam into the religion that exists today.

Umar had a deep insight into the aim and spirit of the Qur'anic message. He had a comprehensive understanding of how the Prophet functioned: his ways of thinking, his character, his attitude to various matters, his handling of particular cases, and his understanding and application of the Qur'anic teachings.[6] Umar had close and direct knowledge of the two most important sources of Islam: the Qur'an and the person and practice of the Prophet Muhammad. He was well versed in the context within which Islam was functioning and developing (including the immediate context in which the Qur'an was revealed), and in which the Prophet functioned religiously, politically, culturally, socially, economically, and intellectually. Given his privileged and unique status, Umar and his legacy provide an important source of information for today's Muslims in understanding the relationship between the Qur'an as a text, the Sunna of the Prophet, and how they were conceptualised and understood in early Islam. Umar should perhaps be considered the second most important figure in Islam, after the Prophet himself, in terms of his socio-political and religious influence and legacy.

Muslim tradition suggests that Umar had a profound insight into the overall message and spirit of the Qur'an and how it should be understood. In particular, there are many reports on Umar's decision-making activities and views on legal matters when he himself became caliph, some of which contradict the literal meaning of the texts of the Qur'an and the Prophet's Sunna. So frequent are the references to Umar's decisions that the texts often refer to *sunnat Umar* (Umar's Sunna) as opposed to *sunnat rasūl Allah* (Sunna of the Messenger of God). The expression *sunnat Umar* testifies to the fact that his views were considered as normative among the Muslims, thus in accordance with the Qur'an and Sunna of the Prophet. The following highlights some of Umar's views, to illustrate that the way Umar interacted with the Qur'an and the Prophet's Sunna reveals important insights into the way in which the first generation of Muslims understood, engaged with, and interacted with the Qur'an.

Recipients of *zakāt*

The first example of a case where Umar's views departed from the literal reading of the Qur'anic text concerns the issue of the categories of people to whom *zakāt* (the alms-tax) should be given. The Qur'an states:

> Alms are meant only for the poor, the needy, those who administer them, those whose hearts need winning over, to free slaves and help those in debt, for God's cause, and for travellers in need. This is ordained by God; God is all knowing and wise.[7]

(9:60)

This verse, in no ambiguous terms, stipulates that *zakāt*, which is prescribed by the Qur'an and confirmed by the Prophet's Sunna, should be given to eight categories of people who are listed in the verse. There was apparently no dispute during the time of the Prophet about the understanding of this verse and its application. Since the Prophet had put it into practice, the Companions of the Prophet were familiar with the interpretation of the verse.

However, during Abu Bakr's caliphate, as adviser to the caliph, Umar made the decision to deny one of the categories of recipients mentioned in this verse their share, namely, those "whose hearts need winning over". According to traditional accounts, this phrase in the verse meant that a portion of *zakāt* needed to be set aside to be paid to some of the leaders of Arab tribes who had not yet accepted Islam, in order to encourage them to join Islam or to keep them on the side of the Muslims. These payments would continue even after the recipients had become Muslim, presumably in recognition of their social status.[8]

During Abu Bakr's caliphate, two tribal leaders came to collect their share of *zakāt* from the caliph, as they had been accustomed to do during the time of the Prophet. Abu Bakr was willing to give their share but Umar, as adviser to

Abu Bakr at the time, refused to pay them. They protested, saying that the Qur'an gave them this right and that this had been the practice of the Prophet right up to his death.[9] However, Umar felt that the Qur'anic text in question had been revealed at a time when Islam and Muslims were weak. The Qur'anic text gave a financial incentive to strengthen the new faith.

Notably, the nascent Muslim community in Medina until approximately two years before the Prophet's death faced a number of real existential threats from different sides. In addition, there were a significant number of religious hypocrites (*munāfiqūn*) in Medina: those who only outwardly professed allegiance to Islam but secretly harboured ill feelings against the Muslims, and were willing to support the enemies of Muslims should the opportunity arise. However, at the time of Umar's rejection of the request of these *zakāt* recipients, the situation was very different. The Muslim caliphate was expanding, with strong armies marching on the Byzantine and Sassanid empires in the north and conquering large parts of the region. Islam and Muslims were no longer weak. This must have been behind Umar's thinking, as he held the view that given Islam's newly dominant status, these tribal leaders who had been sitting on the fence could no longer be permitted to do so. If certain tribal elders wanted to create havoc in the community, the new Muslim state could counter them relatively easily, given the number of armed troops the caliph now had at his disposal. Umar therefore refused to give a share to these tribes, despite this share being very clearly prescribed in the Qur'an, in a verse about whose meaning there had previously been no disagreements.

Umar's reasoning indicates that some Qur'anic rulings, such as this one on the categories of the *zakāt* recipients, may in fact be context-specific and context-dependent. The verse under consideration was not simply a Qur'anic command to be followed literally and regardless of the context. Umar reasoned that if the context changed, the original Qur'anic ruling would no longer be in force, as its original aim and purpose no longer existed.

Distribution of war booty

The distribution of war booty provides another example in which Umar's decision-making contradicted clear Qur'anic verses and the Prophet's Sunna. When the early Muslims fought against hostile groups and defeated them, the question of what to do with the spoils of these battles arose. The Qur'an specifies the rules of distribution for war booty:

> They ask you [Prophet] about [distributing] the battle gains. Say, "That is a matter for God and His Messenger, so be mindful of God and make things right between you. Obey God and His Messenger if you are true believers."[10]
>
> (8:1–2)

> Whatever gains God has turned over to His Messenger from the inhabitants of the villages belong to God, the Messenger, kinsfolk, orphans, the needy, the traveller in need – this is so that they do not just circulate among those of

you who are rich – so accept whatever the Messenger gives you, and
abstain from whatever he forbids you. Be mindful of God: God is severe in
punishment.[11]

(59:7)

Here the Qur'an stipulates distribution of part of the booty to those who partici-
pated in the wars, and this should apply to those of the early Arab Muslim conquests. Importantly, this practice was endorsed by the Prophet himself. Umar,
however, decided not to distribute immovable property as in the case of lands of
Iraq, citing interests of the greater good and benefit (*maslaha*) of society in general.

To make sense of this ruling of Umar, it is important to keep in mind that
during his reign the Muslim armies began to expand Muslim territory into the
area that is today known as southern Iraq. When these lands were conquered,
the Muslim warriors expected that the very fertile lands of Iraq would be distributed among the conquerors, and their inhabitants were to become slaves, in
accordance with the principles stipulated in the Qur'an and put into practice in
a number of cases by the Prophet. Indeed, several Companions of the Prophet
thought this should take place. According to a survey undertaken by one of the
commanders of troops, Sa'd b. Abi Waqqas, each Muslim soldier would receive
three persons as slaves.[12] However, Umar refused to follow the precedent,
reasoning that it should be reinterpreted in the light of the changing situation.
Umar argued that the land should remain the property of the community as a
whole, and that a tax (*kharāj*) should be levied on the conquered lands' produce,
payable to the central government.

His interpretation was based on a consideration of public interest. Namely,
he argued that future generations of Muslims also had an interest in the land
and its produce, and it should therefore not be part of the booty that would
be distributed to the army, or nothing would be left for the future. Similarly,
he reasoned that if no inhabitants were available to work the land, its produce
would soon fail. With this ruling, Umar was making a distinction not found in
the clear meaning of the Qur'anic texts or in the example of the Prophet.

He was opposed in this by many senior Companions of the Prophet,
including Abd al-Rahman b. Awf (d. 32/652), who argued that the land was a
gift from God to the Muslim soldiers. Umar replied:

By God, no territory should be conquered after me to form a great gain,
but be a burden on the Muslims. If we were to divide the land and the
property of Iraq and Syria, how are we going to provide for the towns and
the forts? What is going to be left for posterity and the widows in these
lands of Syria and Iraq?

He then added:

Do you not see that these towns and forts need men to manage their
affairs? Do you not see that these great cities in Syria and Iraq such as

Damascus, al-Jazirah, Kufa, Basra, and Misr need to provide other forts and territories with men and provide for their sustenance?[13]

Finally, when Umar argued that the reference to "those who come after them" in Qur'an 59:10 should be understood to mean the future generations of Muslims, his view prevailed over that of his opponents. Again, Umar had acted on what he considered to be the underlying objective and purpose of the Qur'an and Sunna as a whole, namely, the safeguarding of the public interest. Umar employed this principle as the most important hermeneutical tool in his interpretation of the primary sources, even if it went against the clear literal reading of the Qur'an and the practice of the Prophet himself.

Distribution of the portion of war booty reserved for the Prophet's family

Umar interpreted some other texts of the Qur'an in a similar manner, despite the opposition of key Companions. For example, the Qur'an (8:41) also reserved one-fifth of the spoils of war for the Prophet's "close family". Nu'mani points out that, as with the eight recipients of *zakāt*, the Prophet did not adhere to a rigid distribution among these five categories.[14] Rather, he distributed it as need required: to pay debts, support the poor, and help young people marry. Of his family, he favoured the Hashim and Muttalib clans although they did not receive equal shares; the Nawfal and Abd Shams clans, although equally close to the Prophet's family, did not receive anything.[15]

During Umar's reign some representatives of the Prophet's family, including Ali b. Abi Talib and Abd Allah b. Abbas, argued that this verse of the Qur'an gave them an absolute right to one-fifth of all war gains. However, Umar disagreed, arguing that, like the Prophet, he had the authority to distribute the war gains as the need dictated.[16] Here, Umar was not so much diverging from a clear text as claiming that as head of state he had the same right as the Prophet to determine exactly who would receive funds, which implied that he had the authority to change the precedent set by the practice of the Prophet.

Implementation of Qur'anic punishments

Umar also suspended the implementation of certain Qur'anic punishments for social crimes, and justified this on the basis of the change in the context. For instance, in a year of famine in Medina, known as the "Year of the Drought", Umar suspended the Qur'anic penalty for theft which amounted to amputation of the hand.[17] Notably, the Qur'anic text that provides this particular penalty does not say that it should not be implemented in difficult economic circumstances. However, Umar argued that because of the famine, some people might be forced to steal out of hunger, and it would not be appropriate to implement the penalty of amputation under these circumstances.

Several other accounts of Umar's contextual thinking in implementing Qur'anic punishments exist in tradition. These often occur in cases where a criminal seems to have been forced to commit an offence out of hunger or need. For example, when some young boys stole a she-camel, Umar called on their employer and reprimanded him, saying: "You use them, yet leave them hungry, so that they feed themselves upon illegal gains!" He then ordered him to pay the price of the she-camel to its owner, and let the boys go.[18] On another occasion, a man stole from the *bayt al-māl* (public treasury). Umar responded by saying: "His hand should not be amputated, as he has some right [as a needy person] to that *bayt al-māl*."[19]

In other cases, Umar appears to have felt the need to increase certain punishments beyond the clear instructions of the Prophet. For example, although the Qur'an does not specify a punishment for the consumption of wine, hadith literature states that the Prophet commanded that those who were caught drinking be given forty lashes.[20] By Umar's time, because of the enormous increase in wealth and the easy availability of wine, Muslims seem to have been casual about its prohibition, and were indulging in its consumption on a larger scale than before. Umar, perhaps feeling the need to increase the deterrent, ordered the punishment be doubled to 80 lashes, thereby departing from a clear practice of the Prophet.[21]

Prohibition against Muslim men marrying Jewish and Christian women

Another example of Umar's departure from clear Qur'anic injunction is his prohibition of certain Muslim men from marrying Jewish and Christian women, despite the fact that permission was clearly given for this in Qur'an 5:5. Umar was probably focused on maintaining the purity of the Muslim community, and therefore discouraged this kind of interaction with people of other faiths. Muslims were living in the midst of non-Muslim (particularly Christian) communities, and Umar felt that permitting Muslims to marry non-Muslim women could lead to the dilution of the identity of the Muslim community, despite the permission given by the Qur'an. Thus, he asked the governor of Basra, Abu Musa al-Ash'ari, not to marry a woman of another faith, and furthermore, he asked some Muslims who were married to Christian and Jewish women to divorce them.

Hudhayfa b. al-Yaman (d. 36/656), one of the earliest converts to Islam, challenged Umar to provide the grounds on which he could prohibit something that the Qur'an allowed and the Prophet also practised. Hudhayfa also had a Jewish wife, whom Umar had asked him to divorce. In one report, Umar's answer is: "I fear that other Muslims may follow suit and choose their wives from among the People of the Book for their beauty, to the detriment of Muslim women."[22]

Umar's view regarding this is not necesarily the most "liberal" one from a twenty-first-century perspective. However, from his point of view he was addressing an issue that was important in his context at a time when the identity of the Muslim community vis-à-vis people of other faiths was threatened and he introduced this measure to deal with that issue. The fact that the permission for Muslims to marry Christian or Jewish women was clearly given in the Qur'an and approved of by the Prophet Muhammad did not deter him from his reinterpretation of the relevant text in line with what the new context demanded.

Inheritance law

Umar also made interesting decisions about inheritance law, at times going beyond explicit Qur'anic instructions. In one case, a family came to Umar's court seeking his guidance regarding the distribution of an estate between a husband, a mother, and a sister from both parents. In such a scenario, the prescribed divisions according to the Qur'an (one-half for the husband, one-third for the mother, and one-half for the sister) total more than 100 per cent of the estate.

Umar consulted some Companions of the Prophet, and was advised by some to apply the principle known as 'awl: wherein the shares of each of the heirs are diminished in equal proportion. Many Companions concurred, and the ruling was given.[23] After Umar died, the Companion Ibn Abbas expressed his dissent, saying: "How could God make the estate one-half, one-half, and one-third? If the two halves exhaust the estate, from where would the third come?" He continued: "By God, if he [Umar] prioritized and gave the shares to those mentioned first in the Qur'an, then there would be no need for 'awl to start with." After declaring this view, he was asked: "Why didn't you say this during the time of Umar?" To this, he replied: "He was intimidating and he scared me!"

Ever since this ruling by Umar, Sunni jurists have accepted the principle of 'awl, while their Shi'a counterparts have rejected it on the grounds that it is a violation of the explicit Qur'anic directions.[24] Shi'a scholars contend that, by utilising this principle, the caliph Umar effectively opted to reduce everyone's share from the minimum of the Qur'anic one-twenty-fourth to one-twenty-seventh, which is not a Qur'anic share.

Communal prayer

Muslims, in general, believe that matters of ritual worship cannot be changed at all by anyone other than God or the Prophet. However, after the Prophet's death Umar reintroduced the long, nightly prayers (known as *tarāwīh*) during the fasting month of Ramadan. He argued that Muslims should perform this prayer together, unlike during the Prophet's time. Today, these prayers are a central feature of worship during the month of Ramadan for the majority of Muslims.

During the month of Ramadan, the Prophet would stay in the mosque after the obligatory night prayer (*Ishā*), and offer extra prayers. One night, as the Muslims saw the Prophet offering extra prayers, they also prayed. The following night more Muslims stayed in the mosque after the night prayer to offer extra prayers. On the third night there was a still larger gathering of the Muslims to perform the extra prayers. On the fourth night, when a large number of the Muslims assembled to offer the extra prayers, the Prophet did not offer the extra prayers and retired to his house immediately after the *Ishā* prayers. The following nights the Prophet retired immediately after the night prayers, and gradually the number of Muslims who offered the extra prayers diminished. Then one night the Prophet offered the extra prayers again. When the Prophet was asked about the reason for the break in the extra prayers for some nights he said that he had avoided these prayers lest the Muslims might take them to be an obligation, which might become a burden for the Muslims. The Prophet explained that such prayers were not obligatory, although whoever offered them voluntarily would have the blessing of God. Thereafter it became the practice that some Muslims offered the extra prayers during the month of Ramadan on their own, whereas others did not.[25]

When Umar became caliph, he saw that many Muslims gathered in the Prophet's mosque to offer extra prayers after the night prayers, and noted that there were no specifications about the number of *rak'as* (units of prayer) to be offered. Umar decided that if the prayers were offered in congregation and the number of *rak'as* was fixed, this would be an effective reform. After consulting the Companions, Umar issued instructions that such extra prayers should be offered in congregation under the imamate of a Qur'an reader who should recite a considerable part of the Qur'an each night, so that the entire Qur'an was completed during a week or so. As the hadith below explains, Umar required Muslims to perform *tarāwīh* prayers in congregation:

> Narrated by Abu Hurayra. Allah's Apostle said, "Whoever prayed at night the whole month of Ramadan out of sincere faith and hoping for a reward from Allah, then all his previous sins will be forgiven." Ibn Shihab (a subnarrator) said, "Allah's Apostle died and the people continued observing that (that is, voluntary prayers – *nawāfil* – offered individually, not in congregation), and it remained so during the caliphate of Abu Bakr and in the early days of Umar's caliphate." Abd al-Rahman said, "I went out in the company of Umar b. al-Khattab one night in Ramadan to the mosque and found the people praying in different groups. A man praying alone or a man praying with a small group behind him." So, Umar said, "In my opinion, I would better gather these (people) under the leadership of one Qur'an reciter (that is, let them pray in congregation)." So, he made up his mind to congregate them behind Ubay b. Ka'b. Then on another night I went again in his company and the people were praying behind their reciter. On that, Umar remarked, "What an excellent *bid'a* (innovation) this is … "[26]

Setting free female slaves who have borne children

In another key innovation, Umar decreed that a female slave who bore the child of her master would be set free, although this was not practised during the time of the Prophet or of Abu Bakr.[27] In the Qur'an, the position of the *umm al-walad* (the slave girl who bears her master a child) is undefined.

The caliph Umar was the first to ordain that an *umm al-walad* should become legally free upon the death of her master and no longer liable to be sold or given to another. However, it appears that his ruling was not the final settlement of the matter, as Ali, in particular, diverged from it. This ruling was also controversial among the Companions, with Ibn Abbas notably opposing Umar's decision.[28]

In the dispute that arose around this issue, a number of positions were put forward. Those that disagreed with Umar's ruling argued that the Prophet approved the sale of the *umm al-walad*, while those who sided with Umar cited evidence that the Companions of the Prophet gave approval to Umar's ordinance.[29]

Concluding remarks

Umar b. al-Khattab's reinterpretations of key Qur'anic instructions and commandments provide an important example of how some of the earliest Muslims approached the interpretation of the Qur'an with due regard to the context, and how they interpreted it in relation to changes in this context. For figures like Umar, the Qur'an was a living text, and its guidance required an interpretation that was true to its spirit so that it remains relevant to changing circumstances. Although the ideals of the Qur'an remained, specific applications of some of the teachings (particularly those that were related to changing social, economic, and political circumstances) needed constant reflection. Ideas such as the public interest, the common good, a sense of fairness and justice, and awareness of changing contexts appear to have been at the forefront of Umar's quasi-contextualist thinking when he applied Qur'anic guidance.

Notes

1 Muhammad Muhsin Khan, *Summarized Sahih al-Bukhari* (Riyadh: Darussalam Publishers and Distributors, 1996), 215.

2 Ahmad Ibn Hanbal, *Musnad al-Imam* (Beirut: Alam al-Kutub, 1419/1998), 4/154; Muhammed Abed al-Jabri, *Democracy, Human Rights and Law in Islamic Thought* (New York: I. B. Tauris, 2009), 20; Jalal al-Din as-Suyuti, *The History of Khalifahs Who Took the Right Way* (London: Ta-Ha Publishers, 1995), 114. Indeed, some accounts appear to portray Umar as prefiguring God's commandments in the Qur'an. Mujahid reports that "Umar used to express an opinion and the Qur'an would have it as a new revelation" (as-Suyuti, *The History of Khalifahs*, 114). Umar himself specifies this as happening on three occasions: taking the station of Abraham as a prayer-place (2:125), commanding the Prophet's wives to veil (33:35) and criticising them for their jealousy of each other (*Surat al-Talaq*). See al-Jabri, *Democracy, Human Rights and the Law*, 20. These verses are known in Muslim tradition as *muwāfaqāt Umar:* the "verses where God agreed with Umar".

3 Khan, *Summarized Sahih al-Bukhari*, 716.

4 Under Abu Bakr's leadership, the Muslim community at Medina engaged in *ridda* (apostasy wars) against those Bedouin tribes that had refused to accept Abu Bakr's political leadership and pay taxes to Medina. Some tribes had wanted to go back to their former religion and, more importantly, cease paying tribute to Medina. They argued that,

according to tribal custom, their pledge of allegiance had been with the Prophet, and expired with his death.

5 J. Burton, *The Collection of the Qur'an* (Cambridge: Cambridge University Press, 1977), 138–60; Ahmad Von Denffer, *Ulum ul Qur'an*, http://web.youngmuslims.ca/online_lib rary/books/ulum_al_quran/.

6 With the exception of issues pertaining to women, if we are to believe Mernissi. On the relationship between Umar and the Prophet, see Avraham Hakim, "Conflicting Images of Lawgivers: The Caliph and the Prophet: Sunnat 'Umar and Sunnat Muhammad", in ed. Herbert Berg, *Method and Theory in the Study of Islamic Origins* (Leiden: Brill, 2003), 159–79.

7 Muhammad Abdel Haleem, *The Qur'an: A Modern Translation* (Oxford: Oxford University Press, 2004), 121.

8 Lit. "those whose hearts are won over". The term applied to those former opponents of the Prophet Muhammad who are said to have been reconciled to the cause of Islam by presents of 100 or 50 camels from the Prophet's share (the fifth or *khums* of the spoils of the battle of Hunayn, after the Prophet's forces had defeated the Hawazin confederation). Ed. "al-Mu'allafa Qulūbuhum", *Encyclopaedia of Islam*, second edition (Brill Online, 2012).

9 Muhammad Baltaji, *Manhaj Umar b. al-Khattab fi al-Tashri'* (Cairo: Dar al-Salam, 2006), 151–52

10 Abdel Haleem, *The Qur'an*, 110.

11 Abdel Haleem, *The Qur'an*, 366.

12 Shibli Numani, *Umar* (London: I. B. Tauris, 2004), 93.

13 Al Jabri, *Democracy, Human Rights and the Law*, 23. See also Baltaji, *Manhaj Umar*, 115.

14 Numani, *Umar*, 123–24.

15 Numani, *Umar*, 123–24.

16 Numani, *Umar*, 123–24.

17 The Qur'an (5:38) states: "Cut off the hands of thieves, whether they are man or woman, as punishment for what they have done – a deterrent from God: God is almighty and wise." Abdel Haleem, *The Qur'an*, 71. Reference to suspending the punish-ment is in Ibn Sa'd, *al-Tabaqat al-Kubra* (Beirut: Dar Sader, 1968), 1, 223.

18 S. Al-Tamawi, *Omar Ibn Al-Khattab and the Origin of Modern Politics and Administration* (Cairo: Dar al-Fikr al-Arabi, 1976), 202.

19 Al-Jabri, *Democracy, Human Rights and the Law*, 205.

20 *Sahih Muslim*, "Kitab al-Hudud".

21 Ibn Shabba, *Tarikh al-Madina al-Munawwara*, first edition (Beirut: Dar al-Kutub al-Ilmiya,1417 AH), 2: 731–34.

22 Al-Jabri, *Democracy, Human Rights and the Law*, 25–26.

23 'Ala' al-Din al-Mardawi, *al-Insaf* (Dar Ihya' al-Turath al-'Arabi, 1986), as cited by Ahmad Souaiaia, "On the Sources of Islamic Law and Practices", *Journal of Law and Religion*, 20 (2005), 125–49: 136.

24 Souaiaia, "On the Sources", 125–49.

25 From www.alim.org/library/biography/khalifa/content/KUM/14/1; see also Masud-ul-Hasan *Hadrat Abu Bakr, Umar, Usman, Ali* (Lahore: Islamic Publication), 1982.

26 Sahih al-Bukhari: Hadith 3.227, www.usc.edu/org/cmje/religious-texts/hadith/bukhari/032-sbt.php.

27 Abd al-Salam al-Sulaymani, *Al-Ijtihad fi al-fiqh al-Islami* (Rabat: Wizarat al-Awqaf, 1996), 132–33.

28 J. Schacht, "Umm al-Walad." *Encyclopaedia of Islam*, second edition (Brill Online, 2012).

29 J. Schacht, "Umm al-Walad."

4   A modern form of contextualism
Women's perspectives in interpretation

In the modern period – particularly during the late twentieth and early twenty-first centuries – some significant developments have occurred in the interpretation of a range of Qur'anic texts related to women. A key realisation in this regard is that when the Qur'an (and by extension Sunna) were interpreted throughout the course of Islamic history some violence was done to the original message of the text as understood by the first recipients. Moreover, despite the Qur'an's polysemy as recognised in classical scholarship, the majority of its interpreters were men who lived in patriarchal societies, and who therefore held specific views concerning the nature, norms, and roles of gender in society, and interpreted the relevant Qur'anic texts without necessarily paying attention to the rich possibilities of meaning in those texts.

Some fo the pre-modern interpretations that have been used by Muslims over the last millennium by and large may no longer be considered normative in terms of understanding issues that are related to women, given the radical changes that have occurred in contextual terms, that is, between the context in which the interpretations were produced and the contemporary context of late modernity. In other words, historically prevalent interpretations of the Qur'an did not exhaust all the interpretive possibilities; other interpretations remain possible, partly due to the changes in the interpretive models that were adopted and partly because of the radically different socio-cultural and intellectual background of the late modern interpreters. This chapter explores some of the views about the Qur'an and its interpretation, as held by a number of Muslim scholars of the modern period. These scholars are primarily women, although the ideas of several male scholars are also present in the discourse. The scholars presented in this chapter have put forward significant insights, ideas, and methodological principles for a contextualist interpretation of the Qur'an.

Debates on the emancipation of women

The view that the *interpretation* of the Qur'an and Sunna has been in some cases insensitive to women's perspectives was triggered by the broader debates on women's emancipation that took place from the early twentieth century in a number of Muslim societies.

Juan Ricardo Cole examines the ideas of several Egyptian pro-feminist male Muslim thinkers from the late nineteenth and early twentieth centuries such as Qasim Amin (d. 1908) and Muhammad Abduh (d. 1905) and identifies several ideas upon which these pro-emancipation thinkers generally agreed. These ideas include: more education for women, uncovering of the face and hands of women, the importance of abolishing the practice of women's seclusion, and making both polygamy and divorce more difficult.[1] However, Cole also claims that the real issues were not full veiling and seclusion (on which these thinkers focused); rather that most women were married to their father's choice of bridegroom, subjected to summary divorce, or faced the possibility – however remote – of being relegated to the position of second, third, or even fourth wife.[2]

In the early part of the twentieth century, a number of Muslim women such as Huda Sha'rawi (d. 1947), Nabawiyya Musa (d. 1951), and Malak Hifni Nasif (known as Bahithat al-Badiyah) (d. 1918) – also began to contribute to the debate on women's emancipation. Debates at this time included areas covered by pro-emancipation thinkers mentioned earlier. In short, these women sought some freedom for women to acquire education, employment, and a degree of freedom of movement.[3]

These early Muslim "feminists" argued that it was important for Muslim women to assert themselves, to free themselves from the shackles of the past and unjustified traditions, and to play an important role in society, in the same way as men.[4] These initial gender debates were concerned with the societal condition of Muslim women in Egypt and elsewhere in the Middle East and South Asia. However, this debate then spread to other contexts worldwide.

The debates on women's emancipation at this time did not necessarily engage with sophisticated hermeneutical principles or methods of interpretation. Instead, scholars, activists, and thinkers (both men and women) attempted to go back to Qur'anic teachings and the practice of the Prophet, selectively using a large number of texts that appeared to be relevant to their understanding of women's emancipation. They also highlighted the problems for Muslim societies that arose from keeping half of the population out of sight and excluded from active public roles in society.

Rejecting the status quo, these early twentieth-century scholars argued that the conditions in which women were functioning at that time should not be seen as based on either the Qur'anic or prophetic teachings. From their point of view, such practices and ideas came from the cultural practices of various Muslim societies, and were often justified on the basis of biased interpretations of certain Qur'anic texts and prophetic traditions.

Among these scholars was Tahir al-Haddad (d. 1935) from Tunisia, who, in his published book *Our Woman in the Shari'a and in Society*, argued that the social status of a woman in Muslim society was inferior to their status according to original Islamic teachings and pleaded for improvement in the social and legal positions of women. He was severely attacked by the traditionalist scholars. As a result of this he lost his job, and he died a few years later, a dejected man.[5] Al-Haddad argued that men had "swallowed" women's rights, and that the spirit of Qur'anic message had been betrayed by the selfishness of Muslims: especially the traditional *ulama*, whom he accused of giving tacit approval to the enslavement of women.

From the very beginning of the debate, then, scholars who were familiar with Qur'anic interpretation and Islamic law did not consider that Islam was to blame for the conditions in which Muslim women were functioning.[6] Moreover, in their arguments for reform and change, they made clear efforts to absolve the Qur'an and the Prophet of responsibility for this situation. Their perspective was that the Qur'an and the Prophet were both keen to mitigate the unjust practices against women that were prevalent at the time, by providing new rules, regulations, values, and norms. As evidence of this, they highlighted the reforms made by the Prophet and the Qur'an: including the limitation on the number of women a man could marry,[7] and the assertion that (according to Qasim Amin) the Qur'anic prescription for veiling was specific to the Prophet's women.[8] These scholars also highlighted the fact that the emancipatory reforms introduced by the Qur'an included its provision of a share of inheritance to women (in particular, daughters) in contrast to pre-Islamic practices. In the society of the time, the right to inheritance was essentially limited to males, on the basis that men generated wealth through engagement in war, raids, and business.

However – and perhaps understandably, given the traditional patriarchal attitudes that existed in most Muslim societies at the time these debates were taking place – the ideas of thinkers who supported women's emancipation were strongly criticised. Those who proposed such ideas were often labelled anti-Islamic or were accused of trying to destroy Muslim societies from within. The critique of Qasim Amin is a case in point. Although he was probably well versed in Islamic tradition[9] and expressed his arguments in Islamic terms, his ideas were seen by those following the traditional interpretations of Islam to be constituting a direct attack on Islam and Muslim society. The basic message of Amin's *Liberation of Women* was that women's liberation and participation in national mainstream life were a necessary part of much-needed broader reforms in Egypt, based on the direct positive link between the status of women in society and the degree of development in the same.[10] Many traditionalist critics of Amin argued that his views amounted to the destruction of the traditional norms and values on which Muslim society was based.[11] From the point of view of such critics, the condition in which women were living at the time was in agreement with the two most important sources of Islam (the Qur'an and the Sunna) and was supported by centuries of Islamic legal tradition.

The idea that women should be fully covered and should primarily attend to the needs of their husbands and children at home was, in the opinion of traditionalist critics, an authentically Islamic understanding of gender relations. These critics had little enthusiasm for rejecting the centuries-old tradition of differentiation of rights and obligations between the genders (which were essentially unequal at least in some respects) that had been approved, and by close to a consensus, across all the Islamic schools of law. The kind of restrictions that the Qur'an and the traditions of the Prophet appear to have imposed on women (whether related to women's freedom of movement, obedience to their husband, subjection to male guardians, or a reduced share of inheritance) were taken at face value as examples of the kind of restrictions within which Muslim women had to function. Moreover, the critics believed that arguments for change were unacceptable from a religious point of view, as in their opinion these issues were clearly specified in the Qur'an, the traditions of the Prophet, and in the unanimous positions of Muslim scholars over the centuries.[12]

Influence of colonialism[13]

Traditionalists saw the issue of the emancipation of women as not being driven by Islamic ideas and ideals, but rather by people who were dazzled by Western civilisation. In places like Egypt, the Indian subcontinent, North Africa, and South East Asia, European colonialism was very visible. Traditionalists argued that Europeans began to criticise and denigrate Islam first by suggesting that Islam was responsible for the awful conditions in which Muslim women functioned. According to this argument, Europeans took up the issue of the emancipation of women in order to discredit Islam. Thus, arguably, a number of Muslims had adopted these ideas and began to promote them, accepting the assumption that there were significant problems in Muslim societies that stemmed from an outdated or ill-informed understanding of Islamic teachings. Calls for the emancipation of women were therefore seen by many traditionalists to be a direct assault on the very identity of Muslims and the most important institution in Muslim society, the family. As such, the traditionalists were concerned that the emancipation of women could lead to a complete overhaul of the system in which Muslim society had managed to maintain its norms and values: a family structure based on gender differentiation, where a man remained at the top of the hierarchy.

Debates, arguments, and counter-arguments continued in the first half of the twentieth century, particularly in Muslim societies under colonial rule, where the colonising powers and their representatives on the ground (whether in Egypt, India, or elsewhere) portrayed a sense of the superiority of their culture, tradition, civilisation, and norms. The position of women in European societies, particularly in relation to the level of freedom they had compared with women in Muslim societies, was always shown as an important marker of difference between Europeans and the Muslims under colonial rule.[14]

There is no doubt that the colonial powers brought many ideas and mechanisms that led Muslim societies towards modernisation, including new educational models[15] as well as new systems of governance, bureaucracy, and other institutions. These innovations had an important impact on Muslim societies, including women. The opening up of education (initially at primary, and later at secondary and university levels) was perhaps the most important factor in the emancipation of Muslim women in many Muslim societies.

Modernisation continued at least in some Muslim societies during the first half of the twentieth century, and after the Second World War, with the emergence of a large number of independent Muslim majority states, nation building became an important part of the new ethos. Ideas about the emancipation of women through education and provision of economic opportunities were doubtless facilitated at different levels as part of the nation-building agenda in many Muslim societies. The project of modernisation also had a significant impact on the emancipation of women through the development of new forms of communication, increased travel, and exposure of Muslims to Western societies and increased opportunities for Muslim women to obtain a modern education, either in predominantly Muslim societies or in Western countries. At the same time, the feminist movement in Europe and North America had a significant impact on the emancipation of women project in Muslim societies, taking the debate and discourse about Muslim women to a new level.[16]

Muslim feminist movement

The 1970s onwards saw the emergence of what many refer to as *Muslim feminist scholarship*. Muslim feminism, although it existed in some form at a practical level in much of the Muslim world from the beginning of the twentieth century, began to develop at a more theoretical level towards the end of the century.[17]

However, it would be inaccurate to approach Muslim feminist scholarship as though it were a monolithic entity. Muslim women scholars come from very diverse backgrounds. Some come from traditional Muslim societies; others have undertaken studies in Western universities; still others are indigenous to Western countries, and were either born into Muslim families or are converts to Islam. All of these individuals have very different ideas about how Islamic scholarship should deal with the question of the interpretation of the Qur'an and traditions of the Prophet in relation to issues pertaining to women.

Some scholars, including some of those discussed in this chapter, do not wish to be identified as either feminist or Muslim feminist. Amina Wadud, for example, has refused to allow such labels to apply to her. In her book, *Inside the Gender Jihad*, she describes herself as "pro-faith, pro-feminist", but distinguishes between the Western understandings of feminism (which she believes do not apply to her as an African American)[18] and her own work. She indicates that her pro-faith position arises from her personal Muslim "emphasis on faith and the sacred".[19] Asma Barlas also rejects the idea that she is a feminist. Instead, she argues that she is simply a believer, because "the Qur'an's concern with equality and rights prefigures modern, Western, and feminist discourses, [and is] grounded in a very different ethics and epistemology [to them]".[20] Fatima Mernissi – perhaps the most well known of these scholars in the Arabic-speaking world – has also indicated that she does not wish to be labelled a feminist. Mernissi uses an Arabic term, *nisa'i*, to refer to her work. Although the word is sometimes translated as "feminist", Mernissi defines it differently:

Nisa'i for me is an adjective which designates any idea, programme, project or hope which supports a woman's right to full-fledged participation and contribution in the remaking, changing and transforming of her society as well as for realisation of her talents, needs, potentials, dreams and truths.[21]

For these Muslim women, the term "feminist" probably has some negative connotations, since feminism emerged in the West and was a response to particular Western social and cultural conditions. This legacy makes progress difficult for Muslim women from traditional Muslim societies, who are assumed to have suffered through colonialism and victimised by being labelled as inferior or backward. These Muslim women have also identified the racial overtones of early Western feminism, pointing out that it was primarily concerned with emancipation of white women, and that it did not necessarily criticise Western colonialism and imperialism. For Muslim scholars who argue for change in traditional Islamic views about women, the model provided by Western feminism is not necessarily the right one. Indigenous expressions of feminism are, instead, seen as more authentic and relevant to their arguments.[22]

Another important consideration for these scholars is the context in which they live: if they adopt foreign ideas, concepts, and intellectual tools, it becomes difficult to communicate their ideas convincingly to a Muslim audience. However, some women scholars, such as Ziba Mir Hosseini and Sa'diyya Shaikh, do choose to refer to themselves as Islamic feminist, and this approach is increasingly prevalent.[23] This does not mean that they do not find some support in the views of Western feminist scholarship for their project, as can be seen in the concepts and methodological tools that are borrowed, used, and adapted.

Key ideas and principles

Given the amount of literature available and the diversity of voices that exist in this area of scholarship, a brief summary of the main ideas emerging from Muslim women scholars' contribution to hermeneutics is useful at this stage. Needless to say such a summary may not do justice to the complexity of the arguments presented by these scholars and may even dilute their methods and approaches.

For these scholars the Qur'an is the word of God and should therefore be a key point for debates on women's emancipation. However, they argue that there are different ways of interpreting the Qur'an, and that Muslim men have been interpreting the Qur'an for the last 1,400 years, with the freedom to emphasise certain possible readings and neglect others. Thus, these scholars argue that the Qur'an has been interpreted through a male bias.

Emphasis on the macro context

A recurring point in these debates is that the overall Qur'anic message – when the Qur'an is understood holistically – is a message of justice, equality, compassion, and fairness concerning the relationship between the genders. In order to obtain a better sense of this, due recognition to the context in which the Qur'an was revealed in the early seventh century CE is required. These scholars have often highlighted the fact that the Qur'an was revealed in a specific socio-historical context, and that without this due recognition, the Qur'an can be read out of context, which has important implications for its interpretation. A key aspect of this context is the existing norms, values, and institutions of pre-Islamic Arabia (and even the Arabic language itself) as they are mirrored or reflected in, but not always necessarily endorsed by, the Qur'an. Toward this end, Barlas argues that the role of history is central in determining how Muslims came to read the Qur'an, and it is now necessary to "read *behind* the text" (that is, "to reconstruct the historical context from which the text emerged"), as well as "to read *in front of* the text" (that is, to "re-contextualise the text in light of present needs").[24]

Wadud uses the notion of a *prior text*, which she defines as "a language and cultural context in which the text is read". She identifies that the gender-specific language of Arabic has a role to play in creating particular prior texts that affect the Qur'an's interpretation.[25] This suggests that the Qur'an was partly determined (both in terms of its content and the style of expression) by its historical context, and this is reflected in the text. She notes that the Qur'an objected to many injustices that were perpetrated against women in that society (such as sexual exploitation of female slaves, domestic violence, and the killing of infant girls), and often provided remedies and took significant steps towards change and reform. Wadud acknowledges that despite these reforms the Qur'an was limited by practical considerations in terms of how far it could go toward eliminating discriminatory practices and unjust attitudes.[26]

Emphasis on justice and fairness

This recognition of context is important for the contemporary reading of those texts in the Qur'an that *appear* to be unjust or discriminatory towards women. Wadud argues that the bulk of the Qur'anic text has nothing to do with unjust or discriminatory practices and, in fact, the opposite is true. In many ways, and in many different contexts, the Qur'an emphasised values of fairness, justice, and equality (*musāwa*) between men and women in all aspects of life:

> Full equality is part of Qur'anic intent, because only through a fully established personhood can any human fulfil his or her obligations before God ... To deny full personhood to women is to deny them the full capacity of *khilafah* and to thwart the possibility of their fulfilling the basic responsibility decreed by God for all of humankind.[27]

Put another way, these values can be found in the text by approaching it as a whole, through a process of induction. For example, Wadud makes use of an idea of hermeneutics of *tawhīd*, which emphasises approaches to Qur'anic discourse that are holistic (meaning that they are based upon its textual unity).[28] She further makes a systematic distinction between the unchangeable, "fundamental principles" of the Qur'an, and the changeable "capacity and particularity of … understanding and reflection … within a community".[29] Wadud argues that the Qur'anic text establishes new moral, social, and political trajectories that extend beyond the literal and concrete meaning of the text, and that this requires searching for the underlying rationale for specific Qur'anic injunctions.[30]

Emphasis on non-patriarchal readings

Barlas also emphasises that the Qur'an's image of God is not patriarchal, and argues that God's unity, justice, and incomparability provide the appropriate starting point for reading the Qur'an and understanding its non-patriarchal nature:[31]

> Quite simply, if God is not male, there also is no reason to assume that men alone are made in God's image or are, in any way, ontologically privileged over women; on the contrary, as I will argue, the Qur'an teaches the principle of the complete ontological similarity and equality of the sexes.[32]

Barlas argues that, in its account of the creation, the Qur'an does not prioritise men or male moral agency, and personality.

She uses the following verse to illustrate the way in which the Qur'an holds out the promise of gender equity:

> For Muslim men and women, for believing men and women, for devout men and women, for men and women who are patient and constant, for men and women who humble themselves, for men and women who give in charity, for men and women who fast [and deny themselves], for men and women who guard their chastity, and for men and women who engage much in God's praise, for them has God prepared forgiveness and great reward.[33]

Looking closely at the language of the text

There is also agreement among these scholars on the need to examine Qur'anic language very closely, and in doing so, to keep in mind how this language was read, understood, and interpreted in the tradition, without necessarily being bound by those interpretations. Many scholars agree on the importance of being open to possible readings of the Qur'anic text, although they have also recommended keeping a very close eye on the constraints of the linguistic structures of the text and relevant lexicographical issues. In particular, the syntactic, morphological, and rhetorical aspects of the text need to be looked at very carefully. For example, Wadud identifies *textual silences* (ellipses) in the Qur'an, which can be deduced from the Qur'an's structural and grammatical forms.

Wadud, in this context, pays close attention to the gender-specific language of the Qur'an, especially the grammatical constructs of female and male noun forms the Qur'an employs, and their hermeneutical implications.[34]

Many Muslim women scholars have suggested that where the semantic possibilities of particular terms provide for different interpretations, they should be taken into consideration: readings of the Qur'an should not be constrained unnecessarily, whether linguistically, historically, or in any other way. Barlas suggests that the Qur'anic text is polysemic in nature, and may be read in a number of different contextually legitimate ways. She utilises what could be termed an intra-Qur'anic hermeneutical principle of "reading for best meanings",[35] along with a theory of textual responsibility, to argue that the Qur'an anticipated its patriarchal misreading, and formulated a hermeneutic for its own proper reading.[36] Wadud acknowledges the danger of relativism, but argues that the permanence of the Qur'anic text itself provides the necessary continuity. In addition, Wadud argues that for the Qur'an to function according to its purpose – as a text that changes society – its fundamental principles must be properly understood, and that these must be unchanging.[37]

Reading the Qur'an holistically and intra-textually

Reading the Qur'an in this way does not involve reading it verse by verse. Rather it is about comparing verses with one another within the broad overall textual meaning. Such readings, Hidayatullah urges, should be undertaken in the way that Muslim women scholars have "identified as the Qur'an's overall movement toward advocating justice and equality for all human beings".[38]

Barlas also seeks to "treat the text as a unity" and to read it "holistically, hence intratextually".[39] She observes that Qur'anic exegetes have throughout time been reluctant to read the Qur'an within its historical context:

> Conservatives theorize the Qur'an's universalism (transhistoricity) by dehistoricizing the Qur'an itself, and/or by viewing its teachings ahistorically. This is because they believe that historicizing the Qur'an's *contexts* means also historicizing its *contents*, thereby undermining its sacred and universal character.[40]

Barlas observes that patriarchal readings of the Qur'an often result from a piecemeal and decontextualised reading "by privileging one word, or phrase, or line, or ayah, over its teachings as a whole".[41] She argues that "recognizing the Qur'an's textual and thematic holism, and thus the hermeneutic connections between seemingly disparate themes, is absolutely integral to recovering its antipatriarchal epistemology".[42] She further states:

> I believe that the very nature of divine ontology, or rather, divine self-disclosure (how God describes God)[43] is itself anti-patriarchal in nature and therefore the strongest argument against reading the Qur'an as a patriarchal text.

We therefore need to make God's self-disclosure the epistemological foundation of an anti-patriarchal hermeneutics of the Qur'an.[44]

Azizah al-Hibri also notes the problems of separating a single verse from its context and is concerned with the potential gender bias that can result from an isolated interpretation of a single verse's meaning:

> There is a unified worldview that permeates the Qur'an, and that makes it a seamless web of ideas, so that each verse cannot be properly understood without reference to others. In one sense, this is not a new argument, because ancient jurists have already stated that passages in the Qur'an explain each other.[45]

Wadud observes that the *tafsīr* tradition has not adequately utilised the intra-textual method.[46] To address this issue, Wadud suggests re-establishing the exegetical premise of the Qur'an based on the principle of *tawhīd* (unity) in the Qur'an:

> I propose a hermeneutics of *tawhīd* to emphasize how the unity of the Qur'an permeates all its parts. Rather than simply applying meanings to one verse at a time, with occasional references to various verses elsewhere, a framework may be developed that includes a systematic rationale for making correlations and sufficiently exemplifies the full impact of Qur'anic coherence.[47]

Concluding remarks

This chapter is an example of Muslim scholars (in this case, primarily women) who are attempting to read the Qur'an in a contextualist manner, challenging textualist readings and pre-modern interpretations that support readings that were not favourable towards women. While in the pre-modern period, the macro context in which Muslims functioned for over a thousand years facilitated certain readings of the Qur'anic texts, the changed macro context of the modern period, in particular the twentieth and now twenty-first centuries, requires an approach to the Qur'an that would do justice to contemporary concerns and sensibilities.

These Muslim scholars promote a gender-neutral reading of the Qur'an. In doing so, they rely, in part, on the work of a number of Muslim scholars such as Muhammad Abduh and Fazlur Rahman who provided a range of tools to think about Qur'anic interpretation today, and, in turn, these women scholars contributed their own ideas and made a significant contribution to the field. These scholars emphasise that the Qur'an was revealed in a specific socio-historical context that differs from the context of today. They note that readings of the Qur'an have to be historically contextual, and they recognise that the Qur'an speaks to all Muslims equally and advocates justice and equality, compassion, and fairness and has promoted many positive changes for women.

As women form half of the population in any given society, interpretations that negatively affect them should be a major concern, particularly given the fact that the Qur'an on the whole does not seem to support such negative readings. The entry of a significant number of Muslim women into the field of Qur'anic interpretation, bringing women's perspectives, should be seen as a new and well-deserved contribution that will enrich further the Qur'anic scholarship.

Notes

1 Juan Ricardo Cole, "Feminism, Class, and Islam in Turn-of-the-Century Egypt", *International Journal of Middle East Studies*, 13, 4 (1981), 387–407: 392.
2 Cole, "Feminism", 393.
3 See Margot Badran, "The Feminist Vision in the Writings of Three Turn-of-the-Century Egyptian Women", *British Society for Middle Eastern Studies*, 15 (1988), 11–20.
4 Moja Kahf, "'Huda Sha'rawi's Mudhakkirati: The Memoirs of the First Lady of Arab Modernity", *Arab Studies Quarterly*, 20 (1998), 53–83.
5 Fazlur Rahman, "A Survey of Modernization of Muslim Family Law", *International Journal of Middle East Studies*, 11 (1980), 451–65: 451.
6 Syed Ameer Ali, *The Legal Position of Women in Islam* (London: Hodder & Stoughton, 1912).
7 Michelle Raccagni, "The Origins of Feminism in Egypt and Tunisia" (unpublished PhD dissertation, New York University, 1983), 86, 93, 94. See also Aswita Taizir, "Muhammad 'Abduh and the Reformation of Islamic Law" (unpublished PhD dissertation, McGill University, 1994), 75–76.
8 Qasim Amin, *Tahrir al-Mar'a* (Cairo: Dar al-Ma'arif, 1970 reprinted), 89–91.
9 All of his higher education was in the West (France) and he did not have formal traditional Islamic education. However, he did use Islamic language and sources in his book to argue his points. In his second book, *al-Mar'a al Jadida* (1900), he used more secular arguments. See Margot Badran, *Feminists, Islam and Nation: Gender and the Making of Modern Egypt* (Princeton, NJ: Princeton University Press, 2001), 18–19; Margot Badran, *Feminisim in Islam: Religious and Secular Convergences* (Oxford: Oneworld, 2009), 55–65.
10 As cited in Raccagni, "The Origins of Feminism", 84.
11 For further discussion on Qasim Amin, see Michelle Raccagni, "The Origins of Feminism", 101–4, 144–68. Leila Ahmed shows that Qasim Amin's approach to women is deeply problematic. Amin is secular and Western-educated, yet his book is intellectually muddled, and his view of women is patriarchal and dismissive. Ahmed argues that Amin's book represents the rearticulation in native voice of the colonial thesis of the inferiority of the native and Muslims and the superiority of the European; Leila Ahmed, *Women and Gender in Islam: Historical Roots of a Modern Debate* (New Haven, CT: Yale University Press, 1992), 144–69. For a different reading of Amin see Raccagni, "The Origins of Feminism".
12 Raccagni, "The Origins of Feminism", 94–100.
13 The works by Badran given above are a good reference for this entire section, although her focus is on Egypt.
14 Ahmed points out that the "male establishment" of the colonial powers, while they were appropriating the language of feminism to criticise colonised peoples for their backwardness, were simultaneously opposing the claims of feminism at home and arguing for the Victorian social model: the inferiority of women and the naturalness of female domesticity; Ahmed, *Women and Gender*, 150–51.
15 Some of these were deeply problematic and caused great disruption in society; see John Walbridge, *God and Logic in Islam: The Caliphate of Reason* (Cambridge: Cambridge University Press, 2011), chapter 9.
16 See Badran, *Feminisim in Islam*.
17 See Badran, *Feminisim in Islam*.

18 Amina Wadud, *Inside the Gender Jihad* (Oxford: Oneworld, 2006), 79–80.

19 Wadud, *Inside the Gender Jihad*, 79–80.

20 Asma Barlas, "Globalizing Equality: Muslim Women, Theology, and Feminism", ed. Fereshteh Nouraie-Simone, *On Shifting Ground: Muslim Women in the Global Era* (New York: Feminist Press at the City University of New York, 2005), 107.

21 Cited in Jon M. Armajani, "Islamic Thought in the West: Sacred Texts, Islamic History, and Visions of Islam in a Transnational Age" (PhD dissertation, University of California, Santa Barbara, 1999), 103.

22 See for example, Asma Barlas, *"Believing Women" in Islam: Unreading Patriarchal Interpretations of the Qur'an* (Austin: University of Texas Press, 2002).

23 The terms "Islamic feminist" or "Muslim feminist" are perhaps appropriate, as these Muslim women use Islamic language, sources, and ideas to argue for feminist ideas that they consider to be in harmony with their religion/faith.

24 Barlas, *"Believing Women" in Islam*, 62, 200–203.

25 Amina Wadud, *Qur'an and Woman: Rereading the Sacred Text from a Woman's Perspective*, second edition (Oxford: Oxford University Press, 1999), 5–6.

26 Wadud, *Qur'an and Woman*.

27 Amina Wadud, "Towards a Qur'anic Hermeneutics of Social Justice: Race, Class and Gender", *Journal of Law and Religion*, 12, 1 (1995–96), 48.

28 Wadud, *Qur'an and Woman*, 5.

29 Wadud, *Qur'an and Woman*, 5.

30 Wadud, *Qur'an and Woman*, ix, 7.

31 Balas, *"Believing Women" in Islam*, 205.

32 Asma Barlas, "The Qur'an and Hermeneutics: Reading the Qur'an's Opposition to Patriarchy", *Journal of Qur'anic Studies*, 3, 2 (2001), 15–38: 23

33 A. Yusuf Ali, *The Holy Qur'an* (1975), 1116–17.

34 Wadud, *Qur'an and Woman*, 1.

35 Barlas, *"Believing Women" in Islam*, 15–16, 206–207.

36 Barlas, *"Believing Women" in Islam*, 22–23.

37 Wadud, *Qur'an and Woman*, 5.

38 Hidayatullah, "Women Trustees of Allah: Methods, Limits, and Possibilities of 'Feminist Theology in Islam" (PhD dissertation, University of California, Santa Barbara, 2009), 167.

39 Barlas, *"Believing Women" in Islam*, 16–17.

40 Barlas, *"Believing Women" in Islam*, 50–51.

41 Barlas, *"Believing Women" in Islam*, 168–69.

42 Barlas, *"Believing Women" in Islam*, 8.

43 "I make this qualification since we can only know the nature of God's Being (divine ontology) from how God describes God (the nature of divine self-disclosure)." Barlas, "The Qur'an and Hermeneutics", 21.

44 Barlas, "The Qur'an and Hermeneutics", 21.

45 Azizah al-Hibri, "Divine Justice and the Human Order: An Islamic Perspective", in ed. William Schweiker, Michael A. Johnson, and Kevin Jung, *Humanity before God: Contemporary Faces of Jewish, Christian, and Islamic Ethics* (Minneapolis: Fortress Press, 2006), 238.

46 Amina Wadud, "Qur'an, Gender and Interpretive Possibilities", *HAWWA*, 2 (2004), 331.

47 Wadud, *Qur'an and Woman*, xii, cited in Hidayatullah, "Women Trustees of Allah", 171.

Part II
Key ideas and principles of contextualist interpretation

5 Revelation and contextualisation

Revelation

In order to maintain the transcendence of the divine in traditional Islamic accounts of revelation, Muslim orthodoxy has insisted on the wholly-otherness of the Qur'an when describing the mode of revelation. Thus, Muslims believe that over a period of 22 years, the Prophet received the literal utterances of God, and he experienced these both aurally and visually. Muslim tradition maintains that they were all conveyed to him through the Angel Gabriel, who in turn had received them from the heavenly "Preserved Tablet" (*al-lawh al-mahfūz*). Based on this, the Qur'an is understood to be unfettered by human sounds and letters: it is the exact copy of the "Mother of the Book", which is the archetypal source of revelation. Crucial to this concept is the insistence that the Prophet's role in this process of revelation is confined to relaying these divine words as they were received over more than two decades. As such, he played no role whatsoever in guiding the content or form of the revelation.

Although the majority of Muslim scholars have subscribed to this view, there were a few who – although accepting that the Qur'an corresponds exactly to what God intended to convey to humanity – contended that the Prophet's role in this process may not be likened to that of a mere recipient. Ibn Sina (d. 428/1037) understands prophesy to be an office that the Prophet acquired through his intellectual agency. Other scholars like the famous theologian Ghazali (d. 505/1111) do not go as far, but nonetheless use Ibn Sina's model to explain this revelatory process, arguably in somewhat naturalistic terms. In the modern period, a range of scholars have begun to put forward new ideas that emphasise that the Prophet was much more than just a passive recipient of the revelation. The ideas of some of these scholars are discussed below.

Fazlur Rahman is among the key thinkers of today who argue that the Prophet was not merely a passive recipient of the Qur'an. To him, although Muhammad did not consciously seek out prophethood, he was nevertheless prepared for such a task. Rahman argues that the Prophet, having been an orphan himself, had an acute sensitivity for moral problems from his earliest age, well before the revelation.[1] Rahman maintains that the ultimate source of the Qur'an is God; but he upholds that the character of the Qur'an is both divine and human. As a result, even though Rahman is content to maintain an externality of revelation insofar as its source is concerned, he is steadfast in maintaining that it is internal to the Prophet insofar as its process is concerned. Rahman laments: "Orthodoxy … lacked the intellectual capacity to say both that the Qur'an is entirely the Word of God and in an ordinary sense, also the word of Muhammad."[2] In other words, Rahman believes that the revelation was received from the outside source as mental words that had become intertwined with his heart:

> The words heard were mental and not acoustic, since the Spirit and the Voice were internal to him, and there is no doubt that whereas on the one hand, the Revelation emanated from God, on the other, it was also intimately connected with his deeper personality.[3]

Rahman asserts that Muslim theologians and commentators have misunderstood a number of key terms associated with revelation. In particular, the agent of revelation is not, in his view, an angel as is traditionally understood; rather, it is the Spirit. He argues that although angels (*malā'ika*) are mentioned in the Qur'an, they are not referred to as agents of revelation. Rahman argues that the Qur'an provides ample evidence that the "Revelation and its agent were spiritual and internal to the Prophet".[4] Rahman further posits: "Perhaps the Spirit is a power or a faculty or an agency which develops in the Prophet's heart and which comes into actual revelatory operation when needed, but it originally does 'descend' from 'above'."[5] Furthermore, for Rahman, the heart of the Prophet represents an intermediate realm in which the entire Qur'an is stored. The Prophet's role is to release the Spirit (mental words and visions) clothed in acoustic words (the Arabic language) during the circumstances to which they apply. Although the Prophet may be using his own words, these are hardly his, as they are in conformity with the Spirit (the mental words and images received from above). By making a close connection between the revelation and the Prophet, Rahman provides a strong basis for linking the Qur'an to its immediate context and the person of the Prophet.

Abdolkarim Soroush's theory of revelation[6] is central to his attempts to open new horizons in religious thought in general and specifically in Qur'anic interpretation. Like Rahman, Soroush believes that the Qur'an has an undeniable human aspect, even while its source is ultimately divine. Contemporary Muslims, according to Soroush, need to recognise this human aspect of the revelation: without it they will find it difficult to separate the immutable aspects of religion from those that are mutable. For Soroush, many aspects of religion are not essential, and are therefore mutable. As these aspects are historically and culturally specific, he refers to them as *accidentals*. His thesis argues for rethinking the traditional notion of revelation by accepting a humanistic view of the Qur'an as revealed through the mind of the Prophet, on the grounds that only then can a Muslim be in a position to determine which aspects of the revelation are relevant to their life in the present day.

Central to Soroush's argument is the idea that the Prophet played an active role in the production of the Qur'an. Like Rahman, Soroush makes a case that the process of revelation is internal. He likens it to poetic inspiration, although he acknowledges that the prophetic experience excels, by far, that of the poets or the mystics. When the Prophet receives the revelation, what he actually experiences is only the mental content:

> This content, however, cannot be offered to the people as such, because it is beyond their understanding and even beyond words. It is formless and the activity of the person of the Prophet is to form the formless, so as to make it accessible. Like a poet again, the Prophet transmits the inspiration in the language he knows, the styles he masters and the images and knowledge he possesses.[7]

Thus, for him through the mind of the Prophet, revelation is adapted to its environment; it is also shaped in no insignificant measure by the Prophet's personal history, his life's tribulations and his state of mind during the years of his mission. Given that the Prophet had to function in a historical time, place, and context, many instructions, guidance, and commandments provided in the Qur'an were directly connected to that context.

Soroush suggests that the process of adaptation to the environment is therefore central to any theory of revelation. For him, any responsible hermeneutics or interpretation of the Qur'an has to take full consideration of history, culture, and context of the Hijazi society. The fact that the Qur'an is filled with the issues that the Arabs of the seventh century were grappling with, and rarely discusses events that were happening outside this region constitutes, in his eyes, evidence that "the verses [of the Qur'an] are in keeping with the Arab environment of the time".[8]

Mohammed Arkoun also maintains that revelation was enmeshed within the social, political, and cultural structures of the Meccan and Medinan tribal societies of the seventh century. He highlights that Qur'anic discourse adopts "a paradigmatic semiotic structure to issues peculiar to the Hijazi society" of the period.[9] Therefore, however divine, absolute, and transcendent revelation may be, it also "confirms the role of the social–historical impact in the shaping of a message".[10] Arkoun insists on a contextual as well as a humanistic approach to Qur'anic hermeneutics: "There is no way to find the absolute outside the social, political condition of human beings and the mediation of language."[11]

Abu Zayd is of the view that revelation took place for the purpose of achieving one thing: to engender change in the reality. His argument, however, is that for that to occur, revelation had to embody that reality. In other words, like Soroush, Abu Zayd believes that revelation had to adapt itself to that reality. As revelation is essentially a dialogue, it is required to be commensurate with the cultural, intellectual, and linguistic horizons of its first recipients. Unless this historical context and the elements of this discourse (that is, the historicity of the text) are taken into consideration (*ma'na*), the significance (*maghza*) of the Qur'an and its relevance for us today would be somewhat hidden. He writes:

> Given that humans constitute the ultimate recipients of this revelation, it would be inconceivable to imagine that it would address them except through their particular linguistic system and their cultural framework ... This Revelation is certainly from heaven but it is destined to this world, and thus it does not behove it to be at variance with the laws of reality and all what that entails, such as adapting itself to the structures of this reality, including the cultural ones in particular.[12]

The theories of revelation espoused by Rahman, Soroush, Arkoun, and Abu Zayd are met with suspicion from the textualist scholars, as they go against the traditionally accepted theory of revelation, wherein the Prophet had no role whatsoever in the revelation. In the face of much of contemporary thinking about language, mind, and psychology, perhaps it will be difficult to sustain the traditional theory in the way it is usually presented. Nevertheless, a move to something akin to what these thinkers are proposing would be considered by traditionalist scholars to be heretical. Given this difficult position for many thinkers and scholars who are arguing for a contextualist approach while remaining firmly within the fold of mainstream Muslim theological tradition, there is a need to develop an understanding of revelation that takes into account key aspects of the traditional theory and some of the insights of contemporary scholars like Rahman. In the following I will attempt to provide one way of thinking about revelation that takes context into account seriously.

Levels of revelation

The mainstream Muslim view has been that the Prophet was a passive receiver of revelation, and that this revelation operated at a meta-historical level receiving no direct influence from the immediate context. For this view, the total otherness and externality of revelation – as far as the Prophet is concerned – has to be maintained, with revelation as eternal and independent of any macro context. However, a contextualist approach finds some aspects of this conception of revelation too narrow: it marginalises the organic link between the revelation and its context. Taking into consideration this traditional view, as well as some of the contemporary thinking on the matter, the following approach sets out a broader understanding of the concept of Qur'anic revelation that takes into account both the role of the Prophet Muhammad and the socio-historical context in which he lived.

Here, revelation can be understood as occurring at four different levels. The first level is referred to in the Qur'an as that of *al-ghayb* (the Unseen). In this regard, Muslim theology holds that God revealed the Qur'an first to the Preserved Tablet and then to the Heavens. From there, the Spirit (understood to be the angel of revelation) brought the revelation to the Prophet. Before revelation reached the Prophet it existed at the level of the Unseen, which is beyond human understanding or comprehension. Whatever "code" or "language" was used for the revelation at this level is inaccessible to us as human beings and there is little that can be gained by speculating about the mode or the code.

At the second level, revelation reached the Prophet, and it was revealed to his "heart", as stated in the Qur'an. He then uttered it in an Arabic form for the first time in a human context. His utterance of the revelation in Arabic should also be attributed to the Spirit (*rūh*) and ultimately to God. It is God who enabled the Prophet to express what was revealed to his heart in whatever form it was, if any, in the Prophet's own language, thus making the Arabic Qur'an a "miracle", something the contemporaries of the Prophet found to be beyond their reach in terms of its literary quality. Whether the Qur'an was created, as the Mu'tazilis argued, or not, as their opponents thought, the critical issue is that the Qur'an exists for us, human beings, in a *human* language, addressing our *human* concerns in a form we can relate to and that enables us to connect with the Qur'an. This perhaps should be a sufficient justification for us continuously to relate it to our changing life and its contexts. Hence, the need for interpretation to play an important mediating role.

At the time of the Prophet's utterance of revelation in Arabic it begins to function in history. It was spoken by the Prophet to a community who were subject to various social and historical conditions. God's Word was thus revealed to the heart of the Prophet and then made directly relevant to what was happening in the immediate context. Thus, it addressed initially the concerns, norms, values, customs, and institutions of a specific society. More importantly, it was also communicated using a human language, namely, Arabic.

At the third level, the revelation became a part of the daily lives of Muslims. That is, it was memorised or written down and acted upon. In this way it became a vital, living part of a living community. This "performance" and incorporation of revelation into social life can be termed the *actualisation* of the revelation.

Although changes or additions to the Qur'anic text ended after the death of the Prophet, a fourth level occurred that involved two further dimensions of revelation. Firstly, communities of Muslims continued to add to and elaborate on what the revelation meant. Each subsequent community sought to incorporate what they considered to be the meaning of the Qur'an into their lives. As the activity of interpretation continues, many interpretive communities have emerged among Muslims, and they each carry an element of revelatory authority. When considered together, these interpretive communities can contribute to a better understanding of the Qur'an. Secondly, from a Qur'anic point of view, God continues to provide guidance to those who are conscious of Him and who seek to implement His Word in their lives. Although this latter dimension is not linguistic, it is nonetheless informed by an ongoing interaction with the linguistic forms of revelation that appear in the Qur'an and have been elaborated on by earlier generations of Muslims.

This means that revelation in an indirect sense (in the sense of indirect inspiration), rather than in a linguistic sense, is ongoing through the work of

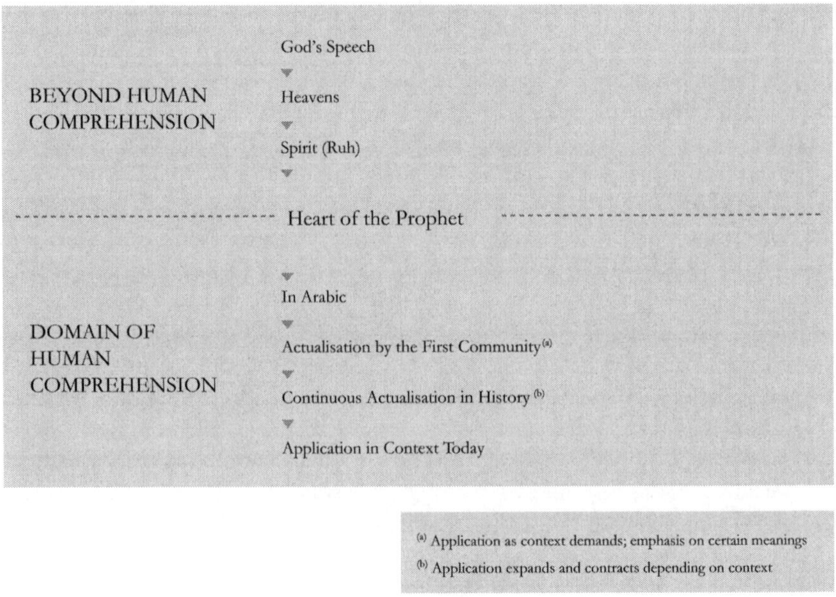

Figure 5.1 Revelation

the ulama (scholars). The accumulated understandings of the Qur'an over time continue to shed light on the text of the Qur'an that was revealed to Prophet Muhammad in the early seventh century. With changes to contexts, new understandings and meanings emerge and are added to the body of accumulated understandings. As these are adopted by the Muslim community (*umma*) they all carry a degree of authority. Thus, a large part of the new interpretations of the Qur'an that are emerging among Muslims today, and continuously being adopted by the *umma*, may be seen as part of the evolving authoritative tradition of Qur'anic interpretation and an indirect expansion of the original revelation.

Macro context of the revelation

The Qur'an makes frequent references to the pre-Islamic beliefs, practices, norms, and customs of the people of Mecca and Medina (Hijaz). The context of the Qur'an also covers aspects of the Prophet's life, and the social, political, and economic conditions of Mecca and Medina. These towns had their own social structures, hierarchies, taboos, and cultures. The region of Hijaz is in a sense a reflection of the cultures that existed in Arabia and surrounding regions. These ranged from Mediterranean (including Jewish and Christian) to southern Arabic, Ethiopian, and Egyptian, all of which, to varying degrees, influenced Hijaz and its people. As a consequence, at the time of the Qur'an the socio-cultural life of the world of Hijaz was diverse. Understanding this fact will help today's interpreter of the Qur'an to make connections between the Qur'anic text and the environment that gave rise to it.

The Qur'an makes many references to various physical characteristics of the geographical environment of Hijaz, the attitudes and responses of the people to the Prophet's message, as well as to the events, institutions, norms, and values of the people in Hijaz and the wider context of seventh-century Arabia. The culture of Hijaz informed the worldview of the first generation of Muslims, and the language of the Qur'an is connected to this specific context. Based on this, several scholars have emphasised the intricate connection between the Qur'an and the context in which it was revealed. Sachedina, for example, identifies tribal culture as a key element of this context:

> The Qur'an did not mark a total departure from tribal culture, whose extremely chauvinistic moral code was at the center of male-dominated tribal dealings … When introducing reforms in Arabian society, the Prophet was aware of the general tribal trends that determined the practical approach to the power structures prevalent in tribal culture.[13]

Sachedina argues that the Prophet's primary mission was not to eradicate all that had come before, but to teach new ideas about God based on the most fundamental principle of *tawhīd* (oneness of God).

Contextualisation

Having established that the initial revelation involved God's Word intertwined with its immediate context, we can begin to consider the implications of this for the contextualist interpreter of the Qur'an, and in doing so outline the process of contextualisation. Broadly speaking, contextualisation involves two essential tasks: it first seeks to identify the basic message (or messages) that emerge from the Qur'anic text from the process of interpretation, and then, to apply that message (or messages) to other subsequent contexts. What the message is determined is based on an understanding of how the Qur'anic text was understood and applied in its original context. The message is then translated to the present context, while keeping an eye on the relevance of the message: both to the original and the new contexts. A clear understanding of this relevance is essential for contextualisation, as there are values and assumptions that exist in modern societies that were not important 1400 years ago when the Qur'an was revealed and when the Prophet undertook his mission in early seventh-century Mecca and Medina.

This process of "translating" the message to the present requires extensive knowledge of both the original and current macro contexts. This knowledge is, in part, about the dominant institutions, values, norms, discourses, ideas, practices, and frameworks that exist in relation to the specific issue at hand. Awareness of these macro contexts allows the interpreter to cultivate an understanding of the similarities and differences that exist between the context

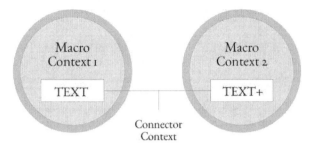

Figure 5.2 Text and context

of the early seventh century and their own context in the twenty-first century. A contextualist reading of a Qur'anic text moves back and forth between these contexts throughout the process of interpretation. An understanding of the context of the Qur'anic revelation in the early seventh century, as well as an awareness of how the context of the early twenty-first century has changed, allows a more appropriate and meaningful interpretation of Qur'anic texts.

Notably, the Qur'an originally functioned in a society whose values it sought to change. For example, some of the discriminatory practices that existed in relation to women in the early seventh century CE, which the Qur'an sought to change, are no longer part of contemporary society, where – at least in general – men and women are considered to deserve equal opportunities, including equal access to resources, education, wellbeing, health, material support, income generation, employment, and power. Teachings of the Qur'an that sought these changes in the seventh century therefore will be applied somewhat differently in this new context, but with the same objective: to make society more equitable.

Limitations of reconstruction of the context

One of the key tasks of the contextualist interpreter is to engage with the history and tradition of a text to reconstruct the context in which the Qur'anic text was revealed. As noted above, this includes an awareness of the dominant values of the time. Given that the interpreter of the Qur'an today has significant chronological distance from the original revelation, there will always be difficulties and problems in this reconstruction. Indeed, the modern interpreter may not be entirely successful in reconstructing the world of the early seventh century in which the Qur'an was revealed. A complete picture of the world then – with all its complexities, its key players, institutions, values, norms, and intellectual and cultural frameworks – does not exist anymore, and may not even be possible to recapture. The Qur'anic interpreter therefore has only limited access to that world, and only a mediated one through other texts, and therefore should not claim that any reconstruction is complete, sacrosanct, or final. Despite all of these limitations, and however inadequate this reconstruction is, from a contextualist perspective it remains an important part of the process of interpretation. Reconstruction therefore needs to be an ongoing project. As more information is gathered about the world in which the Qur'anic text was revealed, the reconstruction will become more accurate. The interpreter of today relies on the existing level of knowledge about that world and does not claim to have a perfect or complete picture of it.

Analysis of the macro context of the modern period

A key part of a contextualist interpretation is an analysis of the macro context of the modern period, with a focus on the specific issue the Qur'anic text is dealing with. This analysis may include relevant political, economic, social, cultural, and intellectual contexts. Perhaps one of the most dominant aspects of the macro context of the modern period is an emphasis on the importance of reason, *ijtihād*, and the avoidance of blind imitation.

Contemporary scholars such as Muhammad Abduh – and those influenced by him – have re-emphasised the role of reason in interpretation of the Qur'an. Indeed, Abduh's hermeneutical approach has been described as a "rational and modern hermeneutics".[14] Abduh emphasises the important role of reason alongside revelation in obtaining human understanding and *hidāya* (guidance).[15] For him, the relationship between reason and revelation is clear: both are important sources, and they should complement each other.[16] Abduh argues that rationality is not antithetical to the Qur'an and Islam; in fact, rationality holds the key to understanding. For Abduh, this distinguishes the Qur'an from other scriptures, as he maintains that the Qur'an is the only sacred text that reasons in a "rigorously deductive and demonstrative way".[17] In his *Risālat al-Tawhīd*, Abduh writes:

> The Book gives us all that God permits us, or is essential for us, to know about His attributes. But it does not require our acceptance of its contents simply on the grounds of its own statement of them. On the contrary, it offers arguments and evidence. It addressed itself to the opposing schools and carried its attacks with spirited substantiation. It spoke to the rational mind and alerted the intelligence. It set out the order of the universe, the principles and certitudes within it.[18]

Abduh's most influential student, Rida, also highlights the role of reason in Islam. For Rida, faith itself is based on this fundamental human ability.[19] According to Campanini, Rida's rationalist and activist attitude is expressed on many levels,[20] including in his "strong critique of the principle of authority and of so-called servile and blind imitation (*taqlīd*)",[21] and his assertion that "Islam is a religion without mystery, particularly with regard to God".[22]

Other scholars who have argued for a similar focus on reason include Muhammad Asad, whose approach to interpreting Qur'anic miracles, such as the healing miracles attributed to Jesus,[23] can be understood in a similar way. For example, he approaches the healing of a blind man and the leper as a metaphorical description of an inner regeneration occurring among people who were spiritually diseased and blind to the truth.[24] Asad does not reject the Qur'anic miracles as such, but explains them rationally to – as Chande suggests – "free them from their mythic context".[25] For Asad, the Qur'an contains legendary accounts[26] that have been used to serve as a medium to express certain eternal truths in the form of parables.[27]

With this emphasis on reason, to some extent, the contextualist interpreter analyses the relevant issues, norms, values, and institutions associated with the issue that the particular Qur'anic text is addressing. This analysis is then compared with that of the macro context of the early seventh century with determine how the Qur'anic message the text is conveying can be translated into the context of the twenty-first century.

Despite the manifest relevance of the macro context for a balanced under-standing of the Qur'an, many Muslims view such an approach to interpreting the Qur'an with suspicion. In general, these Muslims believe that the dominant interpretations of the Qur'anic texts, as received in the tradition, are applicable at all times and in all places and circumstances, regardless of the differences in the subsequent new contexts. From this point of view, the change of context is considered largely irrelevant. In fact, for many Muslims any discussion of the socio-historical context of revelation, especially one that may result in a sig-nificant revision of pre-modern views on issues such as gender and law, is seen as a threat to the religion as well as a threat to the authority of the Qur'an.

However, the Qur'an's articulations on a particular subject may exist in a form that is not easily comprehensible or perhaps applicable today. The Qur'an both mirrored what was relevant and sought to improve the social, political, and cultural practices of the time of its revelation and beyond. Only with such an understanding is it possible to ensure that these Qur'anic texts are relevant for contemporary Muslims. Qur'anic references to slavery, for instance, can be put into this category: an appropriate approach would be to interpret the verses that discuss slavery in the light of prevailing conditions and to examine their underlying objective such as improving the lot of slaves and creating a fairer society.

Although some evidence of a contextualist approach to Qur'anic interpretation exists in contemporary Muslim thinking, the full interpretive significance of this approach for the wide range of issues in the Qur'an that have ethico-legal importance is only now beginning to be extensively explored.

Concluding remarks

What this chapter shows is the close connection between a contextually relevant theory of revelation and contextualisation. While the dominant theory of revela-tion in the Islamic tradition strongly affirms the total "otherness" of the Qur'anic revelation, in the modern period, a number of Muslim thinkers and scholars are attempting to rethink that theory and to put forward some new ideas for that. I do not believe that speculation about the mode of revelation and the code, if any, in which this revelation originally existed before it reached the "heart" of the

Prophet will be particularly helpful. I strongly believe the emphasis should be on the Qur'an as it functioned in history, that is from the time of its utterance by the Prophet, in Arabic in the specific context of his society. Whatever the mode in which it was revealed to the Prophet's heart, he uttered it in a context. The author of the Qur'an is still God and it is God who revealed it to the heart of the Prophet. But it is the Prophet who communicated it to his listeners. Thus the Qur'an enters the realm of history and only then can we relate to that revelation. Contextualisation can build on such an understanding of revelation that is deeply connected to that context.

Notes

1 Fazlur Rahman, *Islam* (Chicago: University of Chicago Press, 1966), 31.
2 Rahman, *Islam*, 31.
3 Rahman, *Major Themes*, 100.
4 Rahman, *Major Themes*, 100.
5 Rahman, *Major Themes*, 97.
6 Abdolkarim Soroush, "The Expansion of Prophetic Experience", in *The Expansion of Prophetic Experience: Essays on Historicity, Contingency and Plurality in Religion* (Brill E-Books, 2013), DOI: 101163/ej.9789004171053.i-355.6.
7 Soroush, "The Expansion of Prophetic Experience"; Michel Hoebink in "Interview with Abdulkarim Soroush", www.drsoroush.com/English/Interviews/E-INT-The%20Word%20of%20Mohammad.html.
8 Interview available online at: www.drsoroush.com/English/Interviews/E-INTIslam,%20Revelation%20and%20Prophethood.html.
9 Mohammed Arkoun, "The Notion of Revelation: From Ahl al-Kitab to the Societies of the Book", *Die Welt des Islams*, New Series, 28 (1988), 62–89: 71.
10 Arkoun, "The Notion of Revelation", 81.
11 Arkoun, "The Notion of Revelation", 81.
12 Nasr Hamid Abu Zayd, *Mafhum al-Nass: Dirasa fi 'Ulum al-Qur'an* (Cairo: al-Hay'a al-Misriyya al-'Amma lil-Kitab, 1990), 64.
13 Abdulaziz Sachedina, *Islam and the Challenge of Human Rights* (New York: Oxford University Press, 2009), 125–26.
14 Aliaa Ibrahim Dakroury, "Toward a Philosophical Approach of the Hermeneutics of the Qur'an", *The American Journal of Islamic Social Sciences*, 23, 1 (2006), 15–51: 22.
15 Dakroury, "Toward a Philosophical Approach", 24.
16 Dakroury, "Toward a Philosophical Approach", 24.
17 Massimo Campanini, *The Qur'an: Modern Muslim Interpretations*, trans. Caroline Higgitt (Abingdon and New York: Routledge, 2011), 14.
18 Muhammad Abduh, *Risalat al-Tawhid* (Cairo: Wuzarat al-Thaqafa wa al-Irshad al-Qawmi, 1960–69).
19 Campanini, *The Qur'an*, 14–15.
20 Campanini, *The Qur'an*, 15.
21 Campanini, *The Qur'an*, 15.
22 Campanini, *The Qur'an*, 15.
23 Qur'an 3:49 and Qur'an 5:110.
24 Abdin Chande, "Symbolism and Allegory in the Qur'an: Muhammad Asad's Modernist Translation", *Islam and Christian–Muslim Relations*, 15, 1 (2004), 79–89: 82.
25 Chande, "Symbolism", 82.
26 These can be traced back to pre-Islamic traditions: for instance, those relating to Solomon's wisdom and magic powers that were part of Judeo-Christian and Arabian lore.
27 Chande, "Symbolism", 82.

6 Hierarchical nature of Qur'anic values[1]

A contextualist interpretation of the Qur'an expects the interpreter to keep a close eye on the hierarchical nature of the values that they encounter in any Qur'anic text. A starting point for thinking about such a hierarchy of values could be the Qur'anic concept of "right action" (al-'amal al-sālih), as this is a concept that is repeatedly mentioned in the Qur'an and on which much of Qur'anic ethical and moral values are based. Although a wide range of Qur'anic values come under this broad concept, these values are not necessarily of the same level of importance. One of the most challenging issues in the contextualisation is determining the degree of importance that should be attached to a particular Qur'anic value or values that have been identified in the text under consideration. Failure to recognise the existence of a hierarchy in the values may lead to interpretations that conflict with the important universal values of the Qur'an. In this chapter, I am using the term "value" in a broader sense, not in the way the term is used commonly. While "value" is often understood to mean standards by which our culture defines what is good or bad, desirable or undesirable, beautiful or ugly, my use of the term here also covers beliefs as well. In a sense, value is about what a Muslim is expected to adopt, follow and put into practice or reject in terms of beliefs, ideas, and practices. To illustrate this, a tentative hierarchy of values is provided here, in descending order of importance. These are not definitive, but may be helpful in a contextualist reading of the Qur'anic text:

1 Obligatory values
2 Fundamental values
3 Protectional values
4 Implementational values
5 Instructional values

In developing this hierarchy of values, I take the following into consideration: the essential beliefs and practices of Islam such as the six pillars of faith including belief in the One God; the five pillars of Islam such as the five daily prayers; anything unambiguously permitted or prohibited in the Qur'an; and values on which there is unanimous agreement among Muslim scholars as far as their importance and applicability are concerned. In a sense, such values form the core of the religion and retain the characteristic of universality. However, many Qur'anic values need to be further examined to determine the degree of universality or particularity that can be associated with them. Below are some tentative comments about various categories of the hierarchy.

Obligatory values

The first level is obligatory values. Such basic values are emphasised throughout the Qur'an. They cover both the Meccan and Medinan periods, and do not seem to be context dependent. In line with this, Muslims of various backgrounds generally consider them to be an essential part of Islam. There are three possible subcategories of such values:

(a) Fundamental beliefs. Examples may include belief in God, the angels, the prophets, Holy Scripture, the Day of Judgement, accountability, and life after death. These are related to what are traditionally known in Islam as the six pillars of *imān* (belief).
(b) Fundamental devotional practices that are emphasised in the Qur'an, such as prayer (*salāt*), fasting (*siyām*), and pilgrimage (*hajj*). Muslim scholars generally consider this category to be '*ibādāt* (prescribed forms of ritual and worship). Since these practices are emphasised frequently, and are not context dependent, they can be taken as universally applicable.
(c) The clearly spelt out and unambiguous specifics of what is permissible (*halāl*) and what is prohibited (*harām*) in the Qur'an and supported in the actual practice of the Prophet. These are also considered to be universally applicable. Where the Qur'an uses the terms *uhilla* or *uhillat* (it has been made permissible) or *ahalla Allāh* (God made it permissible), or *ahalnā* (We made it permissible), this indicates that something is categorically made permissible or lawful. Similarly, the Qur'an uses terms such as *harrama* (God prohibited) and its derivatives to indicate clear prohibition.

In relation to the category of unambiguous *halāl* and *harām*, very few texts of this nature exist in the Qur'an. Although it would be reasonable to argue that such values are in principle universally applicable, this universality applies only to the basic permission or prohibition, rather than the many details associated with the command. Thus, there is often a substantial amount of room for interpreters to develop, expand on, and clarify what a command actually means. An example is *riba* (often translated as "interest" or "usury"). Although the prohibition of *riba* occurs in unambiguous terms, the universality applies to this basic prohibition. Such a universality does not apply to the definition of *riba* or the scope of prohibited transactions, for instance, as there have been significant differences of opinion on such matters. But there is unanimous agreement among Muslims on the prohibition of *riba*. There are a large number of transactions in Islamic law that have been identified by the scholars to be part of the prohibition of *riba* (based on interpretation) but such transactions may or may not come under the universal prohibition as such, as they are most likely dependent on context and interpretation. Thus this subcategory of values is not to be confused with the long lists of *halāl* and *harām* that can be found in standard Islamic legal texts: these are often based on interpretation of the relevant Qur'an and Sunna texts, or are arrived at on the basis of analogical reasoning (*qiyās*) or consensus (*ijmā'*) and may or may not have universal applicability.

Fundamental values

Fundamental values are those values that are emphasised repeatedly in the Qur'an and for which there is substantial textual evidence to indicate that they are among the foundations of Qur'anic teaching. One may not find a particular Qur'anic text saying that the value is "fundamental" or "universal" but the existence of a wide range of texts relevant to the value may indicate the degree of importance attached to the value and therefore its universality.

A survey of the Qur'an indicates that certain values are identified as basic "human" values. Examples may include protection of a person's life, family, or property. Many early scholars were aware of such values and their discussions on them can be found primarily in *maqāsid* (aims and objectives of shari'a) literature. Ghazali (d. 505/1111), for instance, discusses what he calls *al-kulliyyāt* (universals or "five universal values").[2] These universal values refer to protection of life, property, honour, progeny, and religion. For many scholars of *maqāsid*, these values constitute the key objectives of shari'a.[3]

These universal values were arrived at using a method of inductive corroboration by eminent jurists such as Ghazali and Izz b. Abd al-Salam (d. 660/1261), and were then taken up by later jurists and scholars. Although the number of universal values was limited to five by many earlier scholars, and even by Abu Ishaq al-Shatibi (d. 790/1388), in later times such as the contemporary period a number of new values could be developed by following the same method of inductive corroboration and keeping in mind the new context. For instance, a range of new human rights that are important today, such as the protection of the disadvantaged and protection of freedom of religion, can be considered to be universal values today. There are numerous individual verses in the Qur'an that, if inductive corroboration were used, might support the universality of these values.

Following this method, it is possible to arrive at values that protect a range of basic human rights that were not previously identified by the early scholars. This is an area that can be expanded and contracted, based on the needs of the community and the issues and concerns that emerge in a particular context or generation.

Protectional values

Protectional values are values that provide legislative support to the fundamental values. For instance, protection of property is a fundamental value; however, that value has no meaning unless put into practice. This practical application can be performed by means of prohibition, of theft for instance, and the corresponding enforcement. Whereas a fundamental value does not depend on just one textual proof for its existence, the protectional value often depends on only one textual proof. This does not reduce the importance given to it in the Qur'an, since the strength of the protectional value is largely derived from the fundamental value and the specific command relating to the protectional value itself. Since protectional values are essential to the maintenance of the fundamental values, universality can also be extended to the protectional value.

Implementational values

Implementational values are specific measures that are used to implement the protectional values in society. For instance, the protectional value of the prohibition of theft is to be implemented in a society by taking specific measures against those who do not refrain from engaging in such activity. The Qur'an says:

> As to the thief, male or female, cut off his or her hands, a punishment by way of example, from Allah, for their crime, and Allah is Exalted in power.[4]

When the Qur'an decreed measures such as amputation of the thief's hand, it appears to have taken the cultural context of the time into account. Since capital punishment and other forms of bodily punishment and/or communal disgrace were accepted as forms of punishment in seventh-century Arabia, measures that would be highly effective in that context were required.

The specific measure itself (for example, amputation of the thief's hand) does not appear to be a fundamental value or objective of the Qur'an, as the Qur'an almost always indicates in such commandments that the aim is about preventing a person from engaging in unacceptable behaviour: if one has already committed an offence, what is important is that one should repent and refrain from committing further offences. Evidence for this preventative approach can be found in the Qur'an. Immediately after specifying a preventative measure, the punishment, the Qur'an appears to suggest that repentance could lead to a waiving of the measure. The following examples help to clarify this point.

Having stated that the punishment for theft is the amputation of a hand (Q. 5:38), which is the implementational value, the Qur'an goes on to say: "But whoever repents after his iniquity and reforms [himself], then surely God will turn to him [mercifully]; surely God is Forgiving, Merciful."[5] According to Razi (d. 605/1209), repentance could waive punishment.[6] This also seems to have been the view of Shafi'i (d. 204/820)[7] and of Ahmad b. Hanbal (d. 241/855).[8] Ibn al-Qayyim (d. 751/1350) also offered a similar opinion in his well-known work, *I'lam*.[9]

Similarly, having stated that those who engage in *zina* (sexual relations outside marriage) must receive 100 lashes and that those who accuse chaste freewomen of unlawful sexual relations should be given 80 lashes, the Qur'an adds: "Except those who repent after this and act aright, for surely Allah is Forgiving, Merciful."[10]

In the same manner, having specified retaliation for murder, the Qur'an states:

> But if any remission is made to any one by his [aggrieved] brother, then prosecution should be made according to usage, and payment should be made to him in a good manner; this is an alleviation from your Lord and a mercy.[11]

This allows for remission and for following what is right: if the key objective was punishment, further options would not have been given. All of these instances indicate that the measure itself – whether amputation, flogging, or execution – was not the primary objective of the Qur'an in relation to these crimes. More important, from the point of view of the Qur'an, is prevention of the crime in the first place, and then repentance if a crime is committed. Punishment was still needed to deter those who may be inclined to engage in such activities.

Instructional values

Instructional values refer to specific instructions, suggestions, advice, and exhortations in the Qur'an in relation to particular issues, situations, circumstances, and contexts. The bulk of the Qur'anic values appear to be instructional. The texts that deal with these values use a variety of linguistic devices: the imperative (*amr*) or the prohibitive (*lā*); a simple statement indicating the right action intended; or a parable, story, or reference to a particular incident. The following are a few examples of such instructions: instruction to marry more than one woman in certain circumstances;[12] suggestion that men should take good care of wives;[13] instruction to be good to specified people and to be good to parents;[14] instruction not to take unbelievers as friends;[15] and instruction to greet one another.[16]

These instructional values present a degree of difficulty in the contextualisation project. They pose a number of not-so-easy questions to the interpreter: do such instructional values transcend cultural specificity and are they therefore to be followed regardless of time, place, or circumstances? Should a Muslim attempt to "recreate" the circumstances in which the value was given in the Qur'an, in order to put that value into practice in today's world? For instance, the Qur'an refers to slaves and instructs Muslims how to treat them.[17] Therefore, should a Muslim today insist on retaining the social structure in which slaves form an essential part of the Muslim society? More importantly, how should a Muslim at a particular time respond to these instructional values? In many instructional values, does the Qur'an take for granted a certain context against which they are provided?

Given the ambiguities associated with instructional values, they may need to be explored carefully to see if a particular value appears to be universally applicable or binding, and if so, to determine the extent to which this can occur. Through analysis, it is possible to gauge the universality, applicability, and obligatory nature of such instructional values. Three criteria seem to be relevant in this context: the frequency of the occurrence of the value in the Qur'an; its salience during the Prophet's mission; and its relevance to the context (culture, time, place, and circumstances) of the Prophet and the first community of Muslims.

a. Frequency of occurrence

The frequency of occurrence refers to how often an instructional value is mentioned in the Qur'an. This can be measured by identifying the frequency of related core terms. However, this is not a simple task, because a particular value for instance, a value as simple as "helping the poor", can be expressed differently in different contexts in the Qur'an. The interpreter therefore has to survey the Qur'an to identify the related terms or concepts in order to obtain a reasonably accurate estimate of the frequency of occurrence. Once key concepts and associated terms are identified, a frequency check can be undertaken to determine the extent of the occurrence of the value in the Qur'an. The higher the occurrence, the more importance should be given to the value. Naturally, this will still be an estimate, because it is almost impossible to identify all possible associated terms relating to most values.

b. Salience

The concept of salience refers to whether the value in question was emphasised throughout the Prophet's mission. A high salience indicates a high level of significance of the value in the Qur'an. For example, from the beginning of the Prophet's mission, a key value was "helping the disadvantaged". This was an important value in both the Meccan and Medinan periods. However, if a value is mentioned once or twice and then discarded, or if another value that opposes it is supported and promulgated, then the interpreter can assume the value has no particular importance in the overall framework of the Qur'an.

In studying the salience, it is important to use historical reports including hadith that appear to be reliable or stylistic or linguistic features of the text and their immediate linguistic context. This enables the interpreter to determine an approximate dating of the text. The aim is not to arrive at an exact date: rather, to identify chronologically if a value was used or emphasised during a particular period of the Prophet's mission. For instance, the Meccan and Medinan periods each can be divided into early, middle, and late. Based on work already done by Muslim and non-Muslim scholars on the dating of the text, it is then possible to classify the relevant texts into such periods, and to gain a sense of the duration and prominence that the value enjoyed at different times. The higher the salience, the more importance the Qur'an attaches to a value.

c. Relevance

Since the Prophet's mission was initially directed at the people of Mecca and Medina, there is an essential relationship between the mission and the macro context of Mecca, Medina, and the surrounding regions. Clearly the Prophet did not come to abolish all existing cultural precepts, values, and practices. It is therefore reasonable to assume that many of the Prophet's sayings and actions were relevant to the culture of the time. The use of relevance here does not mean that all Qur'anic values are culture-specific: it is a much broader concept, highlighting the relationship between the Prophet's mission and the society it was intended for. In this sense, there appear to be two types of relevance: relevance to a particular culture (which is bound by time and restricted to a particular place or circumstance) and universal relevance to any culture within the orbit of Islam that is regardless of time, place, or circumstance. The second type is of primary interest for identifying universal values.

Some general rules in relation to the instructional values can be derived from the above:

- The more frequently a value recurs in the Qur'an, the more likely it is to be universally applicable.
- The greater the coverage of the value, the more likely it is to be universal.
- The more general the relevance of the value, the more likely it is to be universal.
- If a value meets the three criteria at the extreme positive end of the continuum the value is equivalent to a universal value and its applicability is universal and thus binding.
- If the value meets the three criteria at the extreme negative end of the continuum, the value is a religiously non-universal value (context dependent), and its applicability will be contingent on circumstances.

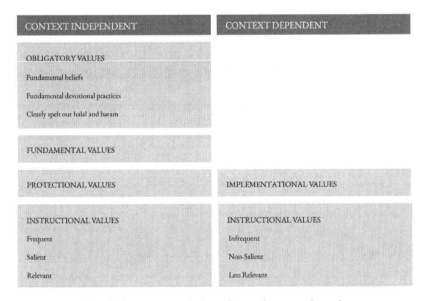

Figure 6.1 Hierarchy of values: Context independent and context dependent

Hierarchy of values in practice

Thinking about various Qur'anic instructions and advice in this manner assists with the project of interpretation. It also enables a degree of stability within the tradition, and allows for reinterpretation of the guidance of the Qur'an in circumstances where the changing context demands this. The core values, beliefs, practices, and institutions from the Qur'an (the fundamentals) retain their importance and continuity in contextualist interpretation. At the same time, this approach allows the interpreter to consider changes in emphasis, shifts in meaning, and – in some rare cases – dropping context-dependent values and practices from the frame of reference altogether.

Depending on the context, certain values that were not seen as particularly important in early Islam can acquire a high degree of importance. The acquired importance of a range of human rights today is an example of this. Some of these rights as understood today were not supported in the Islamic tradition. However, the discourse of human rights is now accommodated into the Muslim tradition in the way that many other religions are adopting them.

Some values and institutions may be dropped altogether because of the changed context. An example is the institution of slavery. Although this existed for centuries in Muslim societies, in the current context Muslims do not wish to maintain or support this institution.

The emphasis on certain values may change as contexts change. An example of this is the institution of marriage. The Qur'an dealt with this in great detail, and reflected, to a large extent, the way that the society of the time functioned, and the relative power of men and women in that society. In a number of Muslim societies, with the reforms in family law, the rules governing marriage are being reconsidered, giving women a stronger say and protection.

In the area of dissolution of marriage, the unilateral power of the husband to declare a divorce without any involvement of the community or the state, for example, is seen as a problem in today's changed context. Such a unilateral approach to divorce made sense in a society where women did not have much power, were dependent on men for economic and financial security, and played a lesser role in the public life of the society. In the present context this imbalance in power between men and women is being addressed with the aim of affording women and men an equal footing. Given this changed context, the powers enjoyed by men in institutions like marriage and divorce do not seem to be fair from a Qur'anic point of view: the Qur'anic sense of justice requires a more equal treatment of both.

Many Muslim scholars are putting forward new interpretations of Qur'anic guidance in such areas, in order to realise the Qur'anic emphasis on fairness, justice, and equity. At a collective level, this can be seen in the ongoing reforms in the area of family law that are occurring in many of the Muslim majority countries. These reforms tend towards curtailing the power of men and giving a stronger say to women. This is justified on the basis of the Qur'an and the overall practice of the Prophet. Similar efforts are being made in other areas also. One example is the reinterpretation of certain Qur'anic texts that have previously been seen to emphasise an antagonistic relationship between Muslims and people of other faiths.

In this ongoing effort, interpreters are guided by the fundamentals of the religion. However, they are also influenced by those values that Muslims and the broader community of human beings consider to be fair, good, and reasonable at a particular time and context; their interpretations are therefore open to changes that follow the changes to context.

Notes

1 This chapter is adapted from my earlier work, Abdullah Saeed, *Interpreting the Qur'an: Towards a Contemporary Approach* (Abingdon and New York: Routledge, 2006), 125–44.
2 Wael b. Hallaq, *A History of Islamic Legal Theories: An Introduction to Sunni Usul al-Fiqh* (Cambridge: Cambridge University Press, 1997), 166.
3 Hallaq, *A History*, 88ff.; Isma'il al-Hasani, *Nazariyyat al-Maqasid 'ind al-Imam Muhammad al-Tahir bin 'Ashur* (Virginia: IIIT, 1995), 46.
4 Qur'an 5:38.
5 Qur'an: 5:39.
6 al-Fakhr al-Razi, *Mafatih al-Ghayb: al-Tafsir al-Kabir*, tafsir of Q. 5:38, www.altafsir.com.
7 Shafi'i, *Kitab al-Umm*, VI, 124.
8 Ibn Qudama, *al-Mughni* (Riyadh: Maktabat al-Riyadh al-Haditha, 1981), X, 311.
9 Ibn al-Qayyim, *I'lam*, III, 15.
10 Qur'an 24:5.
11 Qur'an 2:178.
12 Qur'an 4:2–3.
13 Qur'an 4:34–35.
14 Qur'an 4:36.
15 Qur'an 4:89–90.
16 Qur'an 4:86.
17 See Qur'an 2:177; 4:36; 24:33; 90:12–17.

7 Parallel texts from the Qur'an and dealing with hadith

Parallel texts are those texts that are related to the key messages of a particular Qur'anic text to be interpreted, that exist elsewhere in the Qur'an or in the hadith. While the text being interpreted may appear to communicate a particular message in isolation, when taken together with other similar texts, the interpretation may indicate a significantly different message or messages. Thus a fundamental principle of the contextualist approach to Qur'anic interpretation is to examine not only the verse or verses, which are the direct object of our interpretation, but to consider all of the Qur'anic texts and hadith that are possibly related to these particular verses.

Parallel texts from the Qur'an

A contextualist interpreter looks at additional texts that are related to the text at hand. For instance, when interpreting Qur'an 4:34, the interpreter searches for texts on the theme of gender dynamics in the Qur'an, in order to identify the ideas or values the Qur'an seems to be supporting or providing in the area of gender relations. The intended meaning or meanings of the Qur'an are not always easy to identify in relation to this matter, because the Qur'an makes reference to men and women in a wide range of contexts and issues. Examples can be found, for instance, in the areas of marriage, divorce, inheritance, child support, and spiritual matters. Given the many texts that may exist on a particular topic, only one of those texts may not be used to determine "the Qur'an's view" on gender relations. Thus all available Qur'anic texts on an issue need to be examined and synthesised into a coherent and unified body of knowledge to see whether a dominant pattern of values emerges.

Qur'anic texts that make reference to how women or females in general were treated in society at the time of revelation are helpful for establishing an approach to gender relations. For instance, the Qur'an presents the practice of female infanticide as a gross injustice.[1] It proscribes the practice and condemns those who kill their female babies, regardless of the reason, whether it may be fear of poverty or shame. The Qur'an also criticises the man who is not happy when hearing the news that his wife has given birth to a female baby.[2] Texts that relate to divorce often urge fairness to the woman, and ask the husband to avoid burdening her with unjust demands.[3] This indicates an awareness that the woman was often at a disadvantage in divorce. The Qur'an also rejected the idea that females, especially daughters, should not inherit, and prescribed a share for them,[4] which was a rather radical reform given the nature of pre-Islamic practices related to women, in some cases involving the women themselves being inherited upon their husband's death. In relation to women, there are also a large number of texts in the Qur'an that emphasise equality and egalitarianism.

Qur'anic concerns about the treatment of women in a specific verse thus become evident through an examination of the entire Qur'an and the nature of the immediate revelatory context: social, cultural, economic, and political. These concerns were often related to the dominant values in the society of the time, which the Qur'an critiqued, rejected, mitigated, condoned, or reformed. It often did so by highlighting specific situations in which women were at a disadvantage in the context of seventh-century Hijaz. Although the Qur'an was not attempting to eradicate all unjust practices in a revolutionary manner in that specific society, it was nonetheless reforming and changing the condition of women by means of mitigation and with an apparent long term intention of complete obliteration of those unjust practices.

Related to this is the question of the relative religious and ethico-legal significance that can be attached to the various texts that deal with the issue of women and their roles in society. These texts include the Qur'an, hadith, and accounts of the views of early authorities.

A number of texts in the Qur'an have suggested that there is no difference between males and females as far as issues of belief, spirituality of the person, devotion, worship of God, and God-consciousness (*taqwa*) are concerned. Yet there are verses that seem to suggest that males and females are not necessarily equal in some other respects.

For instance, in the case of one specific type of commercial transaction, the Qur'an (2:282) asks Muslims to have witnesses. Instead of saying just two witnesses are required, it makes reference to males and females, by saying that there should be two male witnesses, or, if that is not possible, one man and two women. The Qur'an gives the reason for having two women, in place of one man, as being that if one woman forgets, the other can remind her.[5] Given the way that society functioned at the time, women in general were unlikely to play the role of witnesses in these types of commercial transaction, as such transactions are public and involve familiarity with business and the social etiquette associated with such activities. In the Qur'an's immediate revelational milieu, those who were usually involved in business were men. Given that the Qur'an was bringing women into this men's world, it probably needed to make some concessions, and was trying to avoid placing unnecessary burdens on women. Nevertheless, the Qur'an was recognising that despite the disadvantage women had in this regard, some women would still be able to play that role. The Qur'an was, if viewed from this perspective, placing confidence in and giving women in that society an opportunity to participate in this very public activity that was otherwise socially denied to them.

An obvious difference can also be identified in relation to inheritance. The Qur'an stated that in certain cases a male relative would receive twice the inheritance of a female relative of the deceased.[6] This is obviously a point of inequality. However, the interpreter of this passage should be mindful of the fact that in that society men often undertook responsibility for the economic and financial wellbeing of the family and for society in general.

When looking at different Qur'anic texts in relation to, for example, the issue of equality of men and women, the interpreter has to decide which Qur'anic texts should be given priority over others: those that do not differentiate between males and females, or those that do. The literature on the interpretation of Qur'an 4:34, for example, shows that most commentators in the past prioritised the texts that, if taken at their face value, seem to discriminate against women. In order to present a reasonably faithful interpretation of the text, however, it is important to recognise that there are different texts in relation to women, and that one text should not be discounted in favour of another. Rather, the question is which texts should be given priority. When a contextualist approach is not adopted, the answer to that question will depend on the dominant values within which the interpreter is functioning, as well as the interpretive approach to be adopted. For example, if the interpreter is functioning in an environment in which the value of equality is strongly emphasised, there would be a natural tendency on the part of the interpreter to prioritise verses that emphasise equality. This could be justified by saying that the verses that do not make that distinction between males and females seem to be more universal. In the pre-modern commentaries on the Qur'an, commentators as a whole gave priority to verses that made a distinction between males and females, and, to varying extents, marginalised the verses that did not discriminate.

Hadith as parallel texts

A particularly difficult problem arises when non-Qur'anic texts are used in interpretation, particularly the hadith texts. Unlike the Qur'an, there is no certainty, even from a Muslim perspective, about the authenticity of a large amount of hadith material to which interpreters have access. Muslim scholars of hadith have debated the issue of authenticity for centuries, and even among those hadith that are considered reliable, their degree of reliability varies. For instance, a hadith that has purportedly come from the Prophet and was transmitted by one or two people is arguably less reliable than a hadith that has been transmitted by a large number of people, as complicity of a large number of people in a lie or an error is less likely. These latter, more reliable hadith are called *mutawātir* hadith. However, even these *mutawātir* hadith are not considered as sharing the same level of reliability as that of the Qur'anic text.

In relation to the example we have been exploring above, there is a much larger body of textual material in the hadith than in the Qur'an. A large number of hadith can be read in what today would be considered to be a discriminatory fashion, and arguably much more support for interpretations that are discriminatory to women can be found in the hadith than in the Qur'an. For example, some hadith seem to reduce the role of a woman or wife to the level of a servant, and there are some hadith that seem to suggest that even spiritually, women have a certain degree of disadvantage.[7] There are, on the other hand, many other hadith that go against those that are discriminatory. Thus, there is a high level of contradictory hadith attributed to the Prophet on the issue. Qur'anic commentators in the past, who were more inclined to support the discriminatory view, used those hadith that portray women in an unfavourable light in their commentaries to bolster the view that women were, and should be, subjected to men's authority. In the modern period, a large number of scholars have marginalised such hadith in their own interpretations.

Dealing with hadith

A key concern for the earliest Muslims was following the normative behaviour of the Prophet and the ethico–religious norms, collectively known as the Sunna. After the passing away of the first two to three generations of Muslims, however, the Sunna came to be gradually equated with the reports known as hadith that purportedly documented this original practice of the Prophet. Many Muslims assume, when interpreting the Qur'an, that if a hadith exists on any issue that the Qur'an directly or indirectly addresses, in the absence of evidence to the contrary, they must follow the teaching contained in the hadith. Furthermore, many believe that any interpretation that does not take such a hadith at face value must be labelled as illegitimate or inauthentic. However, given the many issues surrounding the methods of validating the authenticity of hadith, any interpreter should be cautious when it comes to accepting the vast array of hadith that are available to address ethico-legal issues. The extent of fabrication of hadith in the first two centuries of Islam – as acknowledged by Muslim scholarship itself – and the associated methodological problems, mean that an uncritical reliance on hadith when interpreting the Qur'an is problematic.

Concept of Sunna

Sunna was a well-known concept prior to the coming of Islam, and was understood as a normative action or behavioural system set by an individual worthy of a tribe's emulation.[8] With the coming of Islam, the concept of Sunna was logically transplanted and applied to the Prophet Muhammad as bearer of the revelation himself by those who acknowledged and submitted to his religious authority.[9] Over a period of approximately two decades (610–32 CE), the Muslim community had many opportunities to internalise and absorb the spirit, ethos, and character of the Prophet, which was based upon the Qur'anic norms and worldview.[10] This early understanding of the concept of the Prophet's Sunna has thus been described as the "generally agreed [upon] core of experience which constituted the community's knowledge of what it meant to live as a Muslim".[11]

This early concept of Sunna underwent a major transformation when, in the late second and early third century of Islam, the hadith movement emerged. Associated with this movement are hadith specialists (*muhaddithūn*) who collected hadith and were developing criteria to determine the authenticity of hadith, as well as some jurists who were relying heavily on hadith in developing Islamic law (*fiqh*). The concept of Sunna, as defined by the hadith specialists, is comprised of numerous narratives that document Prophet Muhammad's deeds (*fi'l*), utterances (*qawl*), and approval (*taqrīr*). According to the hadith specialists, these are embodied in various hadith collections, which are considered authentic according to the standards and criteria applied by the discipline of hadith criticism (*ulūm al-hadith*).[12]

Fabrication of hadith

It took some time – over two centuries, in fact – before the hadith were collected in the form of the canonical collections that exist today.[13] The Prophet's Companions did not collect hadith in a systematic fashion. They had access to the text of the Qur'an, with which they were familiar, and they had intimate knowledge of the persona of Muhammad, which ensured that they knew what type of practices, behaviour and values were or were not in harmony with the concept of Sunna. They seem to have been more interested in acting in the spirit of the overall practice of the Prophet, that is, the Sunna as conceptualised prior to its redefinition by the hadith specialists. The Companions' understanding of the concept of Sunna as independent of any written documentation or form of "authentic" hadith, in fact, prevailed, by and large, during the first century of Islam.[14]

During the second and third centuries of Islam, in particular, there were major debates among Muslims about how they should define and understand the Sunna. Some scholars argued that the Sunna should be determined through the standard practices that Muslims had followed, generation after generation, from the time of the Prophet in places like Medina where the Prophet lived for the last ten years of his life.[15] Other scholars argued that if a hadith was attributed to the Prophet, its narrators could be traced and be found reliable, and its chain of transmission appeared authentic, then it should form part of the Sunna.[16]

According to the mainstream Sunni account, numerous hadith indicate that the Prophet actually prohibited his Companions from writing down hadith.[17] The Prophet's rationale might have been that the Qur'an was the very word of God and Islam's primary authority, and there was to be no confusion between God's revelation and the Prophet's own words. Thus, if Muslims had to write down anything it should be the Qur'an. He warned that Muslims could go astray by confusing the word of God with other texts. However, later scholars understood this prohibition to be of a temporary nature on the basis of other hadith explicitly permitting hadith to be written down. Similarly, during the time of the Companions, a senior Companion, Umar, the second caliph, prohibited Muslims from writing down and making collections of hadith, citing the reasons discussed above. Umar was also concerned about those Companions who narrated hadith from the Prophet.[18] On a number of occasions he threatened Abu Hurayra, for example, with punishment if he failed to stop narrating a large number of hadith without being careful about this.[19] Umar's reasoning was that if people were unscrupulously – or otherwise – narrating from the Prophet without being very careful in establishing that these words were indeed coming from the mouth of the Prophet, the situation would have major negative socio-religious and political consequences for the Muslim community. Umar recognised that although what the Prophet said and did was very important, caution was essential when deciding whether or not to accept such reports from certain Muslims. In some cases he would ask for supporting evidence or a witness to verify the report before accepting an account.[20]

Despite cautions from prominent Companions such as Umar, hadith were, eventually, fabricated on a very large scale. Indeed, a range of political forces that had been generated by early Muslim conflicts led to massive numbers of these fabrications.[21] These conflicts included the assassination of the third caliph Uthman and the emergence of competing political groupings: supporters of Ali against those of Mu'awiya; or followers of the Prophet's wife A'isha against Ali. Equally important is the conflict that emerged when Mu'awiya decided to nominate his son Yazid (d. 64/683) as the caliph, opposed by figures like al-Husayn b. Ali (d. 61/680) and Abd Allah b. al-Zubayr (d. 73/692) and their followers. The Muslim community thus was heavily divided: supporters of each faction justifying their claims, at times, based on fabricated sayings attributed to the Prophet praising their faction at the expense of their opponents. Fabrication was not limited to various political factions but extended to some of those who were keen to participate in the hotly debated theological issues of the first and second centuries of Islam as well as those who wanted to develop new forms of religious piety or to enhance existing ones. Given that there was no collection of hadith then – similar to the collection of the Qur'an – it was easy to fabricate and circulate this material.

These political, theological, and sectarian conflicts, which saw the rampant fabrication of hadith, occurred in the first and second centuries of Islam, not too far from the death of the Prophet, before the reasonably sophisticated methodologies that hadith scholars came to develop, during the second and third centuries of Islam, in order to verify chains of transmission.[22]

The demand for hadith was also driven by socio-religious and legal motivations. The early Muslim community had expanded at an incredible pace as a result of military conquests, incorporating into itself people from various religions, cultures, and customs with many who converted to Islam, who had no living memory of the Prophet. Some newly converted Muslims felt the desire to know better the legacy of the Prophet, in part through the collection of hadith. There was also a need to develop a legal apparatus and a body of law that was based on the teachings of the Qur'an and the Sunna. The hadith played a major part in this.[23]

The hadith movement

The hadith movement, known as *ahl al-hadīth*, began to emerge in the second century of Islam. Gradually, the movement came to emphasise the idea that the primary way to understand the Sunna of the Prophet was through hadith. Opposed to them were those who had a sceptical attitude towards the bulk of the hadith material in circulation and collected by the hadith specialists. For the opponents, Sunna had to be understood through the agreed-upon practice of the community going back to the earliest Muslims and the Prophet, for instance, the practice of the people of Medina; the bulk of the hadith material, for them, was not necessarily in line with such practice. However, from the point of view of the hadith movement, hadith, after being considered reliable according to their chain of transmission, should be accepted as part of the Sunna, even if the hadith contradicted what was considered the generally accepted practice of the community.

In the period just before the hadith movement came to prominence, the great jurist, Abu Hanifa (d. 150/767), for example, had his own ideas about what he accepted in terms of authoritative hadith texts as representing Sunna and what he did not.[24] Abu Hanifa's view was that the Qur'an and the generally accepted or agreed-upon practices of the Prophet (in other words, the Sunna) should be relied upon as primary texts, as opposed to the many individual reports that were emerging as hadith which may or may not be supported by the Sunna, and were being collected by hadith collectors.

However, when the hadith movement and hadith acquired an important place particularly in Islamic legal thought, the concept of Sunna also started to change. The Sunna gradually changed from being understood as the generally accepted *practice* of the Prophet as was followed by the earliest Muslim community at large to that of being synonymous with the concept of an authentic (*sahīh*) hadith as defined by the hadith scholars.[25] Even hadith that were obscure, unfamiliar, and sometimes even contrary to both reason and the Qur'anic teachings became equated with Sunna. The argument for equating Sunna with hadith was advanced by people like Shafi'i who argued that all hadith that were deemed authentic based on the criteria developed by hadith scholars must be accepted as normative Sunna, a radical change in the concept of Sunna. The hadith movement's rise and dominance after the demise of the rationalist Mu'tazili movement, in the early Abbasid period provided a strong base for the hadith movement's ideas about what constituted Sunna to become the norm. Sunna then became equivalent to hadith, despite the difficulties associated with the issue of authenticity of the bulk of hadith material circulating then.

General criteria for using hadith in contextualist interpretation

Hadith scholars in the first three centuries of Islam did their best to bring together and collect a large number of hadith, and their efforts should be respected and their collections given due recognition. Bukhari (d. 265/870), whose collection of hadith is considered by Sunni Muslims to be the most reliable, himself is said to have collected approximately 600,000 of the hadith that were circulating at the time, and for each hadith he knew the chain of transmission and the contents of the text. He is reported to have memorised most of them, and after extensive study, critique, and analysis, he selected approximately 3,000–4,000 hadith, some of which are repeated. In his collection, he even put together the repetitions: approximately 7,000 hadith in total.[26] However, despite the achievements of the past, and of figures like Bukhari, there is no guarantee that certain hadith in such collections including that of Bukhari truthfully *reflect* the early concept of Sunna prevalent among the first two or three generations of Muslims.

Therefore, in dealing with the massive amount of hadith material in the contextualist interpretation, systematic methodological criteria are required to be put in place in the light of which the hadith material is to be employed. In the following I will summarise some criteria that can be applied to hadith when using them in a contextualist interpretation of a Qur'anic text.

First, the Qur'an is the foundation of the religion of Islam and hadith can potentially bring additional contextual information about some verses of the Qur'an. Therefore, by and large, hadith should be interpreted in the light of the Qur'an or have a contextualising function.[27] This means hadith must be in accordance with or elucidate some contextually dependent parts of the Qur'an because whatever the Prophet did or said was considered to be in accordance with the Qur'an.[28]

Second, the concepts of Sunna and hadith need to be distinguished. The Sunna (as normative practice of the Prophet) is not large in quantity but it is *the* authoritative source. Fazlur Rahman explains:

> The overall picture of Prophetic biography – if we look behind the colouring supplied by the Medieval legal mass – has tendency to suggest the impression of the Prophet as a pan-legist neatly regulating the fine details of human life from administration to those of ritual purity. The evidence, in fact, strongly suggests that the Prophet was primarily a moral reformer of mankind and that, apart from occasional decisions, which had the character of ad hoc cases; he seldom resorted to general legislation as a means of furthering the Islamic cause.[29]

Given this nature of the concept of Sunna, hadith, much like in the case of the Qur'an, can potentially give us an insight into both the context and content of Sunna of the Prophet *and* probably a large part of the early practice of the Muslim community as well.[30] Much of the hadith material that exists, therefore, should be interpreted in the light of what we know about the actual Sunna (practice) of the Prophet. Hadith that are considered authentic by the hadith scholars may need to be further subjected to critical review if there is a conflict between the actual Sunna and hadith.

Third, hadith should not be interpreted individually but in the light of the other hadith available on an issue by bringing together all such hadith.[31] A single hadith in isolation may not provide the total picture of the issue.[32] The context of a particular hadith should also be explored to determine what the hadith means. Both the text of the hadith and its context should be kept in mind.[33]

Fourth, hadith must be in accordance with collective reason and human nature (*fitra*).[34] Those hadith that go against these two need to be subjected to critique and if shown as contrary to them will be rejected. Thus, a hadith that is abhorrent to the understanding and religious taste of the believers and pious scholars is to be rejected.[35] Similarly, a rare practice which is not in accordance with the customary practice of the Prophet and Muslims may not be accepted.[36]

Fifth, hadith running counter to "conclusive and definite evidence" of the Qur'an and actual Sunna is not to be accepted.[37] Thus hadith which contradict the Qur'an in any manner cannot be accepted as genuine.[38]

Hadith that are solitary (known as *āhād*) may need to be interpreted in line with broad-based values such as justice, fairness, and equity as well as what is generally known to be the standard practice of the Prophet. While acknowledging that such values are often abstract, one also realises that in the context one is living there are certain dominant understandings associated with these values and therefore our sense of being fair, just, and equitable should be an important consideration in interpreting such hadith.

Notes

1 Qur'an 81:8–8.
2 Qur'an 16:58.
3 Qur'an 2:229.
4 Qur'an 4:11,176.
5 Qur'an 2:282.
6 Qur'an 4:11.
7 An example of such a hadith is as follows: Narrated Ibn 'Abbas: The Prophet said: "I was shown the Hell-fire and that the majority of its dwellers were women who were ungrateful." It was asked, "Do they disbelieve in Allah?" (or are they ungrateful to Allah?) He replied, "They are ungrateful to their husbands and are ungrateful for the favors and the good (charitable deeds) done to them. If you have always been good (benevolent) to one of them and then she sees something in you (not of her liking)", she will say, "I have never received any good from you." *Sahih Bukhari*, Volume 1, Book 2, Number 28.
8 Wael b. Hallaq, *The Origins and Evolution of Islamic Law* (Cambridge: Cambridge University Press, 2005), 32–33; cf. Fazlur Rahman, *Islamic Methodology in History* (Islamabad: Islamic Research Institute, 1965), 2–4.
9 The phrase "Sunnah of the Prophet" seems to have emerged immediately after his death. See Hallaq, *The Origins and Evolution of Islamic Law*, 47; cf. M. M. Bravmann, *The Spiritual Background of Early Islam-Studies in Ancient Arab Concepts* (Leiden: E. J. Brill, 1972) 133, 168–74.
10 Adis Duderija, "Evolution in the Concept of Sunnah During the First Four Generations of Muslims in Relation to the Development of the Concept of an Authentic Hadith as Based on Recent Western Scholarship", *Arab Law Quarterly*, 26 (2012), 393–437: 411–12.
11 G. H. A. Juynboll. *Muslim Tradition: Studies in Chronology, Provenance and Authorship of Early Hadith* (Cambridge: Cambridge University Press, 1983), 9.

12 H. A. R. Gibb and J. H. Krambers, *The Concise Encyclopaedia of Islam* (Leiden: Brill, 2001), 552–54.
13 Adis Duderija, "The Evolution in the Canonical Sunni Hadith Body of Literature and the Concept of an Authentic Hadith During the Formative Period of Islamic Thought as Based on Recent Western Scholarship", *Arab Law Quarterly*, 23, 4 (2009), 1–27.
14 Duderija, "Evolution in the Concept of Sunnah", 393–437.
15 Daniel Brown, *Rethinking Tradition in Modern Islamic Thought* (Cambridge: Cambridge University Press, 1996).
16 Adis Duderija, *Constructing a Religiously Ideal "Believer" and "Woman" in Islam: Neo-Traditional Salafi and Progressive Muslims' Methods of Interpretation* (New York: Palgrave, 2011), see especially chapters 3 and 6.
17 Michael Cook, "The Opponents of the Writing of Tradition in Early Islam", *Arabica* (1997), 437–530. See also the hadith: It was narrated from Abu Sa'id al-Khudri that the Messenger of Allah (peace and blessings of Allah be upon him) said: "Do not write anything from me; whoever has written anything from me other than the Qur'an, let him erase it and narrate from me, for there is nothing wrong with that" (narrated by Muslim, *Sahih* "al-Zuhd wa al-Raqa'iq", 5326); "Do not write (what you hear) from me, and whoever has written something (he heard) from me, he should erase it. Narrate to others (what you hear) from me; and whoever deliberately attributes a lie to me, he should prepare his seat in the Fire" (Muslim, *Sahih*).
18 Brown, *Rethinking Tradition*, 96.
19 Brown, *Rethinking Tradition*, 86
20 Brown, *Rethinking Tradition*, 10–11.
21 Ignaz Goldziher, *Muslim Studies*, volume II, trans. C. R. Barber and S. M. Stern (London: Allen and Unwin, 1971); see also Tarif Khalidi, *Arabic Historical Thought in the Classical Period* (Cambridge: Cambridge University Press, 1994), 19.
22 Duderija, "Evolution in the Concept of Sunnah", 393–437.
23 See Duderija, *Constructing a Religiously Ideal*, 28.
24 Brown, *Rethinking Tradition*, 117.
25 Duderija, "Evolution in the Concept of Sunnah", 393–437.
26 Ibn al-Salah, *Muqaddimat Ibn al-Salah*, ed. A'isha bint Abd al-Rahman (Cairo: Dar al-Ma'arifa, 1990).
27 See Qur'an 42:17, 57:25, 5:48
28 Amin Ahsan Islahi, *Fundamentals of Hadith Interpretation* (Lahore: Al Mawrid, 2013), 35–37.
29 Fazlur Rahman, "The Living Sunnah and al-Sunnah wa'l Jama'ah" in *Hadith and Sunnah: Ideals and Realities – Selected Essays*, ed. P. K. Koya (Kuala Lumpur: Islamic Book Trust, 1996), 136.
30 Rahman, *Islamic Methodology in History*, 6, 10.
31 Islahi, *Fundamentals of Hadith Interpretation*, 37.
32 Islahi, *Fundamentals of Hadith Interpretation*, 39.
33 Islahi, *Fundamentals of Hadith Interpretation*, 39.
34 Islahi, *Fundamentals of Hadith Interpretation*, 42.
35 Islahi, *Fundamentals of Hadith Interpretation*, 44–56.
36 Islahi, *Fundamentals of Hadith Interpretation*, 44–56.
37 Islahi, *Fundamentals of Hadith Interpretation*, 44–56.
38 Islahi, *Fundamentals of Hadith Interpretation*, 44–56.

8   Meaning in a contextualist framework

The starting point for exploring the idea of meaning is an understanding that the Qur'an is a communicative act that has a particular purpose. Muslims consider the Qur'an to be God's speech (*kalām*). The Qur'an was intended, in the first instance, for a particular audience: Mecca and Medina in the seventh century CE. The communicative act of the Qur'an therefore remains deeply connected to the specific context in which it first occurred, and the relationships between its speaker (God) and the first recipients (the Prophet Muhammad and his immediate followers). Although the Qur'anic message has been actualised and re-actualised throughout the post-prophetic generations, those new contexts also remain connected to the first context of revelation. Considering the Qur'an as a communicative act helps interpreters to conceptualise a set of ideas about meaning that are appropriate to a contextualist reading. This does not require any new theory of meaning. Rather, this approach builds on a range of theories of meaning that exist in Islamic tradition and contemporary thought. When used together, these assist with the project of determining what a contextualist reading of the Qur'an entails.

Early debates on the Qur'an as speech of God

The Qur'an as the created speech of God

Islamic tradition began to debate very early on the nature of God's speech and whether the Qur'an as speech of God is temporal and deeply connected to humanity and a human language. Among the most well known is the Mu'tazili position according to which the Qur'an is the created speech of God. This current of thought flourished in Iraq in the third century of Islam, although its creative influences continued at least into the ninth century AH.[1] The Mu'tazilis (along with other groups such as Kharijis, most of the Zaydis, and many of the Murji'a and Shi'a) believed that the Qur'an as Word of God was created (*makhlūq*).[2] The Mu'tazilis saw themselves as the true defenders of the Islamic principle of monotheism (*tawhīd*), which led them to argue that the Qur'an was created at a specific time. For them, the Qur'an as an object or a thing cannot be eternal. Believing in the eternity of the Qur'an would lead to idolatry.[3]

For the Mu'tazilis, the Qur'an was the created speech of God, and was a divine act. They distinguished between God's attributes of essence and attributes of action.[4] They understood the former to be integral to God's essence such as life, power, knowledge, and will. These are attributes without which God would not be God. The latter, the attributes of action, encompass those attributes that God may or may not activate, such as creation. The Mu'tazilis believed that divine acts could manifest themselves in the historical world of reality, as opposed to attributes of God's divine essence, which cannot. God's speech belonged to this latter category of attributes because it did not make sense to think of his commandments as existing before the creation of those to whom they were addressed.[5]

Since the Mu'tazilis identified the Qur'an as the speech of God, with speech as a divine act (*fi'l*), for them the Qur'an is a historical phenomenon (*zāhira tārīkhiya*) and a concrete manifestation of God's speech in the human world.[6] Thus the Qur'an itself, although it is the word of God, remains temporal and not eternal. Notably, it was created initially in the "preserved tablet" (Qur'an 85:22) and subsequently recreated in "the hearts of those who memorize it, on the tongues of those who recite it and on the written page".[7] This emphasis on the creation of the Qur'an in a human language has been used in the modern period by a range of scholars to argue for more flexibility in the interpretation of the Qur'an.

Clarity of meaning of the Qur'an

Islamic tradition from the fourth century of Islam gradually rejected Mu'tazili emphasis on the "createdness" of the Qur'an. However, the tradition is rich in debates on the nature of language, whether it is created or not, meaning and how one arrives at meaning, as well as whether language is clear or ambiguous. Thus, in the pre-modern period, a large number of theologians, jurists, and linguists provided a variety of ideas about language and meaning. In the following we will make brief reference to some.

For example, the jurist and theologian Ibn Hazm (d. 456/1064) believed that human beings were able intuitively to understand the meaning of God's speech. He formed the view that rational human beings would be able to understand God's speech naturally.[8] He also argued that revelation as a whole was clear, but that its parts were sometimes ambiguous. For him, revelation consisted of the Qur'an, Sunna, and solitary hadith. These could be used to complement each other in order to reduce ambiguity.[9]

For the Mu'tazili theologian Abd al-Jabbar (d. 415/1025), revelation as a whole was clear, although individual texts could have a combination of unambiguous meaning (*nass*) and apparent meaning (*zāhir*).[10] He argued, therefore, that some expressions required clarification and interpretation through works of *tafsīr*.[11] Abd al-Jabbar saw revelation as a clear indication of God's will, and he asserted that rational inquiry was often needed to determine the meaning of revealed speech. It was on the basis of existing rational and revealed evidence that God's will could be deduced.[12]

Other pre-modern Muslim scholars emphasised a degree of ambiguity in the language and, therefore, in the revelation. Many jurists relied on some form of ambiguity in the language to justify the necessity of interpretation of Qur'anic texts, particularly those of an ethico-legal nature. The ambiguous nature of language necessitated the development of methodological tools by the jurists as part of the principles of jurisprudence (*usūl al-fiqh*). These were used to clarify meaning and maximise the legal value of individual Qur'anic texts. Such tools included, for example, the particularisation of general texts and vice versa, as well as the broadening or limiting of the meaning and application of particular texts by relying on other Qur'anic texts, hadith texts, linguistic analysis, or application of jurisprudential tools. In the juristic debates, jurists often relied on the idea that there was enough ambiguity in the language of the Qur'an and Sunna texts to warrant interpretation. The results of their interpretations were seen as part of the divinely authoritative system of laws even as they continued to adapt those laws to changing social contexts.[13] This pragmatic paradigm came to dominate the discourse among legal theorists and theologians from the fifth/eleventh century and remains dominant to the present day.[14]

Ambiguity of the Qur'anic text was a concern even for the earliest scholars who wrote on principles of jurisprudence. For instance, Shafi'i (d. 204/820), who is considered one of the first jurists to write on principles of jurisprudence and interpretation, devoted a large part of his work to dealing with the question of ambiguity and dealt with that through his theory of *bayān* (explication, interpretation). Like Shafi'i, most scholars of principles of jurisprudence devoted a considerable part of their principles to identifying ways of removing varying degrees of ambiguity from the language of the revelation in their projects of interpretation. Baqillani (d. 403/1013), a prominent Maliki jurist and theologian, believed that even everyday Arabic language could be ambiguous. He devised a way of classifying language in which meaning was conveyed with varying degrees of clarity. He argued that the Qur'an was often ambiguous, and that its meaning can be reached by referring to other texts including non-Qur'anic texts such as hadith.[15] A large part of the concerns of principles of jurisprudence in fact deal with questions of ambiguity, clarity, meaning, and interpretation.

Despite the wide range of theories, ideas, and works on language, meaning, and interpretation in pre-modern Islamic scholarship, the contextualist nature of the Qur'an was not sufficiently recognised at a theoretical level for interpretive purposes at that time. Some recognition was given to the use of contextual information, such as the occasion of revelation texts (*asbāb al-nuzūl*) for certain Qur'anic texts and also the adoption of the concept of the abrogation (*naskh*) of one text or ruling by a subsequent text or ruling. There were also some debates in *usūl al-fiqh* as to whether Islamic law should recognise local custom (*'ādat*) and customary practices; or whether laws should be changed if the customary practices on which the laws are based are changed; and the extent to which *'ādat* is a source of law. However, the approach that a number of scholars today refer to as "contextualist" goes well beyond the limited interest in pre-modern Islamic scholarship. Contextualist interpretation is therefore a rather modern concern though rooted in the tradition.

Meaning in a contextualist interpretive framework

The following are a set of ideas for thinking about meaning in a contextualist interpretive framework. Although many theories of meaning exist, it is beyond the scope of this chapter to outline these theories, given that this is not directly relevant to the discussion. However, it is useful to note that although each theory of meaning may shed light on one or more aspects of meaning, there is unlikely to be a single theory able to function as perfect or complete.

A key focus of a contextualist interpreter is to attempt to relate the meaning of a particular Qur'anic text as it was understood by its first recipients in the early seventh century in Mecca and Medina to emerging contexts within subsequent periods. These new contexts may be political, social, religious, cultural, legal, or economic. Interpreters who adopt this approach aim continuously to renew the original message of the text in relation to newly emerging situations, times, places, and circumstances.

The Qur'an has itself asserted that it was communicated to humanity in the Arabic language as a form of guidance (*hudan li al-nās*). According to the Qur'an, God always communicates to his prophets in their own languages, making it possible for human beings to comprehend and follow the will of God as expressed in their language. So, while maintaining a strong belief in the divine dimension of the Qur'an as God's Word, it is also possible to relate to the this-worldly dimension of the Qur'an. The contextualist interpreter attempts to bridge the gap – even if in a very limited sense – between the divine and mundane, by emphasising that it is possible to understand the text, its meaning, its intention, and what it is communicating, because it has been revealed in a particular language and a specific context.

Human beings cannot comprehend the nature of the divine language, how God communicates, or the mode God uses to communicate, as these all exist in the realm of what the Qur'an refers to as Unseen (*ghayb*), which humans cannot access. Muslims simply accept that the Qur'an has divine origins and that Prophet Muhammad is a recipient of Divine Revelation (*wahy*). The contextualist does not aim to understand thoroughly how God communicates, but instead focuses on the revelation at a historical level. Interpretation therefore begins with the premise that the revelation, meaning, message, and purpose of the Qur'an can be understood simply because the text exists in this world. Language – in terms of signs, symbols, grammatical structures, usage, and functions in society – conveys and constrains meaning. Thus, the interpreter places a high degree of emphasis on the analysis of the language of the text in terms of its morphological, syntactic, stylistic, semantic, and pragmatic aspects.

The contextualist interpreter also acknowledges that the Qur'an is a communicative act that represents the will of God. This act elicited a response that was in harmony with the context of the first recipients (macro context 1).

Any understanding of this message therefore requires a deep awareness of the context in which the message was communicated. This includes an awareness of the way things were: the political institutions that existed, the prevailing ethical and moral values, the issue of power (who had it and who did not, and why this was the case), the prevailing financial and economic conditions, the dominant intellectual currents, and how the people there saw themselves in relation to others around them. This is the sum total of physical, ethical, moral, intellectual, and psychological conditions in which the divine message was communicated.

Historical contexts can never be reproduced or repeated as they were in the first instance. The contextualist understands this limitation, but attempts (using the available data) to arrive at an approximation of the original context as closely as possible and reconstruct the historical context as much as possible. The purpose of the reconstruction is to obtain a better understanding of the purpose and the underlying reasons of the messages that were communicated at the time and place. The interpreter, having reconstructed the original context, even in an approximate fashion, in which the message was communicated, then seeks to identify whether the entirety of the message that was communicated can be understood in that original context.

The interpreter responds to the linguistic text as a message that was understood in a specific way that was appropriate to its original context. This is based on the idea that the recipients of that message (listeners) must have understood, from the message, certain things that they thought were appropriate to them at the time. The overall context in which the recipient relates psychologically, intellectually, and materially to various aspects of the text is not something that the recipient thinks consciously about. Although this is not necessarily a rational decision, any message that is communicated is reduced by the recipient, such that only that which is relevant to the recipient at that particular point in time, situation, and circumstance is heard, understood, or internalised. The interpreter aims to become aware of these omissions and biases better to identify what appears to be the original intention of the message. The intentionality of the message is important in this regard. This intentionality assists the meaningfulness of the message in a significant way.

Meaning emerges out of certain relationships

Based on the above, meaning can be seen as emerging from the relationships between the speaker (God), the message (the text through which God's will is expressed), the recipient, and the context in which the message was given for the first time. The relationships between each of these contribute to the production of meaning, although in each instance the relative importance of the various elements in the production of meaning will vary. Although the role of the speaker is of great importance, the other elements have their place as well and cannot be excluded. The meaning is determined using a combination of all of these elements and their interplay.

The interpreter does not treat the Qur'anic text as if it functioned independent of any context. Such an approach would mean reducing it simply to a linguistic entity that can be understood through the analysis of its morphology, syntax, semantics, stylistics, and pragmatics. Instead, a contextualist meaning extends well beyond what a word or a phrase or a sentence denotes. Meaning is not outside the text or inside the head of the author or the recipient; it emerges out of a complex relationship. Any meaning that emerges out of the relationship between these four elements will change somewhat in subsequent periods and contexts.

There is, however, a degree of stability in the meanings that are historically attributed to the Qur'an, as these are the meanings that appear to have emerged in the first recipient community and transmitted through other texts, practices, and narratives. In particular, this historical meaning is documented in commentaries on the Qur'an, and it is this documentation that has provided a level of stability and continuity of meaning across generations, while allowing for certain shifts in meaning because of changes to contexts in successive generations of Muslims. However, some elements of the message that may not have been emphasised in the original context can become emphasised in a subsequent new context. Likewise, some elements may be de-emphasised as contexts change. Shifts in emphasis occur naturally, because, from a contextualist point of view, the context in which the recipient of the message functions is essential to understanding what the text communicates, and therefore when that context changes, meaning to some extent also changes.

For the contextualist interpreter, as a result of this ongoing emphasis and de-emphasis of certain aspects of the message, the message retains its relevance to its recipients, generation after generation. When understood in this way, meaning involves at least three levels: the first is the purely linguistic meaning, and the second is the linguistic meaning coupled with the emphasis and de-emphasis that existed in the historical context which could be described now as the linguistic meaning *in addition to* historical meaning. These two levels remain in the tradition, and are frequently studied, explored, and examined. The third level is the contextual meaning, which is the linguistic meaning *in addition to* the historical meaning *in addition to* the new emphasis and de-emphasis that are associated with the new context. This contextual meaning is an important part of how the Qur'anic text retains its relevance. This third level of meaning is the focus of this book.

Concluding remarks

Meaning is complex, and therefore a wide range of considerations must be taken into account in understanding the meaning of the Qur'an. Interpretation is not just a matter of understanding the linguistic meaning of the text, as provided for in standard dictionaries, or a literal reading of the text based on historical understandings. Meaning is something that is dynamic, insofar as it emerges in a relationship between the speaker (God), the text (what is said), the recipient (the Prophet and his community), and the context. Although interpreters can be guided by the text, an understanding of what appears to be intended by the message as expressed in the text itself, and an approximate sense of the recipient and the original context, the never-ending changes to context ensure that the meaning of the Qur'an will continue to remain somewhat fluid, despite the elements that provide a degree of stability throughout. The role of the contextualist is to engage with this fluid meaning to identify the values and guidance within God's Word that can continue to guide society through each changing context.

Notes

1 Massimo Campanini, "The Mu'tazila in Islamic History and Thought", *Religion Compass*, 6, 1 (2012), 41.
2 Muammer Esen, "Early Debates on 'The Word of God'" (Kalāmullah/Qur'an), *Journal of Islamic Research*, 2, 2 (2009), 34–45: 39, citing al-Ash'arī, Abul al-Hasan b. Ismāīl, *Maqālāt al-Islāmiyyīn wa Ikhtilāf al-Musallīn*, ed. Helmut Ritter (Istanbul, 1929), II582.
3 Michel Hoebink, "Thinking about Renewal in Islam: Towards a History of Islamic Ideas on Modernization and Secularization", *Arabica*, 46, 1 (1999), 29–62: 33, citing I. Goldziher, *Introduction to Islamic Theology & Law* (Princeton: Princeton University Press, 1981), 88ff.; John L. Esposito, *Islam: The Straight Path* (Oxford: Oxford University Press, 1988), 71.
4 Campanini, "The Mu'tazila in Islamic History and Thought", 44.
5 www.muslimphilosophy.com/ip/rep/H052.
6 M. Sukidi, "Nasr Hāmid Abū Zayd and the Quest for a Humanistic Hermeneutics of the Qur'ān", *Die Welt des Islams*, 49, 2 (2009), 181–211: 186.
7 www.muslimphilosophy.com/ip/rep/H052.
8 Abu Muhammad Ali Ibn Hazm, *al-Ihkam fi Usul al-Ahkam*, (Cairo: Matba'at al-Imam, n.d.) 1:4, 3:9. In the following discussion on meaning in pre-modern scholarship, I rely heavily on the excellent work of David R. Vishanoff in *The Formation of Islamic Hermeneutics: How Sunni Legal Theorists Imagined a Revealed Law* (New Haven, CT: American Oriental Society, 2011), and summarise the research presented in that work.
9 Vishanoff, *The Formation of Islamic Hermeneutics*, 100–101.
10 Abu al-Hassan b. Ahmad Abd al-Jabbar, *al-Mughni fi Abwab al-Tawhid wa al-Adl* (Cairo: Wuzarat al-Thaqafa wa al-Irshad al-Qawmi, 1960–69), cited in Vishanoff, *The Formation of Islamic Hermeneutics*, 123–24.
11 Vishanoff, *The Formation of Islamic Hermeneutics*, 123.
12 Vishanoff, *The Formation of Islamic Hermeneutics*, 142–43.
13 Vishanoff, *The Formation of Islamic Hermeneutics*.
14 Vishanoff, *The Formation of Islamic Hermeneutics*.
15 Abu Bakr Muhammad al-Baqillani, *al-Taqrib wa al-Irshad* (Beirut: Mu'assasat al-Risala, 1998), cited in Vishanoff, *The Formation of Islamic Hermeneutics*, 162–63.

9 "Fundamentals of the religion" and interpretation

One of the most sensitive issues raised by a contextualist approach, for many Muslims, is the question of how this approach might lead to changes in the legal or theological positions arrived at by pre-modern Muslim scholars. Such positions for many Muslims still are equivalent to "fundamentals" or "fundamental principles" (*asl*, pl. *usūl*) of Islam, and must remain unchanged. Often, arguments in favour of a contextualist approach are countered with assertions that a contextualist approach goes against such fundamentals and therefore is an unwarranted approach to the Qur'an. However, from a contextualist perspective, the approach is a principled approach that does not go against the fundamentals of the religion, and in fact, there are enough safeguards in the approach to avoid it being categorised as relativism.

How is the term "fundamentals" used?

Often in contemporary Muslim debates, this term "fundamentals" or *usūl* is used in an ambiguous manner; what it means often is unclear. More importantly, there is no widely agreed-upon understanding of what an *asl* is, as the concept is understood differently within various Islamic disciplines and Muslim interpretive communities. It can be translated as "source" or "foundation", and has a number of other meanings in Islamic legal theory, such as *dalīl* (specific or general textual evidence, or the general principle or foundation upon which analogy is constructed).[1] The term *asl* can also be used to refer to the primary sources (Qur'an and Sunna) and some secondary sources of Islamic law (consensus and analogy).[2] In Islamic theology, *asl* can entail anything from the belief in one God to the belief in life after death. At a very basic level, the six pillars of faith can be understood as *usūl*. These various uses of *asl* require clarification of this concept and how a contextualist approach deals with it.

Asl in a contextualist approach is about the immutables of the religion, that is, what is unchangeable. Such immutables are relatively few and remain the fundamentals of Islam that cannot be changed and are themselves not susceptible to reinterpretation. In a sense, maintenance of such immutables gives the approach a degree of stability whilst still allowing a high degree of fluidity in dealing with the mutables.

Using the framework of the hierarchy of values (see Chapter 6), the immu-tables (= fundamentals) of the religion can be summarised as follows: the obligatory, fundamental, and protectional values as well as the universal values that emerge from the instructional values. Such values appear to be universal and not bound by any specific "context". Muslim scholars throughout the last fourteen centuries have generally considered such values to be essential aspects of the religion. Even in the modern period, they remain sacrosanct, and most Muslim scholars do not argue for changing or reinterpreting these values. What the contextualist approach focuses on is the non-universal (non-fundamental and therefore mutable) teachings. Given the lack of clarity that exists in this area, some explanation is in order.

Among the obligatory values, examples include the six pillars of faith. What is immutable is the basic belief, say, in the one God, prophets, scriptures, and life after death. Whilst there is agreement among Muslim theologians on the very basic beliefs, there are disagreements on the details. Where Muslim theo-logians have disagreements, there is always further room to explore, interpret, and reinterpret contentious areas, and such areas can be considered part of the mutable. In the fundamental rituals and worship, such as prayer and fasting, the basic form of the ritual is immutable, and scholars are in unanimous agreement; where differences exist they should be subject to further interpretation.

Similarly, in the area of *halāl* (what is permissible) and *harām* (what is prohibited) and for which there exists clear, unambiguous textual evidence in the Qur'an (and supported by the Sunna), the immutable is the very *basic* permission or prohibition on which there is unanimous agreement among Muslims, not the details associated with each on which no such agreement exists. The latter should be considered mutable, subject to further interpretation and discussion. For example, if the Qur'an in very clear terms prohibited *riba* by saying "God has prohibited *riba*," then *riba* must remain prohibited. In this circumstance, any interpretation of the relevant text in the Qur'an should not espouse a view that contradicts this prohibition in order to make *riba* permissible. The *asl*, in this sense, is the immutability of the prohibition of *riba*. However, this *asl* remains a general-ity, and many specifics associated with it have to be discovered in order to understand exactly what is specifically prohibited. Interpretation is the only way to discover these details and is obtained by asking key questions such as: what is the nature of the prohibited *riba*? Does *riba* cover interest on consumption loans? What kind of transactions come under the label *riba*? How do we know if we encounter a *riba*-based transaction? What are the criteria to determine what *riba* is? These and many other similar questions are of significant interest to a contextualist understanding of *riba*.

Moreover, in the area of protectional values, the Qur'an prohibits theft (*sariqa*). The prohibition of theft is an *asl*, but it once again operates at a general level. Specifics, such as the legal definition of theft and associated issues, have to be worked out through interpretation. This type of interpretation was central to the legal works of Muslim jurists, and their interpretations, whilst retaining the fundamental principle – that theft is prohibited – led to a range of differing views on the specifics. A contextualist approach will be useful in dealing with such specifics that are appropriate for the contemporary period, and some of the results arrived at by early jurists may need to be rethought as new forms of theft emerge and new ways of tackling theft are developed today.

In the case of instructional values, an example is in the area of family law, where the basic marriage-related laws are seen as *asl* and therefore immutable. For instance, the Qur'an has clearly and specifically stated that a Muslim must not marry one's sister, brother, father, or mother. Such a clear commandment should be followed as an *asl*, and a valid contextualist interpretation should not go against this. Nevertheless, there are many more details about marriage on which no such unanimous agreement exists and which therefore can be subject to further interpretation. For instance, how important is it for a woman to have a male guardian (*waliy*) who gives his approval for the marriage to go ahead, or should the husband have the right unilaterally to bring the marriage to an end, that is, divorce? These are questions on which no universal agreement exists, and based on the realities of today and context, new interpretations can be developed by adopting a contextualist approach.

Any suggestion that early jurists have completed, for all time, all necessary interpretation of texts (such as those that prohibit *riba*, theft, or relate to the issues of marriage or gender relations), and that Muslims of today therefore have no authority to subject these early interpretations to further scrutiny, is untenable. Neither the Qur'an nor the Sunna suggests that Muslims are not permitted to explore, debate, or discuss the nature and purpose behind the fundamentals and the wide range of specific issues associated with such fundamentals, as the juristic works on these areas clearly demonstrate that Muslims never had a problem with such exploration and interpretation. The Qur'an and the Sunna are the most important sources of authority in Islam and must take precedence over any other authority, including the consensus of scholars of any generation on a legal or theological issue on which there is no clear and unambiguous commandment. Anyone who has come after the Prophet, however great that person may be, at least in the Sunni context, must still be considered a fallible individual whose opinions are not binding for all subsequent generations of Muslims.

In Islamic theological and legal literature, there are certain issues on which there seems to be "consensus" among scholars but without the necessary backing from clear and unambiguous Qur'anic texts or the actual practice of the Prophet. One example is the death penalty for blasphemy (*sabb allāh* or *sabb al-rasūl*). There is unanimity among jurists that, in an Islamic jurisdiction, if a person uses foul language concerning the Prophet (*sabb al-rasūl*), that person must be killed. However, there is no clear Qur'anic basis for this unanimous view and the Qur'anic position on this issue is not necessarily supportive of such a view. Many texts of the Qur'an provide details of how obscene language was used against the Prophet by his opponents. He was accused of being a poet, a liar, and a madman. Yet nowhere in the Qur'an is any temporal punishment – let alone death – stipulated for that behaviour. Rather, the punishment for such behaviour, as specified in the Qur'an, is to be meted out on the Day of Judgement. Although the actual act of blasphemy is, from a Qur'anic point of view, a great sin, no death penalty is mentioned in the Qur'an. The presence of consensus in pre-modern juristic scholarship on the death penalty for blasphemy should not therefore deter Muslims of today from critiquing and further examining it, given that the existing penalty in traditional Islamic law is not based on a clear commandment in the Qur'an or in the Sunna. The mere existence of unanimous agreement without a strong basis in the Qur'an and the practice of the Prophet should not be used as a basis for believing the issue to be an "immutable".

A further example can be found in the law of apostasy (*ridda*). The Qur'an and the Sunna express in unambiguous terms that apostasy (renunciation of religion by a Muslim) is a major sin. This can therefore be understood to be an immutable. However, the death penalty for apostasy is not based on the Qur'an and was developed in a particular socio-political context prevalent in the early history of Islam. Debating the death penalty for apostasy does not, therefore, mean that one is going against a fundamental. The death penalty is not specified in the Qur'an, and the actual practice of the Prophet is not supportive of the death penalty either, as there is contradictory evidence on the basis of which pre-modern Muslim jurists constructed the law of apostasy and its punishment. The debate today about the death penalty or how to deal with the issue of apostasy should not be seen as challenging an immutable aspect of the religion.

A contextualist approach therefore is not about destroying religion, its fundamentals, or the foundations of Islam. It is not a free-for-all approach that provides interpretations without any principles. Its careful attention to the linguistic aspects of the text using exegetical tools, its careful consideration of the context in which the Qur'anic text functioned, as well as its concern with preservation of the immutables of the religion, all provide legitimate foundations for a highly principled approach to the interpretation of the Qur'an. Taking the context of the modern period into account in its interpretation will provide a more relevant, appropriate, and spiritually meaningful interpretation for modern-day Muslims.

Notes

1 Imran Nyaze, *Theories of Islamic Law: The Methodology of Ijtihad* (Islamabad: International Research Institute, 2000), 40.
2 Nyaze, *Theories of Islamic Law*, 41.

10 Contextualist interpretation in practice

The Qur'an is an Arabic-language text from the seventh century CE, and, given its cultural and linguistic distance from the present time, a linguistic analysis is required to effectively approach, comprehend, and interpret it. Traditional Qur'anic interpretation has developed a range of concepts, methods, and analyses that relate to morphological, syntactic, stylistic, and semantic aspects of the text. These can be usefully applied to the Qur'an for this purpose. However, many more issues need to be considered before arriving at a proper contextualist interpretation. The following four-step process provides an outline for the process of reaching such an interpretation. I will assume, for the purpose of this exercise, that the interpreter is Muslim. Although much of what I present can be applied to the text by anyone, Muslim or not, the contextualist interpretation of the Qur'an is in many cases a Muslim project and hence the focus on the Muslim interpreter.

As part of providing some examples which will help the reader to understand some of the key elements of the proposal I am putting forward, I focus on the Qur'anic texts that address humans as individuals in society. In particular, I place an emphasis on those texts that refer to the institution of polygamy. For the most part, I rely on the ideas and commentary provided by Fazlur Rahman in his *Major Themes of the Qur'an* concerning these. His approach provides an illustration of how a Muslim interpreter of the Qur'an today would put key elements of this contextualist approach to interpretation into practice.

Step 1: Preliminary considerations

The first step involves taking some time to become familiar with the broader context in which interpretation occurs. Some considerations that will assist with this are outlined below.

Understanding the interpreter's own subjectivity

Each interpreter always brings into interpretation his or her own experiences, ideas, beliefs, values, and presuppositions, and these will have a significant influence on the interpretation. These may include: knowledge about the

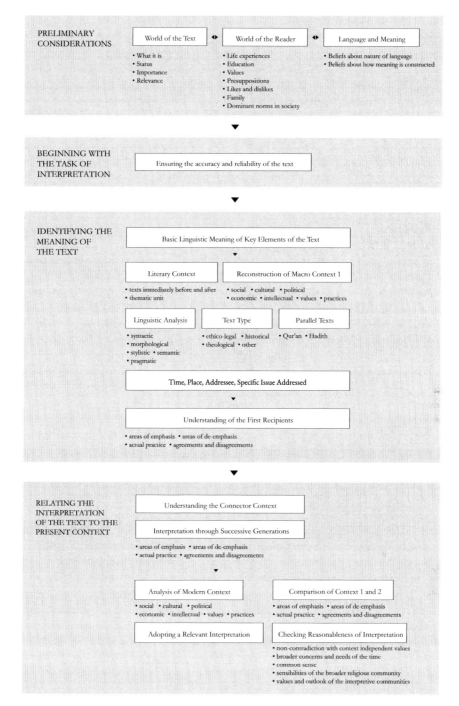

PRELIMINARY CONSIDERATIONS

World of the Text ◆▶ World of the Reader ◆▶ Language and Meaning

World of the Text
- What it is
- Status
- Importance
- Relevance

World of the Reader
- Life experiences
- Education
- Values
- Presuppositions
- Likes and dislikes
- Family
- Dominant norms in society

Language and Meaning
- Beliefs about nature of language
- Beliefs about how meaning is constructed

▼

BEGINNING WITH THE TASK OF INTERPRETATION

Ensuring the accuracy and reliability of the text

▼

IDENTIFYING THE MEANING OF THE TEXT

Basic Linguistic Meaning of Key Elements of the Text

▼

Literary Context | Reconstruction of Macro Context 1

Literary Context
- texts immediately before and after
- thematic unit

Reconstruction of Macro Context 1
- social   • cultural   • political
- economic   • intellectual   • values   • practices

Linguistic Analysis | Text Type | Parallel Texts

Linguistic Analysis
- syntactic
- morphological
- stylistic   • semantic
- pragmatic

Text Type
- ethico-legal   • historical
- theological   • other

Parallel Texts
- Qur'an   • Hadith

Time, Place, Addressee, Specific Issue Addressed

▼

Understanding of the First Recipients

- areas of emphasis   • areas of de-emphasis
- actual practice   • agreements and disagreements

▼

RELATING THE INTERPRETATION OF THE TEXT TO THE PRESENT CONTEXT

Understanding the Connector Context

Interpretation through Successive Generations

- areas of emphasis   • areas of de-emphasis
- actual practice   • agreements and disagreements

▼

Analysis of Modern Context | Comparison of Context 1 and 2

Analysis of Modern Context
- social   • cultural   • political
- economic   • intellectual   • values   • practices

Comparison of Context 1 and 2
- areas of emphasis   • areas of de-emphasis
- actual practice   • agreements and disagreements

Adopting a Relevant Interpretation | Checking Reasonableness of Interpretation

Checking Reasonableness of Interpretation
- non-contradiction with context independent values
- broader concerns and needs of the time
- common sense
- sensibilities of the broader religious community
- values and outlook of the interpretive communities

Figure 10.1 Interpretive framework

world; life experiences; beliefs and values such as belief in God, prophets, scriptures, and life after death; expectations, hopes, likes, dislikes, and priorities; education and training such as knowledge of the language, religion, the Qur'an, and the religious tradition; identities such as gender, ethnic, cultural, linguistic, professional, or family affiliations; attitudes towards political, religious, cultural, or economic issues; and community status and roles in society. As a result of all these factors, the interpreter is already involved with the text on many levels, even before the interpretation begins. Awareness of this frees the interpreter from needing to make claims to finality, as a personal perspective will always be inherent in any interpretation.

The world of the Qur'an

The interpreter also brings a preliminary understanding of several aspects of the text to be interpreted: what it is, what it broadly means, its status and importance in society, its messages and what it is about, and some knowledge about the author of the text, who is God from a Muslim point of view.

Identification and understanding of the following aspects of the Qur'an will assist also with the process of interpretation. First is the Qur'an's positioning as a revelation from God to humanity. The Qur'an is considered by Muslims to be the Word of God, and this infers a particular connection with its Muslim readers. Second is a broad understanding of the concerns of the Qur'an as a text. The central message of the Qur'an and what it aims to convey is about the recognition of the one God as the creator and sustainer of all things. Further, the Qur'an identifies a need for its audience to respond to this message in obedience to this merciful and compassionate God.

According to Fazlur Rahman,[1] even a cursory perusal of the Qur'an would leave most readers with the impression that the text is primarily about God, particularly His infinite majesty and infinite mercy. Nonetheless, it is crucial to remember that God and His nature are not the primary concern of this heavenly document. Rather, "the aim of the Qur'an is man and his behavior, not God".[2] The self-proclaimed reason for the Qur'an is, after all, guidance for humankind.[3] Indeed, even the cosmos – in spite of being another central theme of the Qur'an – is presented as a creation that has surrendered to the will of God. The sole function of the cosmos is to elucidate humankind on their position in the order of being, and it has primarily a moral aspect.[4]

Hence, human beings quickly take centre stage in the world of the Qur'an. Not only are we the ultimate receptor of this divine discourse, we also occupy a unique position in the order of creation. Although we are mere creatures, like any other that God has created, we have nevertheless been endowed with the qualities needed to fulfil the role of God's vicegerent. This represents in the Qur'an the very purpose behind the creation of the universe. Having been endowed with free choice, humans alone can stray from the path and transgress God's limits, the law. Because we have a deep proclivity to be forgetful of this responsibility, the Qur'an is often understood to be a reminder: it awakens in us that moral consciousness (*taqwa*) without which we will not be able to carry out our ultimate duty in life.

Hence, as one prepares to enter the world of the Qur'an, it is essential to remember that this document is squarely aimed at humanity. Furthermore, it "is not just descriptive but is primarily prescriptive",[5] insofar as its aim is to elicit a moral response from both its listeners and adherents. *Taqwa*, in the sense of moral consciousness, means to "be squarely anchored within the moral tensions, the 'limits of God,' and not to 'transgress' or violate the balance of those tensions or limits".[6] *Taqwa* is thus evoked in the Qur'an not only in the context of the proper relationship between humans and their Creator, but also in the context of the proper relationship of humans amongst themselves[7] and even that of the person and his or her self.[8] According to Rahman, *taqwa* "is the most important single term in the Qur'an"[9] and is "as central to Islam as love is to Christianity".[10]

The concepts of moral action in the Qur'an (such as *taqwa* and its opposites) take place only in a social context, as there can be no moral actors aside from those who live in society. The goal of the Qur'an was – and still is – to bring about "an ethical and egalitarian society".[11] Having established this understanding, the following considerations remind us as interpreters of just how these central concerns of the Qur'an were expressed in the socio-historical context of the Hijaz society.

Understanding how meaning is constructed

Meaning is not entirely separate from the interpreter, and it does not exist on its own. Rather, it emerges as a result of the interaction of four elements: God's will (as the author), the text of the Qur'an, the first recipients (the Prophet and the first recipient community), and the macro context of the Qur'an (macro context 1). Several key issues can be considered when identifying meaning in the Qur'an.

The Qur'an is God's speech (*kalam*) and was intended in the first instance for a specific audience in Mecca and Medina in the seventh century. The communicative act of the Qur'an remains deeply connected to the context in which it first occurred. However, a degree of ambiguity is present in the language of the Qur'an, and this as well as the changed contexts of interpretation justify the necessity for its interpretation.

Revelation is God's communication to human beings, and as such, it is always in a human language. As a result, it is possible to understand the text, its meaning, and what it is communicating by studying the text in its context. However, the human languages that facilitate revelation and interpretation contain a certain degree of fluidity and bias. Thus, a complete meaning cannot be obtained simply through reading a text, and more than one approach to interpretation may therefore be necessary.

To arrive at a useful meaning, the interpreter needs to understand how the first recipient community responded to the message and to identify how their response was closely connected to their context. The interpreter may also need to be aware that certain key aspects of the message were considered relevant to the first community and were therefore emphasised at the time.

A key issue is that the meaning of a text can evolve. In different periods and contexts the meaning of the same text can be slightly different as a result of shifts in emphasis in meaning. These changes of emphasis are often the result of changes in contexts. The meaning of a text may have to be "translated", that is, contextualised for a different readership.

Step 2: Beginning the task of interpretation

The second step involves identifying what was originally stated in the text under consideration. Given the widely accepted historical reliability of the text of the Qur'an – at least from a Muslim point of view – the interpreter will generally assume that the text before them is equivalent to what was said and communicated in the early seventh century. There are, however, variations in the text for some Qur'anic verses. The literature on these variations (*qirā'āt* or "variant readings") allows the interpreter to use the details of these variations in their consideration of the text.

The text of the Qur'an that is used for the interpretation should, ideally, be in Arabic. This is the language in which the Prophet Muhammad communicated the Qur'anic message to his followers, and a range of linguistic features of Arabic may not be present in Qur'an translations into languages such as English.

Step 3: Identifying the meaning of the text

In the third step, the interpreter uses exegetical principles, tools, and ideas to arrive at the meaning of the text. This would take into consideration how the text was understood in the early seventh century, and also how it was understood within the *tafsir* tradition.

Reconstructing macro context 1 (early seventh century CE)

Macro context 1 refers to the original social, political, economic, cultural, and intellectual settings of the Qur'anic text under consideration. The macro context encompasses the relevant ideas, values, and views that can be understood by examining the historical information that is available to the interpreter from a variety of sources. The purpose of studying the macro context is to obtain a good sense of the overall setting in which this text was given. This reconstruction may not be completely accurate or perfect, as it is always an approximation. However, this approach allows the interpreter to develop background information for understanding the text.

For instance, when dealing with the verses that relate to polygamy, Fazlur Rahman reminds interpreters that the Qur'an was revealed to an Arab tribal society that was characterised by socio-economic disparities. These differences were the principal reason for the ongoing tribal rivalry and social discord of the time.

To Rahman, polytheism (which the Qur'an routinely criticises) and the segmentation of Arab society at the time, were "the obverse and converse of the same coin".[12] From an economic point of view, Mecca, where the Qur'an was first revealed, "was a prosperous commercial town, but it had a subterranean world of exploitation of the weak".[13] This exploitation was particularly rife in relation to the treatment of girls, orphans, women, and slaves. Thus, it is difficult to obtain a sense of the general message of the Qur'an without keeping in mind some of these aspects of the macro context of seventh-century Arabia, and some of the social ills that the Qur'an was so desperately trying to reform.

Determining the literary context in which the text exists

An effective starting point is to identify the immediate literary context of the text that is the focus of interpretation.[14] This allows the interpreter to identify the themes and messages in that context.

Determining the thematic unit of the text

The Qur'an is not organised thematically and its chapters often contain a variety of themes. More importantly the texts in a given chapter may have been communicated at different points in time during the time of the Prophet.

For these reasons, it is important to understand the thematic unit within which the text under consideration functions. A thematic unit is comprised of the texts that come before or after the verse that is being interpreted, and that are thematically related to the text in question. These texts may range from relatively few to many in number. A careful reading might indicate where the thematic unit appears to begin and where it ends. The interpreter will often find it helpful to put together some notes on the contents of the thematic unit: the ideas, values, messages, and issues it covers, as well as dominant and secondary themes (see also Parallel texts below).

Identifying the specific time and place wherein the text was communicated

The interpreter can then identify whom the text refers to, and to whom it was communicated, for example, a particular group of Muslims or non-Muslims. The interpreter can also identify when the text was communicated. This includes an approximate dating of the text, where possible: early Meccan, late Meccan, early Medinan, or late Medinan. The specific events that appear to have led to the revelation of the text can be identified through the "occasions of revelation" (*asbāb al-nuzūl*) literature and other sources of information, despite the difficulties associated with the unreliability of these sources. Indeed, there is a need to maintain a cautious attitude to such material.

In relation to the verse that discusses polygamy (Qur'an 4:3), Rahman reminds us that the context in which this verse was revealed had to do with the rise in the number of orphans following the death of male soldiers during the ongoing wars. The failure of the guardians to handle orphaned women's properties justly, according to Rahman, prompted the Qur'an to allow the men to marry up to four women, provided that the conditions of the marriage are fair. Interestingly, Rahman corroborates his argument for such a rationale by departing from the traditional literature on *asbāb al-nuzūl* in this regard. Instead, he invokes the following verse:

> They ask you [O Muhammad!] concerning women. Say: God gives you His decision concerning them, and what is being recited to you in the Book *concerning orphan women to whom you do not give their due, but you would rather marry them*, and [also concerning younger] and weaker children.[15]

Although this appears much later in the text, Rahman maintains that it predates verse 4:3.

In summary, Rahman enters the world of the Qur'an, in which equality and fairness are vital. He then considers a wide range of thematically related units and re-examines the precise context and rationale that prompted the polygamy verses. Through this process Rahman is not only able to reveal that the polygamy verse refers to orphaned women, but he is also able to unearth a tension in the text: "Namely the Qur'an's permission for polygamy up to four wives; the requirement of justice among co-wives; and the unequivocal declaration that such justice is, in the nature of things, impossible."[16]

Determining the type of text

The type of text being examined will also influence the interpretation. The interpreter can determine whether the text being studied is a historical text (dealing with past prophets or other people, for example) or an ethico-legal text (related to command, prohibition, instruction, or advice), a parable, or a text related to *ghayb* (the unseen domain related to God, life after death, paradise, and hell). Each of these text types or genres is expressed in a unique way, and the sense of how literal or figurative the text is can be based on the genre of the text. An understanding of the text type allows for a better understanding of the nature of the message communicated in the text.

For example, Rahman noted in relation to the text on polygamy that it is crucial to discern between what he termed "legal enactments" and "moral injunctions". To him, this sort of distinction is essential to unearth the basic *élan* of the "Qur'anic teaching but also solve certain knotty problems with regard, for example, to women's reform".[17] Rahman is firmly of the view that "permission for polygamy was at a legal plane while the sanctions put on it were in the nature of a *moral ideal towards which the society was expected to move*".[18] Rahman laments the fact that although traditional jurists have recognised this legal procedure of the Qur'an, they "generally stuck to the letter of the law and enunciated the principle that 'although a law is occasioned by a specific situation, its application nevertheless becomes universal'", and were thus not able to see that many of the legal verses of the Qur'an are not actually immutable.[19]

Examining the linguistic aspects of the text

A key aspect of interpretation is developing an understanding of the morphological, syntactic, semantic, and stylistic features of the text. This involves identifying why certain linguistic features were used in the text and how these influence meaning. The text may have used certain syntactic or stylistic features to emphasise particular ideas. Certain approaches may have been chosen over others for specific reasons, and asking questions about alternatives may reveal issues that may not always be apparent.

According to Arkoun, it is crucial to examine the language of the Qur'anic text thoroughly, if only because "God appears as the central subject, organizing grammatically and semantically the whole discourse".[20] Features that are specific to Arabic language can be identified at this stage. This process might include inidentification of dominant terms and ideas in the text. This may help to determine which meanings are appropriate in instances where the lexical items are polysemous, or where there is semantic ambiguity. Semantic features such as repetition, use of idioms, irregular or unusual grammatical structures, specific particles and prepositions, the use of definite and indefinite nouns, the presence of ellipsis (*hadhf*), foregrounding (*taqdīm*) and backgrounding (*ta'khīr*), synonyms or partial synonyms, use of tense, choice of singular or plural forms, masculine terms, or use of active or passive participle instead of a verb will all influence the way the text is interpreted. When the interpreter deals with particular words, he or she can cultivate a sense of how these words were used at the time, rather than how they are understood in the present. Major dictionaries such as *Lisān al-'Arab* or Lane's *Lexicon*, as well as *tafsīr* works, will assist with identifying the particular words and their usage at the time.

In the example of polygamy the use of the word "women" is problematic: it may refer to hypothetical women, to women who stand apart from those who are unlawful, or strictly to "orphaned" women. This polysemy has in each case a variety of social and legal implications.

Exploring similar issues in the Qur'an using parallel texts

At this stage, the interpreter can identify other texts that may have some relevance to the primary text under consideration. The interpreter gathers texts from various parts of the Qur'an, for comparison. When they are compared, it is possible to identify the key ideas that emerge from all these different texts; the dominant messages, ideas, and values; how each text relates to other relevant texts; and the chronological sequence of the texts.

When additional Qur'anic texts that are relevant to the text under discussion are identified, the interpreter can examine the messages that they convey. Based on this, the dominant values in the texts can be organised according to a hierarchy of relevance.

The issue of polygamy is a case in point, and clarifies how the idea of parallel texts can be used in a contextualist approach.[21] Contrary to the textualist view, Rahman is of the opinion that the position of the jurists concerning the permission of polygamy was erroneous, not only because it ignored the Qur'an's moral *élan* and its fundamental goal of establishing an ethical and egalitarian society, but also because it failed to assess properly the context of the verses that discuss polygamy in terms of how they were revealed, whom they referred to, and to whom they were addressed.

A key Qur'anic text in relation to polygamy says:

> If you fear that you cannot do justice to orphans, then marry from among women such as you like, two, three, or four. But if you fear you will not be fair [to your wives], then [marry] only one; that is the safest course.[22]

Muslim jurists have often used this verse to justify permission of polygamy. This point is obvious from the approach taken in a number of translations of the Qur'an into English, even those that are the least textualist. When translating this verse, for example, Muhammad Asad adds the word "other" just before the word "women" between brackets, because the traditional sources he consulted seem to point to that meaning, even when these varied in the details. Asad explains that for Zamakhshari and Razi, the verse pertains to women who are outside the prohibited degrees enumerated in Qur'an 4:22–3. He also quotes Bukhari:

> According to an interpretation suggested by A'ishah, the Prophet's widow, this refers to the (hypothetical) case of orphan girls whom their guardians might wish to marry without, however, being prepared or able to give them an appropriate marriage-portion – the implication being that they should avoid the temptation of committing such an injustice and should marry other women instead.[23]

Asad then quotes Tabari, who states that Sa'id b. Jubayr, Qatada, and others indicate:

> The purport of the above passage is this: "Just as you are, rightly, fearful of offending against the interests of orphans, you must apply the same careful consideration to the interests and rights of the women whom you intend to marry."

Rahman argues that one should not use just this text in understanding what the Qur'an is trying to communicate here. For him, the traditional interpretation of the text in question is indicative of an atomistic approach to the Qur'an. He argues that this has hindered the development of an adequate understanding of this verse.

Thus, in dealing with this verse, Rahman considers at least some twenty verses, which he believes are thematically related to the verse in question. He draws attention to those that are most directly related to and in proximity of the verse under consideration, namely: "Render unto the orphans their possessions, and do not substitute bad things [of your own] for the good things [that belong to them], and do not consume their possessions together with your own: this, verily, is a great crime" (Qur'an 4:2). He considers a verse in the Qur'an that takes guardians to task for their dishonest dealings with the properties of orphans (both girls and boys). He also considers others that are far less proximate, including: "You shall never be able to do justice among women, no matter how much you desire to do so" (Qur'an 4:129) to highlight that this permission clashes with the value of justice and morality which are central to the Qur'an.

Rahman also highlights this issue regarding the welfare of the orphans and the poor in general. This was already a central concern of the Qur'an during the earliest part of the Meccan period, and thus Rahman urges the reader of the Qur'an, as they ponder the polygamy verse, also to consider others:

> But nay, nay, [O men, consider all that you do and fail to do:] you are not generous towards the orphan, and you do not urge one another to feed the needy, and you devour the inheritance [of others] with devouring greed, and you love wealth with boundless love!
>
> (Qur'an 89:17–20)

> Have you ever considered [the kind of man] who gives the lie to all moral law? Behold, it is this [kind of man] that thrusts the orphan away, and feels no urge to feed the needy. Woe, then, unto those praying ones whose hearts from their prayer are remote; those who want only to be seen and praised, and, withal, deny all assistance [to their fellow-men]!
>
> (Qur'an 101:1–7)

Equally, Rahman draws attention to other Medinan verses that are thematically related, as they all point to the obligation of looking after the needs of the orphans. For instance:

> And do not touch the substance of an orphan – save to improve it – before he comes of age.
>
> (Qur'an 6:152)

> And Lo! We accepted this solemn pledge from [you,] – the children of Israel: "You shall worship none but God; and you shall do good unto your parents and kinsfolk, and the orphans, and the poor; and you shall speak unto all people in a kindly way; and you shall be constant in prayer; and you shall spend in charity."
>
> (Qur'an 2:83)

True piety does not consist in turning your faces towards the east or the west – but truly pious is he who believes in God, and the Last Day; and the angels, and revelation, and the prophets; and spends his substance – however much he himself may cherish it – upon his near of kin, and the orphans, and the needy, and the wayfarer, and the beggars, and for the freeing of human beings from bondage.

(Qur'an 2:177)

Behold, those who sinfully devour the possessions of orphans but fill their bellies with fire: for [in the life to come] they will have to endure a blazing flame!

(Qur'an 4:10)

Rahman also makes allusion to verses that insist that orphans be treated equitably when wealth is being distributed:

And know that whatever booty you acquire [in war], one-fifth thereof belongs to God and the Apostle, and the near of kin, and the orphans, and the needy, and the wayfarer.

(Qur'an 8:41)

Whatever [spoils taken] from the people of those villages God has turned over to His Apostle – [all of it] belongs to God and the Apostle, and the near of kin [of deceased believers], and the orphans, and the needy, and the wayfarer, so that it may not be [a benefit] going round and round among such of you as may [already] be rich. Hence, accept [willingly] whatever the Apostle gives you [thereof], and refrain from [demanding] anything that he withholds from you; and remain conscious of God.

(Qur'an 59:7)[24]

Exploring hadith texts on the same topic

The interpreter can also identify the texts in the hadith literature that might be helpful for understanding the purport of the Qur'anic text.

Given the difficulties associated with the issue of reliability of a large number of hadith texts, the interpreter may need to approach the hadith material with a degree of caution. A key activity is identifying the degree of reliability of the hadith material available on the issue. This can be based on the criteria developed in hadith criticism as well as criteria developed by Muslim scholars in the modern period.

Hadith are interpreted in the light of the Qur'an. Rather than using a single hadith as textual proof for a particular issue, the interpreter can bring together all or a large number of the hadith available on that issue, as this will help to understand what the hadith material collectively on a particular issue provides.

The overall practice of the Prophet and sayings attributed to him (which may or may not be in line with his overall practice) can be distinguished from any single hadith, as it may be less reliable. Even hadith that are considered by the Muslim hadith scholars to be authentic may need to be further subjected to critical review if there is a conflict between the actual practice (Sunna) of the Prophet and the hadith. In Chapter 7, I provided several criteria that could be used in interpretation.

Exploring how the first recipients understood the text

An interpreter's understanding of how the first recipients of the Qur'an understood the text will be based on the biographical, historical, exegetical, or hadith literature that they have access to, despite the difficulties about historical reliability of some of this material. This information will help to identify the ways in which the first recipients appear to have responded to the message and how they applied the message in their life, the differences among them – if any – in the area of understanding and application, as well as the degree of unanimity among them.

Step 4: Relating the interpretation of the text to the present context

In the fourth step, the interpreter identifies how the *tafsīr* tradition has interpreted the text through successive generations, and then attempts to relate the interpretation to the modern context (macro context 2). The interpreter can then examine if the text has been interpreted consistently throughout the tradition, and can identify the justifications for any competing views, if any. Such competing views could be due to significant differences in the macro context between that of the modern period and the early seventh century.

When significant differences can be identified between the modern and pre-modern macro contexts, the contextualist will have greater flexibility to put forward a slightly different reasonable or even radically different interpretation. The more diverse the tradition of interpretation of the text under consideration, the greater the degree of flexibility available to the contextualist interpreter for providing another reasonable interpretation for the modern period.

Considering the dominant interpretation in a wider context

Certain considerations will assist the interpreter with any examination of the dominant interpretation of the text in the tradition. The interpreter can note if the dominant interpretation of the text in the *tafsīr* tradition is governed by the position of a particular theological school, legal school, or a mystical order. As the dominant interpretation is understood to be one among many other possible interpretations, awareness of the rationale for more marginal interpretations in the tradition will also assist with the interpretation. The more diverse the existing interpretations are, the greater freedom the contextualist interpreter has in adopting a different interpretation.

Relating the understanding of the text in different contexts

The interpreter can then relate the understanding of the text in macro context 1 (early seventh century) to that of macro context 2 (twenty-first century). In relation to this, Rahman writes:

> If the study of early Hadith materials is carried through with constructive purposiveness under the canons of historical criticism and in relation to the historico-sociological background, they take on quite a new meaning. A Hadith, say, in *al-Muwatta*, that Umar did so-and-so, when read as mere Hadith, i.e., as an isolated report, remains a blank and yields little; but when one fully comprehends the sociological forces that brought the action about, it becomes meaningful for us now and assumes an entirely new dimension. There is only one sense in which our early history is repeatable – and, indeed, in that sense it must be repeated if we are to live as progressive Muslims at all, viz., just as those generations met their own situation adequately by freely interpreting the Qur'an and Sunnah of the Prophet – by emphasizing the ideal and the principles and re-embodying them in a fresh texture of their own contemporary history – we must perform the same feat for ourselves, with our own effort, for our own contemporary history.[25]

A grid can be constructed to analyse and summarise the relevant political, economic, social, cultural, and intellectual concerns relating to the specific issue the text is dealing with. This allows the two macro contexts to be easily compared. From this comparison, it is possible to determine the values, norms, and ideas that are specific to each context and to identify any similarities or differences between the two contexts.

The interpreter can then explore if the values the text conveys appear to be universal or particular: in other words, immutable or mutable. As part of this process, it is useful to identify the messages that appear to be specific to macro context 1 (early seventh century); the universal messages that seem to be the objective of the message for macro context 1; and the ways in which the message can be applied to macro context 2 (twenty-first century). This involves taking the similarities of and differences between the two contexts into account.

In the example of polygamy we are exploring, equality constitutes the essence or the *ratio legis* of the legal pronouncement of the text. The latter is upheld provided that it fully, or at least adequately, embodies the former. For Rahman, there may have been a socio-historical background and context that warranted polygamy; when the situation changes or when the law fails correctly to embody the ideal, the law has to be rethought anew.

The greater the similarity between macro contexts 1 and 2, the higher the likelihood that the key message has remained as it was; conversely, wide variances in the two contexts will suggest a greater likelihood of the key message occurring and applying differently in macro context 2, if the value conveyed by the text does not appear to be universal.

Exploring the reasonableness of the interpretation

The new interpretation arrived at may need to be examined to determine if it is reasonable. Several criteria will assist with this evaluation. First, the new interpretation can be assessed to determine if it goes against any fundamental principle (*asl*) or context-independent value of the religion. Second, it is useful to identify if the interpretation takes into account the concerns and needs of the contemporary context, and if it is likely to attract support from a significant part of the community of believers (Muslims). Finally, the interpretation can be assessed to determine if it is in line with common sense or with what believers in general would consider to be reasonable, fair, and just today. Needless to say, these are rather vague. However, in any community, there is always a sense of what is fair, just, and reasonable.

The ideas presented in this chapter will help the contextualist interpreter to think about the key issues associated with the task of interpretation. The steps above take into consideration an understanding of the text as it functioned in the early seventh century CE and the various factors that influence the "translation" of the meaning of the text for the twenty-first century.

Notes

1 Fazlur Rahman, *Major Themes of the Qur'an*, second edition (Chicago: University of Chicago Press, 2009), 1.
2 Rahman, *Major Themes of the Qur'an*, 3.
3 Rahman, *Major Themes of the Qur'an*, 1.
4 Rahman, *Major Themes of the Qur'an*, 2.
5 Rahman, *Major Themes of the Qur'an*, 22.
6 Rahman, *Major Themes of the Qur'an*, 29.
7 Rahman, *Major Themes of the Qur'an*, 28.
8 Rahman, *Major Themes of the Qur'an*, 30.
9 Rahman, *Major Themes of the Qur'an*, 28.
10 Rahman, *Major Themes of the Qur'an*, 29.
11 Rahman, *Major Themes of the Qur'an*, 38.
12 Rahman, *Major Themes of the Qur'an*, 38.
13 Rahman, *Major Themes of the Qur'an*, 38.
14 *Mafhum al-Nass* clarifies as follows: According to some authors, interpreters of the Qur'an today must strive to gain cognizance of the semiotic world associated with the historical context of the Prophet and his direct audience. Abu Zayd, for instance, argues that given the fact that humans constitute the ultimate objective of this revelation, we would be hard pressed to imagine the Qur'an would address them through channels other than their particular linguistic system and their cultural framework. He writes: "This Revelation is certainly from heaven but it is destined to this world, and thus it would be

inconceivable that it should be at variance with the laws of reality. Indeed, it only behooves it to adapt itself to the structures of this reality, including the linguistic ones in particular." See Nasr Hamid Abu Zayd, *Mafhum al-Nass: Dirasa fi 'Ulum al Qur'an* (Cairo: al-Hay'a al-Misriyya al-'Amma lil-Kitab, 1990), 64.

15 Qur'an 4:127, 47.
16 Rahman, *Major Themes of the Qur'an*, 47.
17 Rahman, *Major Themes of the Qur'an*, 47.
18 Rahman, *Major Themes of the Qur'an*, 48 (my emphasis).
19 Rahman, *Major Themes of the Qur'an*, 48.
20 Mohammed Arkoun, "The Notion of Revelation: From Ahl al-Kitab to the Societies of the Book", *Die Welt des Islams*, 28, (1988), 62–89: 68.
21 Rahman, *Major Themes of the Qur'an*, 46–49.
22 Qur'an 4:3.
23 http://asadullahali.files.wordpress.com/2010/09/the-message-of-the-quran.pdf.
24 See also Qur'an 17:34; 2:215, 220; 4:2, 6, 8, 36, 127; and 93:9.
25 Fazlur Rahman, *Islamic Methodology in History* (Islamabad: Islamic Research Institute, 1965), 178.

Part III

Different interpretations for different contexts

Four cases

11 Men's "authority" over women and equality

This chapter is the first of four examples of Qur'anic interpretation which shows how the context influences the interpretation. While in some cases this influence may be very clear, in other cases it can be somewhat subtle. This first example is one where this influence is obvious.

The question of equality of men and women has been one of the most strongly debated issues in contemporary Islamic thought. Many textualists argue that the Qur'an gives men more rights than it gives women. This textualist approach relies heavily on pre-modern interpretations of a few Qur'anic texts. Although such a view of "unequal equality" may have been acceptable in the pre-modern period and would have been in line with the macro context of the period, Muslims who adopt a contextualist framework argue that the macro context of today is so different from that of the pre-modern period that a fresh interpretation is needed of the Qur'anic texts that were used in the pre-modern period to justify inequality of women. This chapter examines approaches to a text of the Qur'an[1] that has been central to debates on issues of gender and equality in Islam. It reads:

> Husbands should take good care of their wives, with [the bounties] God has given to some more than others [*bi mā faddala allāhu baʿdahum ʿala baʿd*] and with what they spend out of their own money. Righteous wives (*sālihāt*) are devout (*qānitāt*) and guard (*hāfizāt li al-ghayb*) what God would have them guard in their husbands' absence. If you fear high-handedness [*nushūz*] from your wives, remind them [of the teachings of God], then ignore them when you go to bed, then hit them. If they obey you, you have no right to act against them: God is most high and great.
>
> (Qur'an 4:34)

The focus of this chapter is the first section of this verse ("Husbands should take good care of their wives, with [the bounties] God has given to some more than others and with what they spend out of their own money"), and it does not discuss the concepts of *nushūz* (highhandedness) or *darb* (hitting) that are introduced in the second half of the verse, except where this provides context for the treatment of the first section.

Context of the text

There are three main approaches to the narrative context for this verse.

Tabari cites a number of accounts of a story which attempts to explain the occasion of the revelation of this text.[2] All of the accounts he uses are transmitted through various commentators of the second generation of Muslims.[3] The story appears to relate mainly to the mention of "hitting" in the second part of the verse. In these accounts, a woman or her family complained to the Prophet after her husband hit her. The Prophet ordered the punishment of retaliation (*qisās*) against the husband, but then – in most accounts – the verse was revealed, so he called the woman or her father back and recited the verse, saying, "I wanted something but God wanted something else."[4]

Later commentators also referred to these narrations, but they added more complete details. For example, none of Tabari's narrations gave the names of the woman or her husband, whereas later versions provided various conflicting possibilities. Two later commentators, Ibn Kathir (d. 774/1373) and Suyuti (d. 911/1505), provide this story. They also provide a second story, in which the Prophet reportedly said: "Do not beat God's [female] slaves," whereupon Umar replied, "They treat their husbands brazenly." In response – according to the story – the Prophet permitted the hitting.[5]

Razi[6] and Qurtubi[7] also refer to the man hitting his wife in the story. They also add certain reports that are connected to the treatment of women elsewhere in the Qur'an. Namely, the verses that appear to give women only half the portion of men in inheritance,[8] as well as the verses immediately preceding the present one.[9] This latter verse also uses the key word *faddala*:

> Do not covet what God has given to some of you more than others [*ma faddala allāhu bihi baʿdakum ʿala baʿd*] – men have the portion they have earned; and women the portion they have earned – you should rather ask God for some of His bounty: He has full knowledge of everything.

According to the narrations cited by Razi and Qurtubi, "some women" (or specifically, the Prophet's wife Umm Salama) asked the Prophet why men had been "preferred" over women in inheritance. Thus verse 4:32 was revealed, presumably to tell women not to covet what men had been given, and to give the reason why men were preferred.

Emphases in pre-modern interpretation

Tabari keeps quite close to the literal meaning of the words of the verse, and puts forward various narrations that are essentially paraphrases of the verse. For example, he cites the view of Ibn Abbas regarding the first phrase in the verse:

> "*Men are qawwām over women*" means "commanders" [*umarāʾ*] of them, that she should obey him in what God has commanded that he be obeyed, and obeying

him means that she is good to his family and protects his property. Thus, God "preferred" [*faddalahu*] him with his spending on her and his labour.[10]

Tabari sums up the narrations related to this first phrase by saying that it gives husbands the right of taking responsibility for the affairs of women: that is, the right to discipline (*ta'dīb*) and command. The reason he gives for this is the financial provision of husbands for their wives, in the form of dowry as well as during the marriage. Unlike some later exegetes, Tabari did not provide a linguistic definition of *qawwām*.

Tabari cites several narrations regarding the phrase that describes "righteous women" (*sālihāt*).[11] Although these narrations use the actual words of the verse as their starting point, they also provide additional details. He interprets the word *qānitāt* to mean "obedient", in the context of obedience to both God and husband. Only one of the seven narrations Tabari gives in support, however, outlines the meaning as "obedient to God and to their husbands". Of the remainder, five simply refer to the meaning as "obedient" (*mutī'āt*), while one places the meaning as "obedient to their husbands".[12] Later commentators have generally taken the view that *qānitāt* refers to being "obedient to their husbands", and omit any mention of God. These later commentators do not attribute their conclusion to any of the seven narrations on this specific word, but rather to Ibn Abbas. This may be a reference to another of the narrations attributed to him: most likely the first narration given by Tabari in his commentary of this verse. Notably, that narration requires women to obey men "in what God has commanded that they be obeyed" (and even specifies this to mean "being good to his family and protecting his property").[13]

The phrase *hāfizāt li al-ghayb* is open to several different interpretations. The narrations given by Tabari indicate that it means that righteous women guard their private parts and their husbands' property in their husbands' absence. Tabari adds that this phrase also requires women to fulfil what is obligatory in the rights given by God to men in other things.[14] In relation to this phrase, Tabari cites a hadith reported by Abu Hurayra, which contains a very husband-centric definition of the ideal woman:

> The Prophet said: "The best of women is the one who, when you look at her, she pleases you, when you command her, she obeys you, and when you are absent, she guards you in terms of her own self and your property." Then he [the Prophet] recited the verse.
>
> (referring to Qur'an 4:34)[15]

Razi is quite patriarchal in his conclusions, although his approach differs from Tabari. Whereas Tabari relied almost solely on the views of earlier authorities, Razi also refers to evidence "from nature" and other provisions of Islamic law regarding male superiority. Although Razi was a proponent of interpretation by the use of reason, he ends up, as is demonstrated below, sounding even more biased than Tabari.

Razi starts out on a more egalitarian note by linking the verse with inheritance, and pointing out that God preferred men over women in inheritance only because men are *qawwāmūn* over women which in this context seems to mean that men pay the dowry and financially support their wives.[16] Thus, for Razi, it is as if there is no *fadl* (preference) at all. He discusses *qiwāma* in terms of "undertaking her affairs", but also of "being concerned with her protection and care" (*yahtammu bi hifzihā*).[17]

However, after establishing this, Razi unambiguously asserts the superiority of men over women.[18] He indicates that men are authorised (*musallatūn*) to discipline women and to "take over their hands". Furthermore, he comments that God made man a commander (*amīr*) over woman[19] and executor over her rights and established for him supremacy (*saltana*) and executive authority (*nafādh amr*) over her. Razi identifies two reasons for men's *qiwāma*, following the structure of the verse: The first is a kind of inherent preference ("with what God has given some of them more than others") and the second is financial ("with what they spend out of their own money").[20]

When Razi discusses the meaning of *fadl* (preference), he identifies that it is comprised of types. The first of these are the essential attributes (*sifāt haqīqiyya*) that make men superior: namely, knowledge and power. For him, there is "no doubt" that men have superior reason and knowledge, and that they can carry out more hard work. Thus, he asserts that men are superior in intellect, resolution, power, writing (in most cases), riding, and archery.[21]

After outlining these essential attributes, Razi presents various examples from religious law or custom to support his view:[22]

- Men are prophets, scholars, have major and minor *imāma* (leadership), and carry out *jihad*.
- Men call for the prayer, deliver sermons, perform *iʿtikāf* (spiritual retreat) in mosques, and bear witness in *hudūd* (prescribed punishments) and *qisās* (retaliation) matters (according to Sunni scholarly agreement), and – according to Shafi'i – in marriage.
- Men have a greater share in inheritance and are preferred in *taʿsīb* (in inheritance). [This refers to the custom of paternal relations receiving whatever is left over after the initial distribution.]
- Men also have liability for blood-money, *qasāma* (swearing that one did not commit murder), guardianship for marriage, divorce, revoking divorce, plurality of spouses, and *intisāb* (the right of affiliation by lineage).

Razi only briefly mentions the second reason for men's *qiwāma* mentioned in the verse, which he describes as "spending out of their own money". He glosses over this as referring to the paying of a dowry and spending of money on wives.[23]

Turning to the phrase regarding "righteous women", Razi firstly defines *qānitāt* as meaning obedient to God, and he defines *hāfizāt li al-ghayb* as guarding the rights of husbands.[24] Tabari, in comparison, had interpreted this to mean "obedient to both God and their husbands".

However, Razi then seems to imply that obedience does in fact relate to the husband. He states that the two descriptions (*qānitāt* and *hāfizāt li al-ghayb*) describe the righteous woman's state depending on the presence or absence of her husband.[25] Thus, "obedience" describes the woman's state when her husband is present. This clearly implies that obedience means obedience to the husband.

Whereas Tabari put forward his view of the meaning of *al-sālihāt*, Razi prefers to state that the grammar of the text (the definite article in *al-sālihāt*) means that every woman who is righteous (*sāliha*) must also be obedient (*qānita mutī'a*). Thus, in her husband's absence, the woman has to guard herself from adultery, protect his property from being lost, and safeguard his house from what is "inappropriate". Razi then quotes the same prophetic hadith cited by Tabari concerning the ideal woman.[26]

Qurtubi's commentary on this verse gives some of the early narrations as well as later juristic interpretations. His views are drawn mainly from the Maliki school of jurisprudence.[27]

Like Razi, he includes a "natural" explanation for the preference of men over women, referring to a biological argument that women are moist and cool, while men are warm and hard. His view of the verse is uncompromisingly patriarchal: women must obey their husbands. When Qurtubi provides the natural reasons, he introduces these by saying "it is said" (*qīla*).[28] Thus, "it is said" that men are superior to women in rationality and management of affairs and that men are more powerful in their selves (*nafs*) and inclinations (*tab'*), because in men the qualities of warmness and hardness (*al-harāra wa al-yabūsa*) prevail, making them powerful and severe, whereas in women moistness and coolness (*al-rutūba wa al-burūda*) prevail, leaving them tender and weak.[29]

Notably, Qurtubi is the first of the commentators examined here to quote a number of hadith whose contents were "demeaning to women" in general:[30] urging women to show utmost respect to their husbands by saying that if anyone is allowed to prostrate to anyone other than God, it would have been to the husband; commanding women to agree to sex even on the back of a camel; and asserting that the angels curse women who leave their husbands' beds. Qurtubi cites several jurists' views to support the idea that husbands need not maintain their wives if the latter are disobedient.[31]

Furthermore, Qurtubi, like Razi, provides several reasons for the preference of men over women. Unlike Razi, he gives the religious reasons first, and he uses a much shorter list to justify this: first, rulers, leaders, and those who fight in battle are men; second, men have to pay the dowry and maintain their wives because of their preference in inheritance.[32]

Similarly to Razi, Qurtubi identifies two reasons why God gave men the right of *qiyām* over women: the religious and natural reasons given above, which Qurtubi equates with the preference (*fadl*); and because of what they spend out of their money (in line with the verse). Qurtubi also argues that this verse indicated that men have the right of *ta'dīb* (discipline) over women. However, he adds that if women safeguard men's rights, men should not mistreat them.[33]

Qurtubi provides a linguistic discussion of *qawwām*. He explains that it is the intensive form of *qiyām*.[34] As such, it means "undertaking" something, having the sole right to make decisions regarding it, and striving to preserve it. Thus the *qiyām* of the man over the woman[35] includes: managing her, educating and disciplining her (*ta'dīb*), keeping her in her house, and preventing her from appearing in public. The woman is obliged to obey the man and fulfil his commands as long as they do not constitute *ma'siya*, a word usually understood to mean "disobedience to God".[36] He summarises that the reason (*ta'līl*) for the obligation to obey husbands is their preference (*fadīla*), maintenance (of their wives; *nafaqa*), rationality (*'aql*), and power (*quwwa*) in matters related to *jihād*, inheritance, and the commanding of good and preventing of evil. Qurtubi also notes that some narrations assert that the reason for men's preference is because men grow beards, but he dismisses this idea, arguing that a man may grow his beard but do none of the things above.[37]

Finally, Qurtubi commented that the ulama understood the phrase "and because they spend on them from their own money" to mean that if a husband no longer provided for his wife, he was no longer *qawwām* over her, and she could break the contract of marriage because the "object" of marriage no longer exists.[38] Thus, if the husband is unable to provide maintenance and clothing the Shafi'is and Malikis hold this to be a sufficient "legal indicant" (*dalāla*) for the annulling (*faskh*) of the marriage. However, the Hanafis do not, because of their interpretation of Qur'an 2:280.[39]

In Qurtubi's understanding of the righteous woman, *qānitāt* is about obedience to the husband (he omits any mention of God) and undertaking (*al-qiyām bi*) to protect her husband's rights and with regard to his property and her self when he is away. He cites the prophetic hadith with the husband-centric definition of the ideal woman, as provided by Tabari.[40]

Ibn Kathir's approach is an attempt, in summary form, to return to the text-centric approach of Tabari. He cites more hadith than Razi and does not engage to as great an extent as Razi or Qurtubi with the extended reason-based explanations of male superiority.

However, Ibn Kathir includes a few general statements that summarise the results of this reason-based approach of other commentators: for example, when interpreting the key phrase "with what God has given to some of them more than others", he states that men are both superior to (*afdal min*) and better than (*khayrun min*) women. Because of this, certain vocations, including prophecy, the highest leadership (*al-mulk al-a'zam*), and the position of judge, were restricted to men.[41] Despite Ibn Kathir's focus on narrations, he provides a very concise version of the nature-based argument used by Razi and Qurtubi.

Regarding the specific meaning of *qawwām*, Ibn Kathir states that it means that a man[42] is a woman's head (*ra'īsuha*), her master (*kabīruha*), her ruler (*al-hākim 'alayha*), and her discipliner (*mu'addibuha*). Indeed, he indicates that man is better than woman "in his essence" (*fi nafsihi*).[43] To support this view he quotes – and was probably among the first to do so in this context – Qur'an 2:228: *wa li al-rijāli 'alayhinna daraja* ("and husbands have a degree [of right] over them").[44]

Ibn Kathir also refers to several hadith that are demeaning to women. He quotes (in connection with the discussion of *qawwām*) a hadith that predicts that a community led by a woman will not prosper.[45] Later, in the section regarding *nushūz*, he cites a number of women-demeaning hadith that echo those chosen by Qurtubi. In his explanation of "what they spend out of their money", Ibn Kathir comments that this pertains to dowry, maintenance, and the "responsibilities towards them that are ordained by God in His Book and the Sunna of His Prophet".[46]

Ibn Kathir cites Ibn Abbas "and others" in support of the view that *qānitāt* means "obedient to their husbands", and, like Qurtubi, does not mention obedience to God. He states that *hāfizāt li al-ghayb* means that the "righteous woman" would guard her private parts and the husband's property in his absence, and he cites the hadith regarding the ideal woman that was discussed above.[47] He also cites the following hadith:

> If a woman prays her five prayers, fasts her month of Ramadan, guards her private parts, and obeys her husband, it is said to her: "Enter the Garden from whatever gate you please."[48]

In this hadith a woman's obedience to her husband is placed on the same level as obligatory acts of worship.

Unlike Ibn Kathir, Suyuti[49] attempts to present his commentary entirely through the words of past authorities. He does not attempt to adjudicate or harmonise between the narrations, and they do not add very much to the general view already conveyed. However, he still manages to be overtly patriarchal, by adducing several pages of hadith and statements of Companions and Successors that encapsulated a reading of the verse that is demeaning to women.[50]

He begins with the hadith of the ideal woman cited above, which he presents with two slightly different wordings. He then cites several pages of texts, which include:

- A report from Umar: "A man does not enjoy anything better after faith in God than a woman of good character, loving and fertile, and a man does not suffer any evil after *kufr* (unbelief) in God than a woman of bad character and sharp tongue."
- A text from Abd al-Rahman: "A righteous woman for a righteous man is like a golden crown on the head of a king, and a bad woman for a righteous man is like a heavy burden for an old man."
- A text from Abd Allah b. Amr: "Shall I inform you of three who are destitute? ... An oppressive leader: if you do well, he does not thank you, and if you do badly, he does not forgive; a bad neighbour: if he sees something good, he covers it up, and if he sees something evil, he spreads it around; and a bad woman: if you see her, she irritates you, and if you are away from her, she betrays you."[51]

The Twelver Imam Shi'i scholar Ali Qummi b. Babawayh Qummi (d. 329/ 939) does not connect the financial maintenance of men with their status, or with a position of authority over women. He comments that wive's duties are to be limited to guarding themselves in their husband's absence. He explains that the last part of the verse indicates that wives are obliged to be sexually available to husbands when men wish to have sex. Qummi does not discuss the issue of qiwāma in relation to authority or innate differences, and he does not discuss or even mention the question of whether "obedient" in the verse meant obedience to the husband or to God.[52]

Modern interpretations of the Qur'anic verse

During the modern period, there have been many examples of interpretation of this verse and the issue of qiwāma. Many still interpret the verse in a highly patriarchal way. However, there are also non-patriarchal interpretations.

Muslim scholars who assert the superiority of men

Some scholars, like some pre-modern commentators, suggest that men's "superiority" over women comes from the innate qualities that men have, which women do not. These qualities include "sound intellect, composure, patience and endurance". Thus, within a marriage the husband's role is "to take care of that which Allah has placed him in charge of", while the role of his wife is "to be obedient to her Lord and to obey her husband".[53]

The modern Shi'i scholar Tabataba'i argues (similar to Razi and Qurtubi) that men have certain natural characteristics such as "stronger rationality than women". They are also stronger in terms of "bearing difficulties" and in performing heavy tasks.[54] In his commentary on this verse, Tabataba'i argues that qiwāma is not a specific rule for a husband's conduct in relation to his wife but a general statement that applies to society at large. He defines al-qayyim as "one who looks after the affairs of another person", and notes that qawwām is an intensive form of qayyim. He interprets the phrase "with what God has given to some of them more than others" as referring to natural characteristics of men, as a result of which men excel over women. In this assertion he includes men's supposedly greater juridical acumen, their greater strength and bravery, and their greater capacity to perform tasks which require perseverance and fortitude; in contrast women are described as "dominated by feelings and emotions" and as embodying "gracefulness and delicateness".[55]

Tabataba'i defines the phrase "what they spend out of their own money" as pertaining to the dowry and financial maintenance; however, he does not make qiwāma conditional on that. Rather, he asserts that men, generally speaking, are collectively the maintainers of women and that the phrase "men are protectors and maintainers of women" pertains not only to the realm of marriage but also to the legal, political, military, and general societal aspects of human life:[56]

Men held politics, military, etc.

Men as a group have authority over women as a group in those common affairs which have more affinity with man's enhanced prudence and hardiness, that is, rulership, judiciary and war.[57]

However, the phrase *righteous women* (*sālihāt*) is interpreted by him to apply only in the context of marriage. He defines *qānitāt* as referring to wives of abiding obedience and submission.[58]

Tabataba'i also acknowledges that a man's authority over his wife should be relegated to a specific domain:

> [A husband's authority] does not negate the independence of woman in her individual will and activities; she decides what she wants and acts as she wishes and man has no right to interfere in any way — except when she intends to do something unlawful ... [The] husband's authority over the wife does not mean that she has lost control over her own self or property or is restricted in her will or action regarding its management; Nor does it mean that woman is not free and independent in safeguarding and protecting her personal and social rights, nor that she is hindered from adopting suitable means to achieve those rights ... It means that when the husband spends his wealth on her in return for conjugal rights, then she must obey and submit to him in all things connected with sexual intercourse (when he is present), and protect him in his absence i.e. she should not betray him behind his back by having unlawful affairs with another man. Also she should not deceive him concerning the property which he gives her by virtue of matrimony as a partner in domestic life.[59]

Here Tabataba'i evidences strong similarities to the pre-modern views. This is also a reference to the traditional Islamic legal position that a marriage contract is analogous to that of a contract of sale, where the husband gives the wife her dowry and maintains her in exchange for sexual rights, a view that is commonly found in the interpretation of the second half of Qur'an 4:34.[60] *Yikes*

Maududi also states that men are superior to women in general:

> Men are superior to women in the sense that they have been endowed with certain natural qualities and powers that have not been given to women or have been given in a less degree, and not in the sense that they are above them in honor and excellence.[61]

And in the family:

> Man has been made *qawwām* (governor) of the family because of his natural qualities and woman has been made his dependant for her own safety and protection because of her natural drawbacks.[62]

Men, naturally gifted more power and control
Women, free but inferior

To support this view, he cites the prophetic hadith about the ideal woman that was commonly mentioned by pre-modern commentators.[63] However, for Maududi, obedience to God is of far greater importance than obedience to the husband and takes precedence over it:

> [T]herefore, it is the duty of the wife to refuse to obey her husband, if and when he orders her to do a thing which amounts to Allah's disobedience. In that case it shall be a sin to obey him.[64]

Some scholars, such as the Council of Ulama of South Africa (a body of traditionalist Sunni scholars), have followed the trend set by pre-modern interpretation in arguing that men are superior to women from the perspective of law. They claim that this is because the Shari'a has established particular roles for men and women that cannot be overturned. The Shari'a accords the husband complete authority over his wife, even to the extent of requiring a man's wife to alter her opinions to those of her husband, and "wholeheartedly submit to his whims and fancies". This is based on the reasoning that God has created a man's wife for "her husband's comfort and peace".[65] These scholars take the position that for a Muslim wife to glance at another man should be considered an act of unfaithfulness and condemned by the husband; whereas the "delicate situation" wherein a man is unfaithful to his wife should be considered by the wife with patience, and that she should attempt to win him back with love and tenderness in order to preserve the marriage.[66]

Non-patriarchal approaches

The idea of *qiwāma* has been seen by some Muslim women scholars in a more balanced way: as giving men a leadership role in a family, while charging them with responsibility over women, including providing for them economically.

Haifaa Jawad, a contemporary British Muslim academic, seems to agree that Qur'an 4:34 gives the husband the right to be in charge of the family. However, she argues the following:

> The headship of the husband should on no account be a license for dictatorship ... if the husband misuses or abuses his status, the wife has the right to interfere to rectify the situation. After all, the whole issue of being a chair-person is to ensure the smooth running of the family.[67]

She also asserts that any neglect by the husband in this responsibility "justifies his replacement by the more able person [the wife]".[68] Jawad clearly sees the verse and the husband–wife relationship differently from most pre-modern and many modern commentators, who did not envisage the wife as actively rectifying a problem caused as a result of abuse by the husband.

Jawad specifies that these verses should be read in the context of the family. She identifies the Qur'anic ideal to be "one of equal partnership", which has been replaced among Muslims by "authoritarianism and dictatorship". She cites the views of the South African Council of Ulama (cited above) as an example of the latter.[69]

Others in the modern period have also perceived *qiwāma* as an economic relationship. According to a document prepared by the Muslim Brotherhood of Egypt,[70] an influential Muslim movement of the modern period, *qiwāma* is merely a matter of leadership and direction in exchange for duties that should be performed. The husband is charged with payment of the dowry in marriage, provision of the house, and meeting the needs of his wife and children. He cannot force his wife to pay for any of these expenses, even if she is wealthy. In most cases, the husband would be older, more socially connected, and the breadwinner of the family. This document also asserts that every type of group, including the family, must have a leader to guide it within the limits of what God has ordained, for there can be no obedience for a human being in a matter involving disobedience to God.[71] *Leaders ordained by God.*

Some interpretations have taken this line of thought further by arguing that *qiwāma* refers to a functional relationship that is economically, socio-culturally, and historically contingent and not inherent. They confine *qiwāma* to an economic relationship, without any inherent idea of male leadership. Riffat Hassan, for example, suggests that *qawwām* is primarily about an economic relationship, that of breadwinner. She points out that Qur'an 4:34, especially the first sentence in the verse, is normative rather than descriptive, because not all men provide for women. She also highlights the fact that although the Qur'an charges the husband with the duty of being the breadwinner, this does not mean that women cannot or should not provide for themselves. It simply means that the Qur'an does not expect women to be breadwinners.[72]

Amina Wadud, Asma Barlas, and Azizah al-Hibri[73] also consider *qiwāma* to be functional, socially contingent, and not inherent in nature. They argue that the man's role as "protector" in the verse is linked to men's economic role as breadwinners and the overall gender dynamics of seventh-century Medina. Thus, in the absence of greater material resources in possession of the husband, there is no *qiwāma*.

Wadud and Riffat Hassan argue that linguistically *qawwāmūn* refers to "breadwinners" or "those who provide a means of support or livelihood".[74] Wadud argues that:

> Even if men are *qawwāmūn* over women based on something else, the verse clearly states that only *some* men are *qawwāmūn*, which is much different than a categorical or essentialist definition of men as better than women.[75]

Al-Hibri rejects the idea that Qur'an 4:34 describes men's innate physical and intellectual superiority, as seen in pre-modern commentaries, since it is not mentioned in the verse; rather, she identifies the basic notion underlying the word *qawwāmūn* as "moral guidance and caring".[76] She refutes the idea that *all* men are *qawwāmūn* over *all* women, saying that it is only in matters where God gave "some of the men more than some of the women".

This highlighting of the word "some" is a key difference of the modern period from earlier understandings of the text, as it emphasises the fact that God's preference cannot be assumed. Thus, for example, if a man knows more than his wife about an area of business she wishes to invest in, he has the right to:

> guide her and protect ... her interests in that matter specifically, but she has the final say. And, if she is "self-supporting", then he has no right to counsel her at all.[77]

In this, al-Hibri clearly envisages a scenario where a woman is likely to be economically independent and intellectually able. This is a contrast to the picture of the passive ideal woman in *some* of the hadith attributed to the Prophet, whose role is primarily to care for the husband's family and guard his possessions and her chastity.

Al-Hibri argues that the Qur'an contradicts the idea of men as inherently superior, as the Qur'an states that "the believers, men and women, are *awliyā'* (supporters, protectors), one of another".[78] For al-Hibri, this verse (9:71) clearly asserts the equal status of men and women. She argues that men cannot be inherently superior to women because women are also their *awliyā'*: "protectors", "in charge", or "guides". She frames her criticism of the idea of men's superiority over women as a question: "How could women be in charge of [the] men who have absolute authority over their lives?"[79]

Fazlur Rahman argues that a wife's economic self-sufficiency and contribution to the household reduces the husband's superiority "since as a human, he has no superiority over his wife".[80] Like al-Hibri, Fazlur Rahman identifies a general principle in the Qur'an that "religiously speaking, men and women have absolute parity".[81] This, he suggests, is indicated by numerous verses in the Qur'an.[82] However, Rahman concedes that the Qur'an seems to "envisage division of labor and a difference in functions", without specifying how.

For Rahman, as for many other modern commentators, Qur'an 4:34 describes a "functional, not inherent superiority".[83] He translates the verse as: "Men are in charge of women because God has given some humans excellence over others and because men have the liability of expenditure [on women]." For him, this means that men are "charged with earning money and spending it on women". He does not take issue directly with the word "some" in the verse but by translating *hum* (in ba'dahum) as "humans" rather than "men", he implies that preference (*tafḍīl*) may potentially apply to women as well.[84]

Rahman connects the functional superiority of men here to other verses in the Qur'an that speak of God's preferring some over others in wealth or power, or of some Messengers over others. Again, these types of superiority are not inherent, but functional. Thus, a wife's economic self-sufficiency and contribution to the household reduces the husband's economic superiority "to that extent ... as a *human*, he has no superiority over his wife [Rahman's emphasis]".[85]

Khaled Abou El Fadl also argues that the status of *qiwāma* is specifically connected to an operative cause (*'illa*): the ability to earn and spend. Thus, it is not an unqualified right that is inherent to men. Like al-Hibri, he argues that a man's *qiwāma* does not exist if he is not supporting his family, if his wife makes an equal financial contribution, or – interestingly – if she has "an equal earning potential that she chose to forgo" presumably to bear and raise children.[86] Abou El Fadl suggests that a husband and wife might equally share the obligation of *qiwāma*.[87]

Abou El Fadl defines *qiwāma* as "service and protection", and specifically denies that it includes the "right to *ta'dīb*" (disciplining), which clearly has a connotation of physical discipline among the specific Muslim communities that he describes. For Abou El Fadl, "a wife is not a child", and thus there is no right to *ta'dīb*, physical or not.[88] This may be compared with the views of Tabari, Razi, and others who clearly saw *ta'dīb* as a central part of *qiwāma*.

Muhammad Shahrur adopts an approach that is based on a close linguistic reading of the passage and a comparison of other Qur'anic instances of the relevant terms. He identifies some passages as embodying overall principles that negate the possibility of a gendered reading of the verse. He therefore takes the possibility of gender equality much further than many other modern commentators.

Shahrur argues that *qiwāma* is not gender-specific, but rather based on certain qualities that both genders could embody.[89] He understands *qiwāma* to mean "to take care of", "to be responsible", or "to be in charge".[90] He reads the words *rijāl* and *nisā'* in the verse as not applying literally to men and women. In the Qur'an, he says, *rijāl* is often used as a term for both sexes, but even more ambiguously, it is used in a sense deriving from its root *r-j-l*, whose general meaning is "to walk" or "go on foot", which both sexes can do.[91] Shahrur suggests that a cultural association between men and walking or public activity may explain the connection.[92] Similarly, he notes that the Arabic root of *nisā'* also expresses an idea of deferment or postponement: here, the cultural association may have been the idea that God created women second, after men.[93] For Shahrur, then, although the term *qawwāmūn 'alā* means "those in charge" or "those with power and competence", the non-gendered nature of *rijāl* and *nisā'* means that the verse is simply saying:

> High competence, moral strength, determination, education, and strong cultural awareness will always put some men *and* women in charge of others who do not excel in these things.[94]

Also, Shahrur asserts that *qiwāma* refers to any guardianship in any aspect of society: not simply those in the family.[95] He also notes the verse's use of the word "some", which for him negates the possibility that it only refers to men and women. Like Rahman, he connects it to passages in the Qur'an with a similar tone.[96]

> See how We have bestowed more on some than on others [*faddalnā ba'-dahum 'alā ba'd*]; but verily the Hereafter is greater in rank and gradation [*darajāt*] and greater in excellence [*tafdīl*].[97]

Shahrur's overall view of the relationship between men and women is based on his reading of Qur'an 2:187, "[Your wives] are your garments [*libās*] and you are their garments." He argues that the term *libās* ("intertwined" or "blended") refers to a symbiosis. Thus the relationship outlined was one of "equality and equivalence".[98]

Drawing on broader Qur'anic principles such as justice, Abu Zayd maintains that if the Qur'an explicitly endorses spiritual equality of the sexes, equality in creation,[99] and equality in performing religious duties and rights, then it could not sanction any inequality in terms of society: thus, in modern society women can also be considered *qawwāmūn*.[100]

Concluding remarks

The various pre-modern commentators on the Qur'an have evidenced a high degree of interpretive convergence. Most regard women as unequal to men and assert that women should be subject to the authority of men. Some commentators, like Tabari, afford women some agency, although others, such as Ibn Kathir, argue that men have been given complete authority over women.

The main reason for the degree of uniformity among these commentators on this Qur'anic verse appears to be that they were functioning in a social, cultural, political, and economic context that strengthened their view that women were subordinate to men. They interpreted the verse through this lens, and thus considered that God had dictated this relationship between men and women. Men were in charge of the religious, political, social, and cultural affairs of the community. They were also the dominant players in the economic sphere. Men were in charge of running the states, managing the armies, and were also part of the armed forces. In comparison, women mostly had domestic roles then.

Similarly, in their societies educational opportunities were predominantly for men, even though nothing was stated in the Qur'an or in the Sunna of the Prophet to suggest that women should be denied education and, in fact, there is evidence to suggest the contrary. Muslim social, cultural, political, economic, and religious norms and values were embedded in the larger late antiquity Near Eastern cultures, which generally shared similar views regarding the role and the status of genders in society. As this chapter has shown, this context meant that the idea that women were to be subject to the authority of men went largely unchallenged, with some commentators going so far as to argue that women were inferior to men intellectually as well as biologically.

However, the twentieth century has seen dramatic changes in all areas of Muslim societies. Women have access to education in most Muslim societies, just like men. Women also have greater opportunities for employment, which has resulted in the active participation of women in the public sphere. Universities accept enrolments from both men and women, with women outperforming men in some areas. In many Muslim societies, women are in charge of major departments of the government, companies, businesses, and social and cultural institutions. In households, it is not unusual for a wife to be more educated than her husband, and also to contribute financially to the welfare of the family. This completely different macro context has impacted on the question of interpretation of the Qur'an as a whole, and particularly texts such as Qur'an 4:34.

The Qur'an seems to have observed that men enjoyed social, cultural, political, and religious authority over women in early seventh-century CE Arabia. It then stated that men were responsible for the upkeep of the family. Such an observation must have seemed natural to the first community of Muslims in line with their social context. For most pre-modern scholars, a verse such as this was not necessarily taking, as a starting point, the prevalent norms and values of its immediate revelational milieu. They interpreted the verse as a general rule that is universally applicable.

However, if the Qur'an was revealed in the twenty-first century, it would, most likely, approach this topic in a different way. Even when the Qur'an made that statement in the early seventh century, it was careful in how it expressed the teaching. For instance, it did not say that *all* men had more advantages over all women. Rather, it said some people had advantages over others, which is accurate: some men have advantages over some women and vice versa. Today, Muslims who are reading this text have to take into account their present context. This will require, at times, radical changes to be introduced to the views held by pre-modern scholars on gender roles, given the opportunities available for both men and women, the degree of political power men and women have, and also the dominant discourses on equality and equal rights that occur as part of the larger discussions on human rights today. It is obvious that in many respects relating to gender roles the macro contexts of the seventh and twenty-first centuries do not match. Therefore, any commentator on the Qur'an has to question if a contextually appropriate Qur'anic observation or injunction for the seventh century should be applied as a general rule in the twenty-first century.

Many Muslim scholars today have argued for interpretations of the Qur'an in the light of the contextual information that exists for the early period as well as for the contemporary period. Failure to do so may lead to interpretations that are not only irrelevant but also inappropriate and obstructive in terms of meeting Qur'anic objectives of justice and fairness, and contemporary sensibilities of Muslims today. Since the original text we are exploring here was contextually relevant, insisting on applying the same interpretation of that verse coming from the pre-modern period in the significantly different context of our time today will be contrary to the actual spirit and intent of the Qur'anic advice, and undermine the Qur'an's claim to universal relevance and guidance.

Notes

1 Qur'an 4:34.
2 Tabari, *Jami' al-Bayan, tafsir* of Q. 434, www.altafsir.com.
3 These included al-Hasan, Qatada, Ibn Jurayj, and al-Suddi.
4 Tabari, *Jami' al-Bayan, tafsir* of Q. 4:34.
5 Imad al-Din Abu al-Fida' Ibn Kathir, *Tafsir, al-Qur'an al-Azim, tafsir* of Q. 4:34, www. altafsir.com; Suyuti, *al-Durr al-Manthur, tafsir* of Q. 4:34, www.altafsir.com.

6 al-Fakhr al-Razi, *Mafatih al-Ghayb: al-Tafsir al-Kabir*, *tafsir* of Q. 4:34, www.altafsir.com.

7 Abu Abd Allah Muhammad Qurtubi, *al-Jami' li Ahkam al-Qur'an*, *tafsir* of Q. 4:34, www.altafsir.com.

8 Qur'an 4:11–12.

9 Qur'an 4:32.

10 Tabari, *Jami' al-Bayan*, *tafsir* of Q. 4:34.

11 Tabari, *Jami' al-Bayan*, *tafsir* of Q. 4:34.

12 Tabari, *Jami' al-Bayan*, *tafsir* of Q. 4:34.

13 Tabari, *Jami' al-Bayan*, *tafsir* of Q. 4:34.

14 Tabari, *Jami' al-Bayan*, *tafsir* of Q. 4:34.

15 Tabari, *Jami' al-Bayan*, *tafsir* of Q. 4:34.

16 Razi, *al-Tafsir al-Kabir*, *tafsir* of Q. 4:34.

17 Razi, *al-Tafsir al-Kabir*, *tafsir* of Q. 4:34.

18 Razi, *al-Tafsir al-Kabir*, *tafsir* of Q. 4:34.

19 Razi uses "women" [*nisā'* or *mar'a*] throughout, even when the context clearly shows that he is talking about wives (as in talking about dowries and enjoying each other's company). He is likely to have conflated these two categories, perhaps seeing women as encapsulated in the category of "wife". Razi, *al-Tafsir al-Kabir*, *tafsir* of Q. 4:34.

20 Razi, *al-Tafsir al-Kabir*, *tafsir* of Q. 4:34.

21 Razi, *al-Tafsir al-Kabir*, *tafsir* of Q. 4:34.

22 Razi, *al-Tafsir al-Kabir*, *tafsir* of Q. 4:34.

23 Razi, *al-Tafsir al-Kabir*, *tafsir* of Q. 4:34.

24 Razi, *al-Tafsir al-Kabir*, *tafsir* of Q. 4:34.

25 Razi, *al-Tafsir al-Kabir*, *tafsir* of Q. 4:34.

26 Razi, *al-Tafsir al-Kabir*, *tafsir* of Q. 4:34.

27 Qurtubi, *al-Jami' li Ahkam al-Qur'an*, *tafsir* of Q. 4:34.

28 Qurtubi, *al-Jami' li Ahkam al-Qur'an*, *tafsir* of Q. 4:34.

29 Qurtubi, *al-Jami' li Ahkam al-Qur'an*, *tafsir* of Q. 4:34.

30 Khaled Abou El Fadl, *Speaking in God's Name* (Oxford: Oneworld, 2001), 209.

31 Qurtubi, *al-Jami' li Ahkam al-Qur'an*, *tafsir* of Q. 4:34.

32 Qurtubi, *al-Jami' li Ahkam al-Qur'an*, *tafsir* of Q. 4:34.

33 Qurtubi, *al-Jami' li Ahkam al-Qur'an*, *tafsir* of Q. 4:34.

34 Qurtubi, *al-Jami' li Ahkam al-Qur'an*, *tafsir* of Q. 4:34.

35 Like Razi, Qurtubi always refers in general to men and women, as the verse does, but clearly envisages husbands and wives in much of his discussion.

36 Qurtubi, *al-Jami' li Ahkam al-Qur'an*, *tafsir* of Q. 4:34.

37 Qurtubi, *al-Jami' li Ahkam al-Qur'an*, *tafsir* of Q. 4:34.

38 Qurtubi, *al-Jami' li Ahkam al-Qur'an*, *tafsir* of Q. 4:34.

39 "If the debtor is in difficulty, then delay things until matters become easier for him; still, if you were to write it off as an act of charity, that would be better for you, if only you knew."

40 Qurtubi, *al-Jami' li Ahkam al-Qur'an*, *tafsir* of Q. 4:34.

41 Ibn Kathir, *Tafsir*, *tafsir* of Q. 4:34.

42 Like the other commentators, Ibn Kathir uses "man" (*al-rajul/al-rijāl*) and "woman" (*al-nisā'/al-mar'a*) throughout, although very often this can be assumed to be in the context of marriage.

43 Ibn Kathir, *Tafsir*, *tafsir* of Q. 4:34.

44 Muhammad Abdel Haleem, *The Qur'an: A Modern Translation* (Oxford: Oxford University Press, 2004), 26.

45 *Lan yufliha qawmun wallū amrahum imra'atan.*

46 Ibn Kathir, *Tafsir*, *tafsir* of Q. 4:34.

47 Ibn Kathir, *Tafsir*, *tafsir* of Q. 4:34.

48 Ibn Kathir, *Tafsir*, *tafsir* of Q. 4:34.

49 Suyuti, *al-Durr al-Manthur*, *tafsir* of Q. 4:34.

50 Suyuti, *al-Durr al-Manthur, tafsir* of Q. 4:34.
51 Suyuti, *al-Durr al-Manthur, tafsir* of Q. 4:34.
52 Ali b. Ibrahim al-Qummi, *Tafsir al-Qummi*, ed. al-Sayyid al-Tayyib al-Musawi al-Jaza'iri (Najaf: Matba'at al-Najaf, 1966/7), v. 1, 137.
53 As-Sa'di, *Taysirul-Karim–Rahman*, cited in M. Shooman, *The Righteous Wife*, trans. Abu Talhah Dawood (London: Al-Hidaayah Publishing and Distribution, 1996), 10.
54 Allama Muhammad Hussain Tabataba'i, *Tafsir Al Mizan*, www.shiasource.com/al-mizan/.
55 Tabataba'i, *Tafsir Al Mizan, tafsir* of Q. 4:34.
56 Tabataba'i, *Tafsir Al Mizan, tafsir* of Q. 4:34.
57 Tabataba'i, *Tafsir Al Mizan, tafsir* of Q. 4:34.
58 Tabataba'i, *Tafsir Al Mizan, tafsir* of Q. 4:34.
59 Tabataba'i, *Tafsir Al Mizan, tafsir* of Q. 4:34.
60 See Ali Kecia, *Marriage and Slavery in Early Islam* (Cambridge, MA: Harvard University Press, 2010).
61 Sayyid Abul Ala Maududi, *Tafhim al-Qur'an: The Meaning of the Qur'an, tafsir* of Q. 4:34, www.englishtafsir.com/Quran/4/index.html#sdfootnote57sym.
62 Maududi, *Tafhim al-Qur'an, tafsir* of Q. 4:34.
63 Maududi, *Tafhim al-Qur'an, tafsir* of Q. 4:34.
64 Maududi, *Tafhim al-Qur'an, tafsir* of Q. 4:34.
65 Cited in Haifaa A. Jawad, *The Rights of Women in Islam: An Authentic Approach* (Hampshire: Palgrave Macmillan, 1998), 38–40.
66 Cited in Jawad, *The Rights of Women in Islam*, 38–40.
67 Jawad, *The Rights of Women in Islam*, 37.
68 Jawad, *The Rights of Women in Islam*, 37.
69 Jawad, *The Rights of Women in Islam*, 38–40.
70 Ikhwan, "Role of Women", www.amaana.org/ISWEB/woman.htm.
71 Ikhwan, "Role of Women"; see also Muslim Brotherhood, *The Role of Women in Islamic Society According to the Muslim Brotherhood* (London: International Islamic Forum, 1994), 8–9.
72 Riffat Hassan, "An Islamic Perspective", in *Sexuality: A Reader*, ed. Karen Lebacqz (Cleveland, OH: The Pilgrim Press, 1999), 337–73: 354.
73 Amina Wadud, *Qur'an and Woman: Rereading the Sacred Text from a Woman's Perspective*, second edition (Oxford: Oxford University Press, 1999), 66–74; Asma Barlas, *"Believing Women" in Islam: Unreading Patriarchal Interpretations of the Qur'an* (Austin: University of Texas Press, 2002), 184–89; Azizah al-Hibri, "A Study of Islamic Herstory: Or, How Did We Ever Get into This Mess?", *Women's Studies International Forum*, Special Issue: *Women and Islam*, 5 (1982), 207–19: 217–18.
74 Barlas, *"Believing Women"*, 186.
75 Wadud, *Qur'an and Woman*, 71.
76 Al-Hibri, "A Study of Islamic Herstory", 217.
77 Al-Hibri, "A Study of Islamic Herstory", 218.
78 Qur'an 9:71.
79 Al-Hibri, "A Study of Islamic Herstory", 218.
80 Fazrul Rahman, *Major Themes of the Qur'an* (Chicago: University of Chicago Press, 2009), 49.
81 Rahman, *Major Themes of the Qur'an*, 49.
82 These include Qur'an 4:124 ("Whoever does good deeds, whether male or female, while being believers, they shall enter Paradise"), Qur'an 40:40, and the famous Qur'an 33:35 (in this verse a long list of the positive traits of the believers is given, and men and women are mentioned separately but as equals); Rahman, *Major Themes of the Qur'an* .
83 Rahman, *Major Themes of the Qur'an*, 49.
84 Rahman, *Major Themes of the Qur'an*, 49.
85 Rahman, *Major Themes of the Qur'an*, 49.
86 Khaled Abou El Fadl, *Conference of the Books: The Search for Beauty in Islam* (Lanham, MD: University of America Press, 2001), 273.

87 Abou El Fadl, *Conference of the Books*, 276.
88 Abou El Fadl, *Conference of the Books*, 246–47.
89 Muhammad Shahrur, *The Qur'an, Morality and Critical Reason: The Essential Muhammad Shahrur*, trans. Andreas Christmann (Leiden: Brill, 2009), 272–92.
90 Shahrur, *The Qur'an, Morality and Critical Reason*, 273.
91 For example, Qur'an 22:27 states, "[the pilgrims] will come to you on foot [*rijālan*]".
92 Shahrur, *The Qur'an, Morality and Critical Reason*, 274–75.
93 Shahrur, *The Qur'an, Morality and Critical Reason*, 276.
94 Shahrur, *The Qur'an, Morality and Critical Reason*, 280.
95 Shahrur, *The Qur'an, Morality and Critical Reason*, 280–82.
96 Shahrur, *The Qur'an, Morality and Critical Reason*, 280.
97 Qur'an 17:21.
98 Shahrur, *The Qur'an, Morality and Critical Reason*, 272–73.
99 Qur'an 4:1.
100 Nasr Hamid Abu Zayd, "The Nexus of Theory and Practice", in *The New Voices of Islam: Rethinking Politics and Modernity, A Reader*, ed. Mehran Kamrava (Berkeley and Los Angeles: University of California Press, 2006), 153–76: 163–64.

12 Crucifixion and death of Jesus Christ

Whether Jesus Christ was crucified and died on the cross has been a key "theological" issue that Muslims have been debating from the first century of Islam. Although the Qur'an does not elaborate on this issue, and makes a brief reference to it in only one or two verses, Muslim theology and Qur'anic interpretation have strongly maintained the idea that Jesus was neither crucified nor killed. In fact, this has been the dominant position throughout much of Muslim history. This is likely to be an example of a theological position that was adopted very early on in Islam and has exerted a strong influence on how pre-modern Muslim commentators have interpreted the relevant Qur'anic texts. In a wider sense, it is an example of a dominant theological position that is pushing for a particular interpretation. How Muslims arrived at such a theological position is not within the scope of this chapter: what is relevant for the purpose of this inquiry is that the macro context of the pre-modern society favoured ideas such as the miraculous saving of a prophet from death, substitution of someone else for him, or raising him in body and spirit to the heavens. Although "miracles" can occur, other readings are possible for the relevant verse. In the macro context of the pre-modern period such alternative readings were not generally entertained even though one can find a degree of uneasiness on the part of some commentators about accepting the traditional narratives on this issue (for example, Razi). However, in the modern period, within a scientific worldview that is influenced by ideas such as reason and critical examination of theological positions, it is possible to rethink such positions particularly if there are no clearly spelt out texts in the Qur'an or in the *mutawātir* hadith (a hadith whose authenticity is beyond any doubt, according to hadith scholars) to support the position. Thus, although the premodern theological position regarding the crucifixion and death of Jesus is still dominant, other ideas are also emerging. This chapter will give the reader a sense of how Muslims interpreted the key phrase of Qur'an 4:157 in the pre-modern period and some of the variety of ways in which commentators are approaching the question today, in a different context.

Although Jesus himself is mentioned or referred to in almost a hundred separate verses of the Qur'an, his crucifixion is treated directly in only one,[1] and referred to obliquely in one other.[2] This chapter examines the most important of these verses: Qur'an 4:157, which says, "And they did not kill him, nor did they crucify him, though it was made to appear like that to them." The interpretation of this part of the verse is by no means uniform: interpretations range from outright denial of the crucifixion and death of Jesus (in the pre-modern period) to simple affirmation of the historicity of the event (in the modern period) at least by some Muslim scholars.[3]

Virtually all of the pre-modern Muslim commentators agree that God, in a miraculous manner, rescued Jesus from being crucified, and that someone else was substituted for Jesus on the cross; this is known as the "substitution narrative".[4] This explanation found its way into Islamic tradition very early on. The substitution narrative is based on various narrations (reports) that are ascribed to a number of early Muslims. Such narrations are traditionally held to be from anonymous Jewish and Christian sources and often referred to as "the stories of the Israelites" (*Isrā'iliyyāt*). This chapter first presents the main pre-modern interpretations of the verse using a range of Sunni and Shi'a sources. This is followed by discussion on modern interpretations of the same verse.

The relevant text

For our purposes, the most important verses on the crucifixion and death of Jesus are the following:

> And because they [the Children of Israel] disbelieved and uttered a terrible slander against Mary, and said, "We have killed the Messiah, Jesus, son of Mary, the Messenger of God." They did not kill him, nor did they crucify him, though it was made to appear like that to them [*wa lākin shubbiha lahum*]; those that disagreed about it are full of doubt, with no knowledge to follow, only supposition: they did not kill him, certainly [*yaqīnan*]. No! God raised him up to Himself. God is almighty and wise.[5]

These verses arise in the context of a broader moral discourse in chapter (*sūra*) 4. The verses, generally held to be from the Medinan period, discuss and criticise the Prophet's Jewish interlocutors. At various times during the Medinan period, there was religious and political tension between Muslims and the Jews in Medina, and the Qur'anic critique of certain Jewish people needs to be understood in that context. Here, the Qur'an criticises what it calls "faithlessness" (*kufr*)[6] in the history of the Jews when they "killed their prophets without justification"; slandered Mary, the mother of Jesus, defaming her virtue; and boasted that they had killed the Messiah.[7]

The reference to the crucifixion arises almost in passing, and is not the main subject of the verses.[8] The verse lists it as one of the examples of the moral failings of these particular Jews. It does not place any weight on the issue of crucifixion, which had by then become a central doctrine of the Christian Church. Rather it moves on to other aspects of the discussion. Viewing the entire set of verses in this context, one could come to the conclusion that the

Qur'an was probably less interested in rejecting a Christian theological position than in denouncing the ability of people who are rebellious towards God to act against God's will.

The crux of the verse, for the present discussion, arises when it describes what had actually happened to Jesus. The verse does not seem to say that Jesus was not killed: only that the Jews did not kill him. When the verse describes what actually happened, it does so using the passive verb *shubbiha*. The active form of this verb, *shabbaha*, can be translated as "rendered similar", "made to resemble", or "made confused". Used in the passive form, it is not clear which of these meanings is intended, and whether it refers to a person or the crucifixion as a whole.

In a clear example of the role of translation in interpreting the Qur'an, the following major English translations of the Qur'an present a range of interpretations. Translators who assume the phrase *shubbiha lahum* refers to the crucifixion translate as follows:

YUSUF ALI: but so it was made to appear to them ... [9]
MUHAMMAD ASAD: but it only seemed to them [as if it had been] so ... [10]
PICKTHALL: but it appeared so unto them ... [11]
ABDEL HALEEM: though it was made to appear like that to them ... [12]

Translators who assume that the phrase refers to Jesus adopt the following translation:

SAHIH INTERNATIONAL: but [another] was made to resemble him to them.[13]
SHAKIR: but it appeared to them so (like Isa) ... [14]   ↳ made to look like Jesus.

The latter interpretations are in line with the substitution narrative that was favoured by the majority of Muslim commentators in the pre-modern period.

Although this is the key verse in relation to the issue of Jesus' crucifixion, the raising (*raf'*) of Jesus is also mentioned twice more in the Qur'an. These verses are given here, to allow for further context:

O Jesus, indeed I will take you [*inni mutawaffika*] and raise you to Myself and purify you from those who disbelieve and make those who follow you superior to those who disbelieve until the Day of Resurrection. Then to Me is your return, and I will judge between you concerning that in which you used to differ.[15]

The key issue here is the interpretation of *mutawaffi*: the active participle of the verb *tawaffa*. This verb is most often used to mean "to cause to die", and in general its passive form, *tuwuffiya*, means "he passed away". However, the issue of whether or not Jesus died is relevant to the present discussion.

Another relevant verse contains a statement that the Qur'an presents as the words of Jesus:

Disbelief is huge w/ Islam.

So peace is on me the day I was born, the day that I die, and the day that I shall be raised up to life (again)![16]

There are also several verses in the Qur'an that argue that Jesus was mortal:

Say, "Who could avail ought against God if He wanted to destroy Jesus the Son of Mary and his mother … ?"[17]

The Messiah Jesus son of Mary [was] only a messenger. Messengers have passed away before him.[18]

Then when You received me [i.e. caused me to die], You were the watcher over them.[19]

[Jesus = messenger to Islam]

Muslim conception of Jesus

Demonstrate truth.

The Qur'an identifies Jesus as having a special importance as a prophet, by saying that God sent him with a range of miracles to support and demonstrate the truth of his mission.[20] These miracles included: sending the disciples a "table" laid with food,[21] creating a living bird from dust,[22] healing the blind and sick,[23] giving life to the dead,[24] and having knowledge of what people had eaten and what was in store for them in the coming days.[25] The Qur'an distinguished Jesus from the rest of humanity, referring to him as *kalimatuhu* ("His Word"), a term that it does not use to refer even to Adam.

Very early on then, Muslim commentators on the Qur'an and theologians appear to have adopted the idea that Jesus was – in a number of ways – different from other human beings. According to this conception, first, he was brought into this world without any human father and was "created" directly by God. In this way, he was similar to Adam, although he was created in the womb of Mary, whereas Adam had no biological father or mother. Furthermore, Jesus was able to "speak" while he was an infant in the cradle. This is shown in an incident when the relatives of Mary and the leaders of the community questioned Mary, accusing her of an unchaste act resulting in the birth of a child. Mary pointed to the child Jesus, who in turn spoke from the cradle.[26] By the time of Tabari's (d. 310/923) writings, these ideas had come to form an important part of the Muslim conception of Jesus. Given that Jesus was so different from other people and so unique, it seemed unlikely that his life ended in the way described in the Gospel accounts, namely, with crucifixion and death. Muslim tradition therefore elaborated on the statements of the Qur'an. According to some, Christ was replaced by a double, whereas according to others, his replacement was Simon of Cyrene or one of the Apostles (specifically, Judas).[27]

Pre-modern exegetical views

There are clear differences between each of the commentators examined here. Tabari's treatment of the verse 4:157 characteristically anchored itself in a presentation of transmitted narratives, and did not go into a close analysis of the grammatical construction of the verse or its precise inner workings. In this he differs from the approach taken by other commentators considered here, who were separated from him by several centuries: Zamakhshari (d. 538/1144), Razi (d. 605/1209), and Shawkani (d. 1250/1834). Of these later commentators, Zamakhshari and Razi in particular took a much closer look at the grammar of the Qur'anic verse, especially the difficult phrase *shubbiha lahum*. Also, following common practice in the Qur'anic exegetical tradition, these commentators incorporated the material of preceding commentators to a large extent. Often, this incorporation was verbatim and without attribution.

The substitution theory and "shubbiha lahum"

Tabari's Qur'anic commentary, *Jāmi' al-Bayan*, reveals that by the third century of Islam many Muslims had come to the view that it was not Jesus who was crucified. His commentary identifies two narratives regarding the crucifixion, and each narrative has multiple versions. Both narratives suggest that it was not Jesus who was crucified, but rather another man. Tabari relates two versions of the first narrative,[28] both of which found their way into Islamic tradition through the Yemeni figure Wahb b. Munabbih (d. c. 110/728), who was a member of the generation who succeeded the Prophet's Companions (that is, a Successor). Wahb is well known in Islamic tradition for having conveyed many *Isrā'iliyyāt* (Judeo-Christian) narratives.

According to Tabari's first version, when the Jews besieged Jesus and his disciples, God made all the disciples resemble Jesus. When the Jews demanded that Jesus show himself, Jesus said to his disciples, "Who among you is ready to sell himself today in return for Paradise?" and one of his disciples volunteered for martyrdom. Since this disciple had been made to resemble Jesus, the Jews took him and crucified him.[29]

The second version is a longer account. In some ways it parallels the Gospel accounts; however, it has some unique features. For example, according to this account Jesus was informed by God of his imminent death, and because of this – even though the Muslim position sees him saved from death in the end – he became worried and afraid. Inviting his disciples to eat, he served them, washed their hands, and wiped them with his clothes. When they objected, he said: "He who objects to anything that I do tonight is not from among my followers." After the meal, Jesus made an unusual request:

What I have done for you tonight of food, service and washing your hands, is simply a good example for you to follow. Indeed, you see that I am the best one of you, so do not be proud with each other. Instead, sacrifice yourselves for each other as I have sacrificed myself for you. As for the matter I need you to help me with, it is that I ask you to pray to God, and [indeed] exert yourselves fully in prayer, so that He will postpone my death.[30]

Yet, the story goes that his disciples found themselves overtaken by a strange feeling of inability to do anything, and could not pray or even remain awake. Lamenting this, Jesus said, "The shepherd will be taken, and the sheep will scatter."[31] As the account continues, the reader familiar with the Gospel accounts will notice key elements of similarity: namely, a prophecy that one of his disciples will deny him before the rooster crows, and an account of Jesus being sold for a few dirhams by an unnamed disciple. The story relates that after this, the disciples "went out and dispersed".[32] Then, as prophesied, one of the disciples betrayed Jesus, and the miraculous intervention by God took place.

The narrative describes the Jews taking "him"[33] – although the identity of him in the sentence is unclear, and could refer to either Jesus or another – tying him up, mocking him, and finally taking him to the place of crucifixion.[34] Then, finally, "God raised him up to Him", and the Jews then "crucified someone that had been made to resemble [Jesus] for them [*salabū mā shubbiha lahum*]".[35]

There are two ways to understand this: either another person was made to resemble Jesus, and the Jews took the other person, tied him, and crucified him, in which case the phrase "God raised him up" refers to Jesus in another place being raised up. In this respect, this is the same as the first account. Alternatively, it could mean that Jesus was the one who was taken, tied up, and then placed on the cross but was then rescued, and another person was substituted at the last moment.

Tabari also introduces a second series of accounts,[36] which seem to resemble the first two narratives closely.

After presenting the various narrations, Tabari customarily added his opinion. In this instance, he states a clear preference for the two narrations reported by Wahb b. Munabbih.[37] Recapping the first where all the disciples are transformed, and a volunteer goes out to the Jews, Tabari indicates that this account is more convincing, as if only one of the disciples had been transformed, the rest of the disciples would have known which one of them it was. Whereas, he suggests, they in fact were in confusion.[38] Presumably, this relies on the phrase in the verse, "And those who differed among themselves are in doubt concerning it", which, perhaps, refers to the disciples. Somewhat confusingly, Tabari also provides an interpretation of this same phrase – "those who differed" – and gives its meaning as "the Jews".[39] After the event, when the disciples were – presumably – returned to their original forms, one would expect that they would have been able to ascertain which one was the martyr.

Regardless of this problem, Tabari continues with his commentary, indicating that it is possible that the second Wahb narrative (where the disciples left Jesus in the evening) is also a true account.[40] He reasons that at least one of the disciples had remained with Jesus and that this was the one who was made to resemble Jesus, was captured, and crucified. The disciples, remembering Jesus' lamentations the previous night, thought his prophecy had come true and that he had been killed.[41] Interestingly, Tabari comments on the accounts of the disciples, and by implication, of the Christian narrative of the crucifixion: "They do not deserve to be called liars" for they were only "relating the story according to the truth they knew" [*hakaw mā kāna 'indahum haqqan* even though the reality was different].[42]

All the narratives provided by Tabari, including the ten he relegates to a second preference,[43] confirm that Jesus was neither killed nor crucified. The differences between them are in other details. For example, the identity of Jesus' substitute, and the way the Jews were deceived. The accounts thus present a remarkable degree of conformity on the key issue of the survival of Jesus, yet manage to preserve a variety of details and historical difference because of the variation in other, less significant details.

The approach of the famous Mut'azili commentator, Zamakhshari, is most often characterised by a focus on the linguistic features of the text to be analysed. His analysis of the phrase *shubbiha lahum* is no exception. Zamakhshari initially presents a narration similar to Tabari's, although it differs from that of Tabari in several respects. First, Zamakhshari – like the later commentaries examined in this chapter – does not give the full chain of transmission (*isnād*) of the narrative, but rather simply prefaces it with the expression *ruwiya* ("it was narrated").[44] Second, whereas Tabari's narrations confine themselves mainly to the events of the day in question, and thus seem to be interpretations (or elaborations) of Qur'an 156–58 only, Zamakhshari's narration is more of a "back story" account, which appears to furnish an explanation for the crucifixion in the first place. Perhaps this is because by Zamakhshari's time Muslims were no longer familiar with the story and needed to be reminded of it in more detail. Also, unlike the accounts of Tabari, Zamakhshari's story attempts to make links between several Qur'anic verses.

Zamakhshari's story begins with "a group of the Jews" cursing Jesus and Mary. Jesus then asks God to curse those who curse him and his mother, with the end result being that those Jews were turned into monkeys and pigs. Seeking retribution, the Jews sought to kill Jesus, but – the story continues – "God informed [Jesus] He would lift him up to Heaven and purify him from the company of the Jews." Jesus then asked his disciples which of them was ready to be made to resemble Jesus (corresponding to the second series of narratives from Tabari). One disciple volunteered and was killed.[45]

Zamakhshari then narrates a second version, wherein one of the disciples attempts to betray Jesus. However, instead of Jesus being killed, he was raised to the heavens and the traitor made to resemble Jesus (*ulqiya shibhuhu 'ala al-munāfiq*). When the Jews entered the house, they assumed that the traitor was Jesus and had him crucified.[46]

Next, Zamakhshari discusses the crucial passage in this verse (*wa lākin shubbiha lahum*), and examines it grammatically. For example, in relation to the question, "'What is the grammatical subject (*musnad*) of *shubbiha* [made to resemble]?"[47] he asserts the following:

> If you say the grammatical subject is the Messiah, then [I say] the Messiah is the one who is resembled [*mushabbah bihi*] and not the one who is made to resemble [*mushabbah*].[48]

Zamakhshari argues that, strictly speaking, the verb *shabbaha* ("to make some-thing resemble another") has two objects according to Arabic grammatical custom: the primary object, that which is made to resemble another thing (the *mushabbah*); and the secondary object, that other thing which is resembled (the *mushabbah bihi*). In the passive form of *shubbiha*, the primary object becomes the subject, not the secondary object. Here, Jesus is the one resembled, and so cannot be the subject of *shubbiha*.[49] Zamakhshari continued:

> And if you make the grammatical subject the one that was killed, he has not yet been mentioned [in this verse].[50]

Zamakhshari's argument here is: how can a verb in the passive voice be used with a subject who has not yet been mentioned? He provides his own view, which involves two possibilities. For the first possibility, he writes:

> I say that the grammatical subject is the following genitive particle and pronoun (*lahum*, "for them"), as you would say, "it appeared to him that" (*khuyyila ilayhi*). This is as if [the verse] said: "the resemblance affected them."[51]

Interestingly, this is precisely the interpretation that many modern commenta-tors on the Qur'an have taken for this verse when rendering it in English. Mostly, they translate the subject of the verb as "it", suggesting that "it" refers to "the situation", "the crucifixion", or "the death of Jesus", rather than to Jesus or to the one presumably killed in his place.

The second possibility is that the subject is indeed the one killed – although this contradicts Zamakhshari's earlier statement – as the reference earlier in the verse is to someone who has been killed (that is, when the Jews said, "We have killed"). This suffices to be a first reference to the one killed – who is not Jesus, despite the claims of the Jews – thus the verb *shubbiha* may indeed have him as a subject.

The famous theologian Razi wrote only a few decades after Zamakhshari also adopted a linguistic approach, with close attention to theological matters. He incorporates much of the traditional view, including Zamakhshari's inguistic analysis. However, Razi's overall approach is quite different to that of his predecessors.

In an approach that is common to much of the *tafsir* tradition, Razi incor-porates substantial amounts of Zamakhshari's discussion of this passage into his own. He does so sometimes verbatim, but always without attribution, although, as noted above, Zamakhshari himself also quite possibly derived much of his analysis from previous commentaries. Razi deals with the crux of the verse – was Jesus killed? – in the opposite order from Zamakhshari. Razi begins by presenting the grammatical argument, and then examines the traditional narrations.[52] He identifies two problems. The first is – like Zamakhshari – the subject of the passive verb *shubbiha*. In this, his analysis reproduces

Zamakhshari's almost verbatim.[53] The subject is neither Jesus nor the one killed, for the reasons given by Zamakhshari. Again, there are two possibilities: the first is that the subject is the genitive particle and pronoun *la hum*, rendering the verse as "the resemblance affected them", and the second is that it does in fact – despite the earlier denial of this possibility, as with Zamakhshari – refer to the one killed other than Jesus.[54]

Having established those approaches, however, Razi departs from Zamakhshari in a way that indicates some misgivings about the traditional narrative wherein another person was miraculously made to resemble Jesus. Thinking through the logical consequences of this traditional approach, he states:

> [If it is possible to say] that God Most High may make a person resemble another it opens the gate of sophistry. It means that if we see Zayd, it may be he is not Zayd, but has had Zayd's appearance cast upon him. If this is the case, then marriage, divorce, and the right of possession all perish. It would also undermine the [epistemological standard] of *tawātur* (widespread transmission of a report beyond the possibility of error), for a *tawātur* report derives its authenticity from the fact that the narrators physically met each other. So, if this taking on of resemblances was accepted for tangible matters, it would invalidate *tawātur*. This, in turn, would undermine all the Laws (*sharā'i'*). And one cannot reply that this [type of occurrence] was confined to the time of prophets, peace be upon them, for [our knowledge of them] is only known by evidence and proofs, and he who denies knowledge of such evidence and proofs cannot say anything definite concerning any tangible matters, or rely on any *tawātur* reports.[55]

Razi then makes a curious point, which indicates that he was writing in a context where saintly miracles (*karāmāt*) were an accepted reality:

> Moreover, [you may argue that] there are no miracles in our age, yet there are still *karāmāt* (special spiritual powers bestowed on holy people and saints). Thus this [idea of resemblance] is possible in any age.[56]

Razi seems to be arguing that if such a miracle happened in the time of Jesus, then there is no reason it would not continue to happen today, given that saints can and do perform miracles, just as they did in the time of the prophets.

He sums up this argument by again returning to the logical impossibility of such a miraculous occurrence, and indeed, the threat that it poses to the entire rationalistic edifice of Islamic epistemology:

> All in all, leaving the door open for this [possibility of one person being made to resemble another] would undermine *tawātur*, which would undermine the prophethood of all the prophets, peace and blessings be upon them. This is a subsidiary issue (*far'*) that [if permitted] would undermine all the fundamentals [*usūl*]; therefore, it should be rejected.[57]

Razi offers a solution for explaining the narrations, which he attributes to "many of the dialectic theologians (*al-mutakallimīn*)".[58] Namely, that the Jews, on seeing that Jesus had been raised to the Heavens, feared that the populace would riot, and hence chose someone else to crucify, claiming to the mob that this person was Jesus. This narrative does not appear in the commentaries of Tabari or Zamakhshari, and it seems to find favour with Razi because "there is no problem" regarding how the miraculous resemblance might have occurred. Presumably, he would then say that the meaning of *shubbiha lahum* is "it was made to seem so to the Jewish masses by their leaders".[59]

However, the idea of a miraculous casting of resemblance upon another person appears to have been a strong one. Despite his earlier misgivings of this concept, Razi feels compelled to relate the various permutations of this possibility, grouping them together under "the second answer:" where he provides four stories that more or less correspond to the main narratives already related by Tabari:

1   That one of the Jews sent to bring Jesus out from the house was made to resemble Jesus, and then killed by his fellows.
2   That the Jews appointed a man to spy on Jesus, and when Jesus ascended a mountain and was raised to heaven, the spy was made to resemble him, and was killed by his fellows.
3   That, on being besieged in the house, Jesus asked his disciples for a volunteer to "buy Paradise by bearing my resemblance".
4   That one of Jesus' disciples sought to betray him, but was made to resemble him and was killed.[60]

Perhaps indicating his lack of interest in these stories, Razi does not indicate which one he prefers, and ends the section by saying: "And these possibilities are mutually contradictory and mutually opposing [*muta'ārida mutadāfi'a*], and God knows best the truth of matters."[61]

Shawkani was, arguably, one of the key scholars who emerged just before the modernist movement. In general, he provides a summary, fairly doctrinaire version of all the discussions that have gone before, but without Razi's rationalist and speculative digressions.

Shawkani explains the phrase *shubbiha lahum* in only a few terse lines, summing up the traditional view and presenting it as settled doctrine:

> The true condition of the matter is that [the Jews] did not kill [Jesus] nor crucify him, "though it was made to appear like that to them [*wa lākin shubbiha lahum*]," meaning, "his likeness was cast upon another person."[62]

Shawkani also presents a narrative, introduced with *qīla* (it is said): that the Jews did not know Jesus' appearance, which explains how they were deceived.[63]

In brief, examining the approaches of these four pre-modern commentators reveals several similarities, but also some differences.

The first three – Tabari, Zamakhshari, and Razi – all seem to allow for much more ambiguity than Shawkani who is writing at a much later time, in that they include a range of views that sometimes seem contradictory. In some cases, it is clear which view they prefer. At other times, it is necessary to read between the lines: this is especially important in the context of Razi, who includes traditional narratives while at the same time criticising them and seeming to prefer other explanations.

All the traditional narratives examined above agree that Jesus was not crucified, and that another person,either a disciple or one of the Jews seeking to kill him, was the person actually crucified. Only Razi seems to indicate a second possibility, with perhaps some sympathy for the Christian view, and this is that Jesus was in fact crucified but that his body's death did not afflict his soul, which was immediately transported to the realm of Majesty (*'ālam al-jalāl*) where it experienced only delight and happiness. In his discussion on the phrase "those who differed" in the verse, Razi goes beyond the traditional view of complete denial of crucifixion and death, though indirectly. In his comments on the Nestorian Christians' view of the matter, Razi says that the Nestorians claimed that Jesus was only crucified in his human aspect (*nāsūt*), and not his divine aspect (*lāhūt*).[64] Razi then embarks on an interesting digression. In brief, he puts forward a view that he attributes to the *hukamā'* (the philosophers), who he says hold views that are similar to this: namely, that the human being is "not limited to this physical form (*haykal*)", and thus the killing of Jesus only affected his physical form, and not his soul (*nafs*).[65] In response to a counter-argument, Razi confirms the unique nature of Jesus, whose soul is "holy, exalted, and heavenly, tremendously illuminated with divine light, and extremely close [in nature] to the spirits of the angels".[66]

Therefore, instead of suffering at death, such a soul is transported directly to "the vastness of the heavens and the lights of the realm of Majesty, where it experiences only delight and happiness".[67] According to Razi, this was a mark of Jesus' uniqueness, for such souls are very few.[68]

Although he does not state it explicitly, Razi appears to have some sympathy for this view. Rather than the traditional narrative of a miraculous substitution, this view seems to accept that Jesus was crucified, but rather than suffering along with his physical body, his exalted soul was directly raised to the heavens. This view coincides with Razi's tendency towards rationalist explanations, and his misgivings about the traditional narrative. Razi then provides a cursory description of the Melkite and Jacobite views, each of which only received a brief mention. Both of these, although using differing terms, held the view that the crucifixion affected Jesus' spirit as well as his body, and as such these ideas seem to hold little interest for Razi.[69]

The Qur'anic interpretation from the time of Tabari seems to be fairly consistent in asserting that there was no killing and no crucifixion of Jesus. The commentators were by no means unanimous in the interpretation of the verse under discussion, and, as demonstrated above, their interpretations ranged from an outright denial of the crucifixion of Jesus to *sympathy* for a simple affirmation of the historicity of the event. However, the substitution narrative is by far the most dominant and frequent, and this explains why it has had such on-going influence.[70] One way to account for this remarkable consistency in Muslim exegetical literature on the death and crucifixion of Jesus is to approach it from within a strictly Muslim context. For Muslims, the miraculous nature of Jesus himself – his conception, his birth, his growing up, and then his ministry – all occurred within a miraculous frame of reference. Thus, his end should also occur within that context. Given that this conception of Jesus probably came to dominate the thinking in the second and third centuries of Islam, and that Muslim theology had accepted this conception of Jesus, it was very easy for that theological position then to dominate the thinking of Muslim commentators in relation to Qur'anic texts. That theological position therefore came to provide a decisive framework for interpretation of this very ambiguous Qur'anic verse.

Interpretation in the modern period

Throughout the modern period, the majority of Muslim commentators on the Qur'an continued to function within the pre-modern interpretive framework. The Muslim conception of Jesus that developed in the early period of Islamic history, therefore, remains the most powerful frame of reference for Muslims, even in the modern period.

Abul Ala Maududi refuses to recognise any death or crucifixion of Jesus that corresponded to the accounts in the Gospels. He suggests that although the trial and sentencing was for Jesus, and that Jesus was in attendance, when the penalty was to be implemented God rescued Jesus:

> This verse is explicit on the point that the Prophet Jesus Christ was rescued from crucifixion and that the Christians and the Jews are both wrong in believing that he died on the cross. A comparative study of the Qur'an and the Bible shows that most probably it was Jesus himself who stood his trial in the court of Pilate who sentenced him to death, but they could not kill or crucify him, for Allah raised him to Himself.[71]

This rescue was achieved by means of a substitution. Thus, Maududi, following the pre-modern tradition, also subscribes to the substitution narrative saying the "one who was crucified afterwards was somehow or other taken for Christ".[72] However, Maududi does not provide a tenable answer to the issue of how God made the matter "doubtful for them", aside from saying:

> As regards the matter how "it was made doubtful for them" that they had crucified Jesus, we have no means of ascertaining. Therefore it is not right to base on mere guesswork and rumours an answer to the question how the Jews were made to believe that they had crucified him, whereas in fact, Jesus, the son of Mary, had escaped from them.[73]

Sayyid Qutb also accepts the substitution theory. He states: "What we know for certain is that they neither killed nor crucified him. Instead, another victim was made to appear similar to him."[74] Qutb rejects the positions of both Jews and Christians. In fact, he labels their claims as "false" and as having "no basis other than in their own suspicions".[75] Unlike Maududi, who does not refer to the so-called Gospel of Barnabas, Qutb appears to be relying on this Gospel to support his case. For Qutb, the Gospel accounts of Mark, Matthew, Luke, and John could not be relied upon, as they:

> were all written after a lengthy lapse of time which also witnessed the persecution of Christianity and the Christians. In such an atmosphere of secrecy, fear and persecution, it is exceedingly difficult to be certain of the truthfulness of the reports that circulated.[76]

However, Qutb was happy to accept the position of the Gospel of Barnabas insofar as it confirmed the Qur'an's position. Qutb states that: "One of the many Gospels written in this period was that of Barnabas which gives an account of the story and crucifixion of Jesus that is at variance with the four recognised Gospels."[77] Qutb is not the first modern Muslim to rely on this Gospel to interpret the Qur'anic position on the crucifixion and death of Jesus. Before him, Rashid Rida also relied on this Gospel.

Qutb, however, is more circumspect about the issue of Jesus being "raised" to heaven:

> The Qur'an does not give any details concerning how Jesus was raised or whether it took place in body and soul together in this state of life, or in soul after death. Nor does it tell us when and where his death took place, if at all.[78]

Although the substitution theory is dominant in Islamic exegetical tradition, some voices do seem to reject the idea that there was no crucifixion or death of Jesus. Abu Zayd states that: "Since [the reference to the crucifixion] exists only in the context of responding to the Jewish claim, the discourse structure suggests it was denying the capability of the Jews to have done this depending on their own power."[79] Abu Zayd thus emphasises that the Qur'an was not denying Jesus' death or crucifixion as such, but the attribution of these to the Jews, who were boasting that they had killed Jesus. Interestingly, Rida also makes a comment that is not too far from what Abu Zayd says. According to Rida:

> The actual fact of the crucifixion is not itself a matter which the Book of God seeks to affirm or deny, except for the purpose of asserting the killing of prophets by the Jews unjustly, and reproaching them for that act.[80]

Also among those who reject the idea of death and crucifixion are Ahmadis (Qadiyanis), who believe that Jesus died a natural death and in fact left his birthplace and settled in Kashmir in India.[81] However, Muhammad Ali, an Ahmadi scholar, disagrees with the idea that the words "they did not crucify him" mean that Jesus was not put on the cross. Rather, Ali suggests that these words simply mean that Jesus did not die as a result of the experience. The phrase "they did not kill him certainly", therefore, would mean that the people did not know without doubt that Jesus had been put to death on the Cross.[82] Ali refutes the story that someone else was made to look like Jesus and to suffer in his stead, and argues that the words mean that the matter became dubious to the disciples.[83]

The Shi'a scholar Muhammad Husayn Tabataba'i interprets the words *shub-biha lahum* as "seizing someone else unknowingly".[84] He argues further that although a literal reading of the words, "Rather, God took him up to Himself", may suggest a bodily ascension, "God actually meant a spiritual and not a formal ascension, because the Exalted One has no place of the kind occupied by bodies."[85] In this, Tabataba'i followed a time-honoured tradition in Mu'tazili and Shi'i thought, which sought to explain metaphorically all anthropomorphic references to God in the Qur'an. Even – he concludes – "if the text indicates literally bodily ascension, heaven means only the locus of proximity to Him and His blessing".[86]

In contrast, Mahmoud Ayoub provides an allegorical interpretation of Jesus' ascension. He suggests that, instead of referring to a literal man, the Qur'an was speaking about the Word of God who was sent to earth and who returned to God. Thus, the denial of Jesus' killing is a denial of the power of men to destroy the Divine Word. Hence the words, "they did not kill him, nor did they crucify him". Ayoub's suggestions go far deeper than the events of human history to the heart and conscience of human beings. The claim of humanity to have this power against God is only an illusion as exemplified in the Jewish society of Christ's earthly existence: "They did not slay him ... but it seemed so to them ... they only imagined doing so."[87] The words *wa lākin shubbiha lahum* (it was made to appear like that to them) therefore can be seen as an accusation or judgement against the human sin of pride and ignorance, stemming from a lack of certainty or firm faith.[88] They are, Ayoub suggests, an affirmation that God is greater than human powers and empty schemes: "They did not kill him, [that is, Jesus the Christ and God's Apostle] with certainty, rather God took him up to Himself, and God is mighty, and wise." Indeed, the phrase, "and God is Mighty and Wise", contrasts human limitations with divine power and infinite wisdom. The same verse presents Christ the Word as a challenge to human wisdom and power, and as a judgement against human folly and pride. Men may:

> wish to extinguish the light of God with their mouths, that is, with their words of foolish wisdom, but God will perfect His light in spite of our foolishness and obstinacy.[89]

The commentaries examined here in relation to the crucifixion and death of Jesus show a remarkable similarity between the views of various pre-modern and modern commentators on the Qur'an, and this similarity can be sum-marised as the denial of the crucifixion of Jesus. This denial is largely based on certain reports that were transmitted by second-generation Muslims and are not necessarily based on any particular tradition of the Prophet that is considered to be "authentic".

Commentators understood certain texts of the Qur'an on this question rather literally to mean a complete and categorical negation of the killing of Jesus Christ and his crucifixion. However, their view is based very much on a literal reading of the text, and relies on specific theological positions adopted by early Muslims with regard to Jesus. Virtually all commentators have suggested that the Qur'an indicates that another person, a substitute, was crucified in place of Jesus.

In the past, scholars from different theological, legal, and mystical traditions have, by and large, agreed on this same conclusion; this convergence of opi-nion has changed, however, in the modern period to a certain extent. Many scholars of today emphasise the importance of reason in interpreting the Qur'an. Using approaches based to a certain extent on reason and taking into consideration that there are other possible interpretations, a number of Muslim scholars today argue that there is nothing theologically difficult in accepting the idea that Jesus was crucified and that he was killed. There are many other prophets who are mentioned in the Qur'an as having been killed by their opponents, and Jesus was not an exception. Rejecting the Christian claims about Jesus and the New Testament narrative of Jesus' death largely based on a few sayings from the second-generation Muslims is highly problematic from the point of view of such contemporary Muslim scholars.

It could be argued that nothing would be compromised in Islamic theology if Muslims adopted the view that Jesus was crucified, and as a consequence of this died just like many other prophets who are mentioned in the Qur'an. Such a view does not detract from the high esteem in which Jesus is held in the Qur'an and the traditions of the Prophet.

Differences in context

We are now in a position to determine the new insights that the contextualist approach can provide in relation to the interpretation of the verses that relate to the crucifixion and death of Jesus, as compared with the textualist approach that has been dominant in the tradition.

It is essential to note that the contemporary context of the modern scholar differs significantly from the pre-modern context. The textualist approach relies on a theological position about the nature of Jesus Christ and his death, derived from early Islam. This position does not appear to have any strong textual evidence either from the traditions of the Prophet that are universally accepted as historically reliable, or from the Qur'an. Instead, the theological position may have been influenced by debates between early Muslims and Christians of the time about the relative merits of each religion and which of them is "true". There is evidence to suggest that such theological debates occurred between

Christians and early Muslims even as early as the first century of Islam in places like Damascus.[90] Christians must have put forth various theological arguments about how Jesus Christ was crucified and resurrected, and the ways in which the meaning behind this provided a foundation for some of the most important Christian beliefs. It is possible that Christians engaged in debate with Muslims using Qur'anic references to Jesus that denote Jesus as an exemplary human being. In the Qur'an, for example, Jesus is referred to as the "Word", and Jesus' birth and many of his acts are depicted as miraculous.

The Qur'an only mentions the death or crucifixion of Jesus in passing. In this, rather than a critique of Christian theology or dogma, the Qur'an was perhaps making a comment to rebuke the Jewish community in Medina and as part of a critique of how certain Jewish groups treated the prophets sent to them, including Jesus. In all likelihood, in the very early period of Muslim expansion into largely Christian areas outside Arabia, these passing references in the Qur'an may have become important proof texts for Muslims in Muslim–Christian debates on the question of which religion was true and authentic. By rejecting the very basis on which important Christian theological positions were based, early Muslims were, perhaps, indirectly attempting to discredit the very foundations of Christian theology. However, the textual basis of this position held by Muslims does not appear to be very strong. Most of the views attributed to early Muslims on the question of death and crucifixion are actually from the second generation of Muslims, if not later, and not directly attributed to the Prophet or the first generation of Muslims.

As texts that deny the death and crucifixion of Jesus were most likely over-emphasised in early Muslim polemics, and later became the standard Muslim theological position in relation to Jesus, in subsequent centuries it became very difficult to question such positions. From the fourth and fifth centuries of Islam, standard creeds became a permanent features of the Muslim theological landscape. In this, a number of ideas relating to people of other faiths came to be accepted as standard. The people of the book (Jews and Christians) were also constructed as "unequal" to Muslims in the body politic of Muslim states. Similarly by this time, the view that the scriptures of Jews and Christians were distorted, unreliable, and historically problematic also gained credence. The development of these positions was based on the idea that Islam was superior to other religions, and those religions as well as their scriptures and key theological positions were seen as "inferior" to that of Islam. The positions that emerged from this period have been carried over for centuries, right up to the modern period. By and large, in standard theological texts, no obvious interest in approaching other religions in ways other than to the original polemical attitude of early Islam has been exhibited since then, until recently. However, this is not solely a Muslim issue: other religious traditions have portrayed their religious "others" as being completely disconnected from the truth. Religious traditions, historically, have often claimed exclusivity by stating that there is only one way to God and truth. This hostility between Islam and Christianity on the theological front thus continued into the modern period.

However, a number of changes have occurred in our context of today. In the modern context, there is a much stronger emphasis on mutual understanding between people of different faiths or religious traditions. This is particularly the case in multi-religious and plural societies. The move toward greater interfaith understanding is a project in which people of all religious traditions are participating, and which manifests in a wide range of interfaith activities and discussions. This is illustrated in statements given by prominent religious leaders about the importance of understanding between faiths. Importantly, with the intellectual freedom that exists in large parts of the world today, scholars, thinkers, and theologians have the freedom to examine and re-examine theological positions and interpretations, and to question how such positions originated, how they developed, and from which sources (textual or other) they were derived. In the modern context, major theologians and other leaders of both Islam and Christianity are often engaged in friendly discussions and debates, which occur in seminars, conferences, and symposia privately and publicly. A spirit of inquiry at the scale we find today did not exist in the pre-modern period, at least in relation to interreligious understanding.

One key characteristic of the modern period is also globalisation. Today people live in a globalised world and interact with people of different faiths much more frequently than in previous generations. In this context, borders are no hindrance. The need to live harmoniously together through mutual understanding is an unavoidable issue. In addition, Muslim thinkers and scholars have the opportunity to examine and explore some of the theological positions and interpretations that have little or no clear textual basis in the tradition, and are obstacles to mutual understanding in line with the contemporary critical spirit.

All of this has led a number of Muslim scholars to bring aspects of Qur'anic interpretation that seemed to have been fixed for centuries back into question. Thus the interpreter of the Qur'an can think and critically evaluate theological positions that have been taken for granted, despite the absence of a strong textual basis for them in the Qur'an. If the historical or textual basis of a particular theological position is not strong, a space is opened, in which it becomes possible to rethink these interpretations and to find guidance in the Qur'an that is useful to the contemporary context, and a contextualist framework appears to be particularly suitable for this task.

Notes

1 Namely Qur'an 3:55 (which refers to the lineage of Mary); see Todd Lawson, *The Crucifixion and the Qur'an: A Study in the History of Muslim Thought* (Oxford: Oneworld Publications, 2009), 14.
2 Qur'an 19:33.
3 Lawson, *The Crucifixion*, 12.
4 Lawson, *The Crucifixion*.
5 Qur'an 4:156–58.
6 Lawson translated this as "faithlessness", although it can also be translated as "unbelief", "ungratefulness", and "denial of the truth".

7 Lawson, *The Crucifixion*, 9.
8 The same point was made in Lawson *The Crucifixion*, 10.
9 The Qur'an, 4:157, trans. Yusuf Ali, www.islam101.com/quran/yusufAli/QURAN/4. htm.
10 The Qur'an, 4:157, trans. Muhammad Asad.
11 The Qur'an, 4:157, trans. Mohammed Marmaduke Pickthall, www.sacred-texts.com/ isl/pick/.
12 The Qur'an, 4:157, trans. Abdel Haleem (Oxford: Oxford University Press, 2005), 65.
13 The Qur'an, 4:156, Sahih International, http://tanzil.net/#trans/en.sahih/4:156.
14 The Qur'an, 4:157, Shakir, www.comp.leeds.ac.uk/nora/html/4–157.html.
15 Qur'an 3:55.
16 Qur'an 19:33.
17 Qur'an 5:17.
18 Qur'an 5:75.
19 Qur'an 5:117.
20 Qur'an 2:87.
21 Qur'an 5:112–15.
22 Qur'an 3:49.
23 Qur'an 3:49.
24 Qur'an 3:49.
25 Qur'an 3:49.
26 Qur'an 19:27–31.
27 Georges C Anawati, "Īsā", in *Encyclopaedia of Islam*, second edition, ed. P. Bearman, Th. Bianquis, C. E. Bosworth, E. van Donzel, and W. P. Heinrichs (Leiden: Brill, 2011).
28 Tabari, *Jami'*, *tafsir* of Q. 4:157, www.altafsir.com.
29 Tabari, *Jami'*, *tafsir* of Q. 4:157.
30 Tabari, *Jami'*, *tafsir* of Q. 4:157.
31 Tabari, *Jami'*, *tafsir* of Q. 4:157.
32 Tabari, *Jami'*, *tafsir* of Q. 4:157.
33 Tabari, *Jami'*, *tafsir* of Q. 4:157.
34 Tabari, *Jami'*, *tafsir* of Q. 4:157.
35 Tabari, *Jami'*, *tafsir* of Q. 4:157.
36 Tabari, *Jami'*, *tafsir* of Q. 4:157.
37 Tabari, *Jami'*, *tafsir* of Q. 4:157.
38 Tabari, *Jami'*, *tafsir* of Q. 4:157.
39 Tabari, *Jami'*, *tafsir* of Q. 4:157.
40 Tabari, *Jami'*, *tafsir* of Q. 4:157.
41 Tabari, *Jami'*, *tafsir* of Q. 4:157.
42 Tabari, *Jami'*, *tafsir* of Q. 4:157.
43 Tabari, *Jami'*, *tafsir* of Q. 4:157.
44 Jar Allah al-Zamakhshari, *al-Kashshaf 'an Haqa'iq al-Tanzil*, *tafsir* of Q. 4:157, www. altafsir.com.
45 Zamakhshari, *Kashshaf*, *tafsir* of Q. 4:157.
46 Zamakhshari, *Kashshaf*, *tafsir* of Q. 4:157.
47 Zamakhshari, *Kashshaf*, *tafsir* of Q. 4:157.
48 Zamakhshari, *Kashshaf*, *tafsir* of Q. 4:157.
49 Zamakhshari, *Kashshaf*, *tafsir* of Q. 4:157.
50 Zamakhshari, *Kashshaf*, *tafsir* of Q. 4:157.
51 Zamakhshari, *Kashshaf*, *tafsir* of Q. 4:157.
52 al-Fakhr al-Razi, *Mafatih al-Ghayb: al-Tafsir al-Kabir*, *tafsir* of Q. 4:157, www.altafsir.com.
53 Razi, *al-Tafsir al-Kabir*, *tafsir* of Q. 4:157.
54 Razi, *al-Tafsir al-Kabir*, *tafsir* of Q. 4:157.
55 Razi, *al-Tafsir al-Kabir*, *tafsir* of Q. 4:157.
56 Razi, *al-Tafsir al-Kabir*, *tafsir* of Q. 4:157.

57 Razi, *al-Tafsir al-Kabir, tafsir* of Q. 4:157.
58 Razi, *al-Tafsir al-Kabir, tafsir* of Q. 4:157.
59 Razi, *al-Tafsir al-Kabir, tafsir* of Q. 4:157.
60 Razi, *al-Tafsir al-Kabir, tafsir* of Q. 4:157.
61 Razi, *al-Tafsir al-Kabir, tafsir* of Q. 4:157.
62 Muhammad b. Ali al-Shawkani, *Fath al-Qadir, tafsir* of Q. 4:157, www.altafsir.com.
63 Shawkani, *Fath al-Qadir, tafsir* of Q. 4:157.
64 Razi, *al-Tafsir al-Kabir, tafsir* of Q. 4:157.
65 Razi, *al-Tafsir al-Kabir, tafsir* of Q. 4:157.
66 Razi, *al-Tafsir al-Kabir, tafsir* of Q. 4:157.
67 Razi, *al-Tafsir al-Kabir, tafsir* of Q. 4:157.
68 Razi, *al-Tafsir al-Kabir, tafsir* of Q. 4:157.
69 Razi, *al-Tafsir al-Kabir, tafsir* of Q. 4:157.
70 Lawson, *The Crucifixion*, 17.
71 Sayyid Abul Ala Maududi, *Tafhim al-Qur'an: The Meaning of the Qur'an, tafsir* of 4:157, www.englishtafsir.com/Quran/4/index.html#sdfootnote194sym.
72 Maududi, *Tafhim al-Qur'an, tafsir* of Q. 4:157.
73 Maududi, *Tafhim al-Qur'an, tafsir* of Q. 4:157.
74 Sayyid Qutb, *In the Shade of the Quran, tafsir* of 4:157, trans. Adil Salahi, Vol. 3, 317–18, http://islamfuture.files.wordpress.com/2009/12/volume_3_surah_4.pdf.
75 Qutb, *In the Shade of Q. the Quran, tafsir* of Q. 4:157.
76 Qutb, *In the Shade of Q. the Quran, tafsir* of Q. 4:157.
77 Qutb, *In the Shade of Q. the Quran, tafsir* of Q. 4:157.
78 Qutb, *In the Shade of Q. the Quran, tafsir* of Q. 4:157.
79 Nasr Hamid Abu Zayd, *Rethinking the Qur'ān: Towards a Humanistic Hermeneutics* (Amsterdam: Humanistics University Press, 2004), 34.
80 Sayyid Muhamad Rashid Rida, *Tafsir al Manar*, second edition (Cairo: Dar al-Manar, 1367 AH), VI, 18–19.
81 Muhammad Ali, *The Religion of Islam* (Lahore: Ahmadiyya Press, 1936), 247.
82 Ali, *The Religion of Islam*, 247.
83 Ali, *The Religion of Islam*, 247.
84 al-Sayyid Muhammad Hussain al-Tabataba'i: *al-Mizan fi Tafsir al-Qur'an* (Beirut: Muassasat al-Alami, 1970), *tafsir* of Q. 4:157.
85 Tabataba'i, *al-Mizan, tafsir* of Q. 4:157.
86 Tabataba'i, *al-Mizan, tafsir* of Q. 4:157.
87 Muhammad Ayoub, "The Story of the Passion", *The Muslim World*, 70 (1980), 91–121: 117.
88 Ayoub, "The Story of the Passion", 91–121.
89 Ayoub, "The Story of the Passion", 117.
90 See, for instance, David Richard Thomas, *Syrian Christians under Islam: The First Thousand Years* (Leiden: E. J. Brill, 2001), 19.

13 *Shūra* and democracy

Shūra or consultation is a central concept in contemporary Muslim political thought. In fact, it is seen as the foundation for thinking about governance in an Islamic context. A distinctly Islamic approach to governance is supposed to translate this concept into all aspects of management of Muslim societies. In contemporary debates on how to achieve this, one specific Qur'anic verse (3:159) and its interpretation is central; however, in the pre-modern period the significance of such verses was somewhat marginal. Although the works of some pre-modern scholars, such as Abul Hasan Ali b. Muhammad b. Habib al-Mawardi (d. 450/1058) and Abu Hamid al-Ghazali (d. 505/1111), discuss how a Muslim society may deal with consultation, their descriptions lack the kinds of understanding that commentators in the modern period seem to attach to the concept. Their political context and the systems of governance in place then did not leave much room to broaden the concept of consultation to include the kind of ideas that Muslims today attach to the notion of "consultation". Today, Muslims, like others, often see democratic systems of governance in which the citizens participate as among the most appropriate, and often want to justify that based on Qur'anic ideas and texts, in particular the verses that deal with the concept of "consultation". Thus, the new context of the modern period has given the interpretation of the relevant verses much more significance than seems to have existed in the pre-modern period.

This chapter explores how pre-modern Muslim commentators on the Qur'an examined and interpreted the concept of *shūra* (consultation), with particular reference to Qur'an 3:159. It also provides a brief overview of how *shūra* has been equated with democracy by some Muslim scholars, and how this approach has been contested by other Muslim thinkers in the modern period. A comparison of the pre-modern and modern interpretations of these verses shows the degree of divergence in how Muslims interpret these texts and the relevance of context for the interpretation of the verses in both periods.

The text

The command "Consult with them about matters ... " (*wa shāwirhum fial-amr*)[1] is part of a longer sequence of verses that were revealed in the context of the

Battle of Uhud (3/625) between Muslims and their Meccan opponents in which Muslims were narrowly defeated.[2] Central to this verse is the idea of *shūra* (consultation), where God commanded the Prophet to consult with his Companions. There has been substantial debate among Muslim commentators surrounding the context and meaning of this command.

Context of the verse

Tabari's treatment of the verse suggests that he considers it to be addressed only to the Prophet.[3] In his discussion of the meaning of *shūra*, he asserts that it is most correctly understood as a command from God directed at the Prophet to consult his Companions in matters relating to war (thus obliquely referring to the Battle of Uhud) and that this was intended by God to set a precedent.[4]

Zamakhshari makes two references to the context of the verses in question. In the first, he obliquely refers to war,[5] in a similar way to Tabari's.[6] In the second, he cites a view that if the Bedouin chiefs did not mutually consult, things would not go well with them.[7] Thus, Zamakhshari argues that God had commanded the Prophet to consult the Companions so that his views would be more easily accepted and would not create division and paralysing disagreement.

Razi and Qurtubi both briefly summarise the context of the verse, and identify that the Prophet spoke gently to his people after the events of Uhud and that God praised him for it.[8]

Interpretation in the pre-modern period

Most early commentators do not give a strongly political interpretation of the verse. Instead, they focused on the theological implications arising from God's command to the Prophet to consult with his Companions. They also seem to have limited the scope of *shūra* to matters of war. Their concern in interpretation seems to be limited to identifying what the Prophet was commanded to consult upon, rather than delineating the scope of what Muslims should seek counsel on.

Tabari emphasises the original context of the verse, and identifies that the Prophet was asked to consult his Companions about matters of war. He provides one narration that regards the Qur'an's command as setting a precedent for the believers "where there had not come to them [the believers] any tradition from the Prophet".[9] He also notes that the Prophet did not need to consult his Companions, and supports his position with three views[10] that suggest that the purpose behind the command for consultation was to please the hearts of the Prophet's Companions (*tatyīban li anfusihim*).[11]

Tabari is not as political as some later commentators, and his emphasis is clearly on the Prophet. At one point, he states that the Companions and Successors would consult each other and proclaim what "the gathering of their leaders had reached consensus upon".[12] However, this is the closest he comes to an overtly political conceptualisation of the meaning of the verse. Although he does acknowledge that this consultation would take place in both matters of religion and in the more mundane matters of daily life, his focus was on the believers' intention of seeking the guidance of God.[13]

Zamakhshari expresses the view that consultation applied to matters of war and the like, and that the verse was revealed in order to soothe the hearts of the Prophet's Companions and to honour them. However, Zamakhshari also remarks that consultation allowed the Prophet to seek support or assistance from the opinions of his Companions.[14]

Razi's commentary, although it encompasses many more areas, is only marginally more political than that of Tabari.[15] Moreover, it is not nearly as political as that of Qurtubi (see below), despite being of similar length. Razi focuses on the character of the Prophet and his relationship with his Companions. His main aim seems to have been to explain why God would command the Prophet to consult his Companions, given that the Prophet should have little need to consult them.[16] Razi identifies a number of sub-issues in relation to this, and emphasises the following reasons for *shūra*:

1   The Prophet's consultation with his Companions is evidence of his excellence of character (*husn al-khuluq*).
2   Although the Prophet was the most perfect of created beings, the knowledge of any created being is finite, so that it is "not impossible" that a good idea can come to another human being, particularly in the mundane affairs of the world.
3   The Prophet was commanded to consult in order to set an example.
4   God commanded the Prophet to seek counsel to show that there were no ill feelings in his heart after Uhud (the Prophet was not intended to benefit from the views or knowledge of his Companions).
5   It is to demonstrate that the Companions have a worth (*qīma*) with God.
6   Finally, it is to show that the Companions should depend on God's favour and His pardoning of them.[17]

Razi then discusses the legal aspects of the verse, stating that the scholars agree that the Prophet could not consult in matters where there was a clear text (*nass*). To address the question that arises if there is no clear text, he cites a number of scholars, who had suggested that this situation was only relevant in matters of war.[18] Razi also cites two examples from the biography of the Prophet (*sīra*). In two separate incidents, both of which related to battles, a Companion was said to have asked the Prophet whether an action of the Prophet was commanded by God, or whether it was a "matter of strategy" or "done for their sake".[19] In both cases, once the Prophet clarified that his actions were not commanded by God, the Companions gave their counsel, which the Prophet followed. Razi also cites Shafi'i who, using an analogy, holds the view that *shūra* is recommended, rather than obligatory.[20] However, Shafi'i does not clarify whether this only applies to the Prophet, or to others as well.

In the pre-modern period, Qurtubi was perhaps the most political, and the most willing to see *shūra* as a command for all Muslims and particularly the rulers. He cites the greatest range of textual evidence to support this view, including some hadith that are sometimes of questionable authenticity, poetry, the precedents of the Companions, and anonymous "wise sayings".[21] Most interestingly, he cites two jurists who hold the view that *shūra* is obligatory for rulers. Similarly, Qurtubi provides several texts that explicitly connect *shūra* with the concept of ideal government, and make it obligatory.[22] Of the commentators examined thus far, he is generally the most in favour of the merits of *shūra*.[23]

Qurtubi then moves to the political implications of *shūra* and the concerns of his contemporary context. To examine this issue, he cites a range of views. One such view is:

> *Shūra* is one of the foundations of the *sharīʿa* and one of the most important of legal rulings. [If a ruler] does not consult the people of knowledge and religion, his expulsion is obligatory. And on this there is no dispute. Indeed, God has praised the believers by saying: "And they conduct their affairs by mutual consultation [Qur'an 42:38]."[24]

Qurtubi identifies a saying, attributed to "a Bedouin", which asserts that the Prophet would never be deceived because he always consults them; as well as two other brief sayings that praise the taking of advice and criticise those who esteem their own opinion.[25]

He also cites the Maliki jurist Ibn Khuwayz Mindad (d. c. 390/1000) whose views on *shūra* can be deduced from the following statement:

> It is incumbent on those who have power [*al-wulāt*] to consult the scholars of religion in what they do not know, and in what they find difficult to understand in the affairs of religion. Likewise, [it is compulsory for the rulers] to consult the military in matters relating to war, and the people in matters relating to [their] welfare, and the bureaucracy, state advisers, and the tax collectors in matters relating to the welfare of the land and its prosperous development [*masālih al-bilād wa ʿimāratiha*].[26]

Qurtubi also mentions a poem that praises those who consult on the basis that God commanded his Prophet to do so. He goes on to discuss the possible ways of dealing with *shūra*, and provides a range of views regarding the attributes of those to be consulted including trustworthiness, knowledge, piety, and wisdom; and experience and favourable disposition toward the one who seeks counsel.[27] For him, *shūra* was founded on the idea that people have divergent views. He argues that this divergence should be carefully examined, in order to take what is "closest to the Book [Qur'an] and the Sunna".[28]

Interpretation in the modern period

Moving to the modern period, Maududi and Qutb are examples of scholars who examine the role of *shūra*.

In his interpretation of this verse, Sayyid Qutb focused[29] on moral exhortation, the spiritual significance of the Battle of Uhud for the believers, and the lessons to be drawn from that in terms of the development of the community.[30] In one sense, this approach is also political, as it sees the community as a single entity and speaks of particular moral lessons that God was giving through Uhud and these verses. This reflects Qutb's pan-Islamic views. Indeed, Qutb criticises nationalism and, at one point, speaks of Islam as the true "identity card" of the Arabs. He uses universal language regarding the importance of *shūra*, and asserts that it is the basis of Islam's political order and that without it no system is "truly Islamic". He supports this by citing the fact that God commanded *shūra* even after the disastrous result of its application at the Battle of Uhud.[31]

Qutb's treatment reflects his overall spiritual-moral focus as well. He sees *shūra* not merely as a technical principle of government, but as something that must permeate all aspects of the life of the Muslim community. He relates the act of obeying God including implementing *shūra* in order to succeed in the mundane world. Unlike the pre-modern commentators examined above, Qutb is not troubled by the question of why God would command the Prophet to seek counsel. For him, it is clear that *shūra* serves to set an example for the community and to establish the "fundamental principle" of community life. He forms the view that the argument that the Prophet could have dispensed with *shūra* is "totally false". His analysis identified *shūra* as quite necessary for the community to attain political maturity and responsibility. As can be seen above, this opinion is in stark contrast with many of the pre-modern commentators, who implied that the Prophet, being infallible, could certainly have done without *shūra*.[32]

Maududi does not provide any detailed interpretation of this part of this verse, rather he reserves this for Qur'an 42:38.[33] In his interpretation of Qur'an 42:38, Maududi's approach is highly political. He uses the discussion of this verse as a starting point to develop his theory of the Islamic government. For him, *shūra* had gone from a general linguistic term to become a fully fledged political concept. He praises *shūra* in very general terms, as "the best quality of the believers" and "an important pillar of the Islamic way of life". For him, abandoning *shūra* would be "an express violation of the law prescribed by God". Importantly, he understood *shūra* to be obligatory on the Muslim community (*umma*). He cites the following reasons for its importance. First, the decision of one person according to his or her own opinion is injustice when the interests of many are concerned. Second, arbitrary action is morally detestable, as it is only the result of felt superiority or usurping of others' rights. Third, deciding in matters of common interest is a grave responsibility, so consultation is needed to share the burden.

Maududi also indicates that *shūra* extends beyond government and should permeate all aspects of Muslim life. He suggests, for example, that husband and wife should mutually consult, and that in a tribe or city there should be a committee of representatives, just as it is the case for a political ordering of a nation-state. He specifically criticises the act of obtaining power by force or deception as being un-Islamic and even criminal.[34]

Maududi identifies a number of elements that he considers to be necessary to the concept of *shūra*:[35] freedom of opinion and freedom of information; the appointment of representatives by free consent rather than by coercion, bribery, or fraud; that advisers to the head of state should not have gained their positions using coercion, bribery, or fraud; that advisers should have freedom of expression and should advise based on knowledge, faith, and conscience, not according to duress or party philosophy; that advice given by "consensus of the advisors" or supported by "the majority of the people" must be accepted and implemented. Maududi ends the interpretation of the verse by upholding the principle of legislative sovereignty of God, citing the Qur'an.[36] The implication of this is that Muslims can consult in order to come up with the most correct ruling in legal matters, but not give independent judgement in settled matters.

This section can be concluded by noting that the pre-modern commentators on this verse, by and large, saw the main issue of *shūra* to be about why God commanded His infallible Prophet to consult with the Companions who were highly esteemed but very fallible. These commentators generally resolved this by arguing that the Prophet was commanded to consult in order to soothe the Companions' hearts. The view that the purpose of *shūra* was to set a precedent did exist, but was usually relegated to a minor role in discussions, and was not analysed in any depth. The more politically minded commentators of the period, like Qurtubi, accepted this, but also argued for a widening of the scope of *shūra* to include a relationship to the rulers and politics, and how *shūra* was to be conducted. In the modern period, scholars like Maududi and Qutb have moved away from pre-modern interpretations which did not attach much political significance to the verse and emphasised a strongly political interpretation of the verse as their context demanded such a reading today. These views are in stark contrast with the views of the pre-modern commentators, who, with the possible exception of Qurtubi, tended to see it merely as flattery for the Companions.

Shūra **and democracy in the modern period**

Democracy is an idea that is subject to negotiation within particular social, cultural, and political contexts. Religion and religious beliefs that are based on specific texts and traditions can be used to justify arguments either for or against democracy. This section discusses the differing views among Muslim scholars when it comes to equating *shūra* with democracy. It outlines some of their views about democracy, and identifies a range of approaches used to justify arguments both for and against democracy. In many cases of contemporary Muslim political activism, democracy has been described as a godless rule based on the will of the people rather than the Divine law. For some, democracy is equivalent to *shirk* (polytheism).[37] This association of democracy with *shirk* clearly identifies democracy as un-Islamic and as against the fundamental principles of Islam and as such democracy and Islam cannot co-exist. It is seen also as human intervention in the business of legislating, which should be reserved solely for God. Some political Islamists argue against identifying parallels between *shūra* and democracy simply on the basis that, for example: "Democracy is a defiled Western word that has no place in Arabic and in Allah's religion."[38]

Although his approach is comparatively more moderate than that of some other political Islamists, Maududi is also vocal in his argument that democracy is incompatible with Islam. He argues that Muslims should vote for a head of state who could then interpret the Qur'an and Sunna. The head of state's interpretation of the Qur'an and Sunna would be aided by an advisory council. This council (*majlis-i-shūra*) would be made up of members selected by the head of state, rather than democratically elected by the people. This is a clear retrogression from the pre-modern Sunni theory of the state, since according to that theory the "shūra council" or "the people of loosening and binding (*ahl al-hall wa al-'aqd*)" have to elect a head of state and therefore preexist him. The ruler, however, would not have to take the advice given by the council. For Maududi, any Islamic conception of democracy was to be the antithesis of secular Western democracy which transfers *hākimiya* (God's sovereignty) to the people.[39]

In contrast, the Shaykh of al-Azhar of Egypt, Ahmad al-Tayyib, issued a statement in 2011 regarding the goals of shari'a, which were identified as follows: to promote knowledge and science, to establish justice and equity, to protect liberty and human dignity, to uphold moral values as held by Islam, and to practise democracy as it protects the dignity of all. The Shaykh argued against despotism on the grounds that it leads to numerous social problems.[40]

Some thinkers are open to different forms of governance in Islamic societies. Abou El Fadl, for example, notes that the Qur'an does not prescribe a particular form of government, but rather that it identifies a set of social and political values that are central for Muslim polity. He indicates a number of values that are of particular importance, such as pursuing justice through social cooperation and mutual assistance,[41] establishing a non-autocratic and consultative method of governance, and institutionalising mercy and compassion in social interactions.[42] He asserts that Muslims today must endorse the form of government that is most effective for promoting these values.[43] Abdolkarim Soroush, a contemporary Iranian Muslim thinker, goes further, as he argues that Western democracy is the most appropriate "shura-based system of government".[44]

Muhammad Imara proposes that *shūra* is a form of democracy. In his view, leaders should be elected, supervised, and then dismissed if they do not fulfil their tasks in a system of *shūra*. Even a document from the Muslim Brotherhood also equates *shūra* with democracy, arguing that the Islamic form of governance is "the essence of democracy". Moreover, the list of "promises" guaranteed by the Muslim Brotherhood includes "a government elected by the people, political plurality, and freedom of the press".[45] One may argue that this is perhaps part of the Muslim Brotherhood's apologetics which attempt to show the superiority of what Islam has to offer even in the area of democracy.

Hasan al-Turabi, a contemporary Sudanese Muslim thinker, notes that *shūra* has never been a conceptual or practical synonym for democracy; however, he argues that Muslim thinkers must do just that and link it again to Islam's foundational texts of the Qur'an and Sunna. Turabi distinguishes between four types of *shūra*: (1) universal *shūra*, which is also the highest and strongest form of *shūra*, demonstrated, for example, in referendums and general elections. This type of *shūra* constitutes a kind of *ijma'*, a consensus within the nation that is legally binding, so long as it does not contradict the Qur'an and the Sunna; (2) *shūra* that is based on the people's representatives in government; (3) *shūra* that is based on experts; and (4) *shūra* that is based on opinion polls.[46]

Other Muslim scholars have also made strong comparisons between *shūra* and democracy. Ali Shariati is quoted as saying, "I consider democracy to be the most progressive and even the most Islamic form of government."[47] Rashid al-Ghannushi of Tunisia also regards the "Islamization" of democracy as the closest to implementing the Islamic concept of *shūra*.[48] Muhammad Shahrur, a leading contemporary Syrian intellectual notes that, "democracy, as a mechanism, is the best achievement of humanity for practicing consultation".[49] M. S. Zafar stresses that, "as long as the human intellect cannot create any institution better than parliament, there should be no problem in adopting this institution".[50]

Sadek J. Sulaiman, an Omani scholar, suggests that democracy and *shūra* are synonymous in conception and principle, although he notes that they may differ in how they are applied. Indeed, he notes that both *shūra* and democracy reject "any government that lacks the legitimacy of free elections, accountability, and the people's power". He also notes that:

> the logic of shura, like the logic of democracy, does not accept hereditary rule, for wisdom and competence are never the monopoly of any one individual or family. Likewise, shura and democracy both reject government by force, for any rule sustained by coercion is illegitimate. Moreover, both forbid privileges – political, social, and economic – claimed on the basis of tribal lineage or social prestige.[51]

Abul Kalam Azad also identifies compatibility between democracy and community deliberation and consultation, which are key aspects of *shūra*. He writes that one of the best qualities or attributes of Muslims mentioned in the Qur'an was their tendency to consult with each other. He notes that the Prophet himself used to consult with his Companions on matters related to state and administration. Then, during the period of the Rashidun Caliphs (632–60 CE), *shūra* was made into the very basis of government.[52] Likewise, Mufti Shabbir Ahmad Uthmani emphasises that, "Allah likes working through deliberations, whether in worldly affairs or in religious ones … the very foundation of Pious Caliphate was laid on the Shura". However, he stresses that deliberation and consultation are only valid for those matters "about which there are no clear injunctions in [the] Qur'an and Sunna".[53]

Concluding remarks

The concept of *shūra* is directly raised in the Qur'an, and Muslim commentators have explored this in some detail. Although most early commentators did not provide a strong political interpretation of *shūra*, some later commentators have argued for a wider understanding that includes the political dimension. New ideas about governance, the ruler and ruled, and the necessity of implementing *shūra* in the governance of an Islamic state were introduced by commentators such as Qurtubi, in line with the debates and needs of his time.

In the modern period, concepts of *shūra* and democracy remain strongly contested among Muslim scholars and thinkers. The preceding discussion has shown that attitudes towards *shūra* exist very much on a broad continuum. Some thinkers and activists of today argue for a return to the pre-modern understanding of *shūra*; while others provide a new and quite different understanding of *shūra* by equating it with democracy. The examples given in this chapter show that treatments of the concept range from hostility to the notion of democracy to caution to the assertion that *shūra* and democracy are compatible. Many thinkers have identified a degree of crossover between the values of *shūra* with those of democracy, and for some thinkers there is no exclusivity in the application of ideas, whether they come from Islamic or Western sources. Overall, some reformist Muslim thinkers are working toward a new interpretation of *shūra* that is in line with contemporary understanding of what is acceptable in the governance of Muslim states.

This chapter has shown that in the early period of Islam and in the early interpretations of the *shūra*-related verses, there was very little emphasis among the scholars on the idea of *shūra* as an important concept for the governance of Muslim societies. For the early commentators *shūra* was regarded as an informal concept and not of great religio-legal or socio-political significance. *Shūra* was understood simply as a piece of advice to the Prophet, and there was nothing obligatory or compulsory about it. Again, this interpretation was very closely related to the specific context of the time. In the tribal system of the time, a person could not simply impose their view on the rest of the community, particularly on important matters such as political issues, or issues related to war and peace. Any understanding as to the appropriate action needed for a particular issue had to be reached through consultation with various important figures, and via some kind of consensus.

After the first few centuries of Islam, the governance of Muslim societies became largely authoritarian. Many rulers did not usually accept advice from subordinates, and Muslims did not develop the idea of using *shūra* as an essential part of governance. The way in which Qur'anic commentators interpreted *shūra* was very closely aligned with their own circumstances. There was no obligation to establish *shūra* as an important or an essential institution for the governance of the society. *Shūra* was instead seen simply as a voluntary institution for the ruler to be adopted according to the whim of the ruler. *Shūra* as a mechanism was not used for consultation on important issues. Given the context, it would have been difficult to argue for *shūra* in any other way. The nearly absolute power of the ruler as a "shadow of God on earth", as the famous tradition puts it, meant that he would not have easily accepted the idea that a group of people be given, in the name of *shūra*, the authority to provide advice that would be religiously binding to him.

In the modern period, however, there is a dislike for strong authoritarian rule as has been clearly demonstrated by the recent Arab uprisings. Moreover, there is a growing sense of the importance of equality for citizens' rights, and the idea that all citizens have the right to choose their political leaders and their parliamentary representatives is now deeply embedded in Muslim thinking. In the modern period this is represented by notions of democracy, and is evidenced in the prevalence of democratic institutions, including parliaments elected by the people. This changed context has influenced many contemporary commentators on the Qur'an and Muslim thinkers who have begun to argue that the Qur'anic concept of *shūra* is very closely connected to the kind of ideas, values, and institutions of democracy and participatory systems of governance.

Since the twentieth century, Muslims have been slowly but surely reinterpreting the concept of *shūra* as being akin to democracy and democratic institutions. Some traditional interpretations of *shūra* remain, but the general trend is to interpret it in the light of the new social, political, economic, and cultural contexts, highlighting the contextualist nature of Qur'anic interpretation.

Notes

1 Qur'an 3:159.
2 This series of verses begins at Qur'an 3:121 and ends at around Qur'an 3:175.
3 Tabari, *Jami' al-Bayan, tafsir* of Q. 3:159, www.altafsir.com.
4 Tabari, *Jami' al-Bayan, tafsir* of Q. 3:159.
5 In his paraphrase of *wa shāwirhum fial-amr*, he states *ya'nī, fi amr al-harb*.
6 Jar Allah al-Zamakhshari, *al-Kashshaf 'an Haqa'iq al-Tanzil, tafsir* of Q. 3:159, www.altafsir.com.
7 Zamakhshari, *Kashshaf, tafsir* of Q. 3:159.
8 al-Fakhr al-Razi, *Mafatih al-Ghayb: al-Tafsir al-Kabir, tafsir* of Q. 3:159, www.altafsir.com; Abu Abd Allah Muhammad Qurtubi, *al-Jami' li Ahkam al-Qur'an, tafsir* of Q. 3:159, www.altafsir.com.
9 Tabari, *Jami' al-Bayan, tafsir* of Q. 3:159.
10 From Qatada (d. 117 AH), al-Rabi (d. 139 AH), and Ibn Ishaq (d. 150 AH).
11 Tabari, *Jami' al-Bayan, tafsir* of Q. 3:159.
12 Tabari, *Jami' al-Bayan, tafsir* of Q. 3:159.
13 Tabari, *Jami' al-Bayan, tafsir* of Q. 3:159.
14 Zamakhshari cites various texts: (a) Al-Hasan, who states that God commanded *shūra* to set an example for the Companions; (b) a Prophetic hadith that states that when a people consult, they are guided to the best of their decisions; (c) statement of Abu Hurayra: *mā ra'ayta ahadan akthar mushāwaratan min ashāb al-rasūl*; (d) a text (*qīla*) about the Bedouin chiefs; and (e) the (exegetical) reading: *wa shāwirhum fi ba'd al-amr*. Zamakhshari, *Kashshaf, tafsir* of Q. 3:159.
15 Razi, *al-Tafsir al-Kabir, tafsir* of Q. 3:159.
16 Razi, *al-Tafsir al-Kabir, tafsir* of Q. 3:159.
17 Razi, *al-Tafsir al-Kabir, tafsir* of Q. 3:159.
18 Razi, *al-Tafsir al-Kabir, tafsir* of Q. 3:159.
19 Razi, *al-Tafsir al-Kabir, tafsir* of Q. 3:159.
20 Razi, *al-Tafsir al-Kabir, tafsir* of Q. 3:159.
21 Qurtubi, *al-Jami' li Ahkam al-Qur'an, tafsir* of Q. 3:159.
22 Qurtubi, *al-Jami' li Ahkam al-Qur'an, tafsir* of Q. 3:159.

23 Qurtubi, *al-Jami' li Ahkam al-Qur'an, tafsir* of Q. 3:159.
24 Qurtubi, *al-Jami' li Ahkam al-Qur'an, tafsir* of Q. 3:159.
25 Qurtubi, *al-Jami' li Ahkam al-Qur'an, tafsir* of Q. 3:159.
26 Qurtubi, *al-Jami' li Ahkam al-Qur'an, tafsir* of Q. 3:159.
27 Qurtubi, *al-Jami' li Ahkam al-Qur'an, tafsir* of Q. 3:159.
28 Qurtubi, *al-Jami' li Ahkam al-Qur'an, tafsir* of Q. 3:159.
29 Sayyid Qutb, *Fi Zilal al-Qur'an, tafsir* of Q. 3:159 in Sayyid Qutb, *In the Shade of the Quran*, trans. Adil Salahi, Vol. 2, 220–23, http://islamfuture.files.wordpress.com/2009/12/volume_2_surah_3.pdf.
30 Qutb, *Fi Zilal al-Qur'an, tafsir* of Q. 3:159.
31 Qutb, *Fi Zilal al-Qur'an, tafsir* of Q. 3:159.
32 Qutb, *Fi Zilal al-Qur'an, tafsir* of Q. 3:159.
33 See www.englishtafsir.com/Quran/3/index.html.
34 Sayyid Abul Ala Maududi, *Tafhim al-Qur'an: The Meaning of the Qur'an, tafsir* of Q. 42:36, www.englishtafsir.com/Quran/4/index.html#sdfootnote194sym.
35 Maududi, *Tafhim al-Qur'an, tafsir* of Q. 42:36.
36 Qur'an 42:10 and Qur'an 4:159.
37 Salah Eldeen al-Gorshy, "Deepening Democracy: A New Mission Ahead of Islamic Thought", *Al Arabi*, 456 (1997).
38 Abu Basir, *Hukm al-Islam fi al-Dimuqratiyya wal-Ta'adudiyya al-Hizbiyya*, www.tawhed.ws/r?i1/41478&c1/45306, cited in Uriya Shavit, "Is *Shura* a Muslim Form of Democracy?", *Middle Eastern Studies*, 46, 3 (2010), 349–74: 361.
39 Abu A'la Maududi, *Political Theory of Islam*, trans. Khurshid Ahmad (Lahore: Islamic Publications, 1976), 13, 15–17, 38, 75–82.
40 For brief accounts of his speech in English, see "Al Azhar Sheikh Calls for a Speedy Transition to Democracy", Islamopedia (16 Feb. 2011), www.islamopediaonline.org/news/al-azhar-grand-sheikh-calls-speedy-transition-democracy; "Al-Tayeb: Al-Azhar Supported Revolution", Newspusher (16 Feb. 2011), www.newspusher.com/ES/post/1298400531-2/ES-/al-tayeb-al-azhar-supported-revolution.html.
41 Qur'an 49:13; 11:119.
42 Qur'an 6:12, 54; 21:107; 27:77; 29:51; 45:20.
43 Khaled Abou El Fadl, "Can Individual Rights and Popular Sovereignty Take Root In Faith?", www.sistersinislam.org.my/news.php?item.43.46.
44 Abdolkarim Soroush, Mahmoud Sadri, and Ahmad Sadri, *Reason, Freedom, and Democracy in Islam: Essential Writings of Abdolkarim Soroush* (New York: Oxford University Press, 2000).
45 Muslim Brotherhood, "Barnamij Hizb al-Ikhwan al-Muslimin," 7, 13–24, www.islamonline.net/arabic/Daawa/2007/08/ikhwan.pdf cited in Shavit, "Is Shura a Muslim Form of Democracy?", 357–58.
46 Hasan al-Turabi, *Nazrat fi al-Fiqh al-Siyasi* (Um al-Fahim: Markaz al-Dirasat al-Mu'asira, 1997), 117–18, cited in Ahmad S. Moussalli, "Hasan al-Turabi's Islamist Discourse on Democracy and Shura", *Middle Eastern Studies*, 30 (1994), 52–63.
47 Ali Shariati, "Iqbal Muslih-i Qarni Akhir", in *Majmu'ah-i Athar*, Vol. 5 (Teheran: Husayniyah-i Irshad, 1979), 48, cited in Forough Jahanbakhsh, "Islam Democracy and Religious Modernism in Iran (1953–97): From Bazargan to Soroush" (PhD thesis, McGill University, 1997), 202.
48 Shaykh Rashid al-Ghanuchi, "Self-Criticism and Reconsideration", *Palestine Times*, 94 (1999).
49 Mohammed Shahroor, "A Proposed Charter for Muslim Activists", August 1999, cited in Graham Fuller, *Future of Political Islam* (New York: Palgrave Macmillan, 2003), 61.
50 S. M. Zafar, "Accountability, Parliament, and Ijtihad", in *Liberal Islam: A Sourcebook*, ed. Charles Kurzman (New York: Oxford University Press, 1998), cited in Fuller, *Future of Political Islam*, 61.

51 Sadek J. Sulaiman, "Democracy and Shura," in ed. Charles Kurzman, *Liberal Islam: A Sourcebook* (New York: Oxford University Press, 1998), 97, cited in Fuller, *Future of Political Islam*, 61.
52 Mawlana Abul Kalam Azad, *Tarjaman al-Qur'an* (New Delhi: Sahitya Academy, 1966), 334–35, cited in Tauseef Ahmad Parray, "Text, Tradition, and the Interpretations of the Shura: A Study of the Views of Modern Indo-Pak Mufassirun (Exegetes)", *Hamdard Islamicus*, 34 (2011), 7–22: 14.
53 Mufti Shabbir Ahmad Uthmani, *Qur'an Majeed* (New Delhi: Taj Company, n.d.), 632, cited in Parray, "Text, Tradition, and the Interpretations of the Shura", 14–15.

14 *Riba* and interest

Riba (often translated as "interest" or "usury") is one of the hotly debated issues in the modern period. While the Qur'an unambiguously prohibited *riba* there have always been debates among Muslim scholars on what constitutes *riba*, and these differences can be found in pre-modern *fiqh* and Qur'anic interpretation as well as in modern day debates on the same issue. Naturally, the debates are often influenced by particular contexts in which the scholars find themselves. In the early seventh century CE, the Qur'an condemned and prohibited *riba* and seemed to have been primarily concerned about exploitation of the poor and needy through interest on debts they owed to their creditors. The focus shifted to a large extent in Islamic jurisprudence (*fiqh*), where the primary interest was in determining largely what kind of barter transactions would come under the label *riba*, based on what a number of hadith appear to have said on the issue of *riba*. In fact, the bulk of *fiqh* discussions are about such transactions, and relatively little emphasis was on what the Qur'an prohibited as *riba*. In the modern period, the context has changed significantly, and given the widespread use of lending and borrowing based on interest, the focus shifted primarily to "interest" and whether certain forms of interest can be considered *riba* while others not, and whether interest as such should be considered *riba*.

This chapter will explore the different ways in which pre-modern and modern scholars have approached the question of *riba* and show the kind of emphasis that exists in the interpretation of *riba* in both periods. Unlike the previous chapters, this chapter will not look at the interpretation of one particular verse on *riba*. However, much of the emphasis is on the sentence, "*wa harrama al-riba*" (and [God] prohibited *riba*) in Qur'an 2:275.

Riba-related verses and interpretation

The first verse of the Qur'an to contain the term *riba* appears to have been revealed during the very early period of the Prophet's mission in Mecca: most probably in the fourth or fifth year – 614 or 615 CE – but perhaps earlier.[1] This verse reads:

> And, whatever you may give out in *riba* so that it may increase through other people's wealth, does not increase in the sight of God; but whatever

you give by way of charity seeking God's pleasure, will receive manifold increase.[2]

Having referred to differences in individual wealth among people in previous verses,[3] the Qur'an commands Muslims to provide financial support to those in need, which includes relatives, the destitute, and wayfarers.[4] It then clarifies that support should be on the basis of charity rather than *riba*, and states that those who give on the basis of charity will have their reward manifold in this world or the hereafter.[5]

The condemnation of *riba* in this very early period of the Prophet's mission appears to be consistent and contemporaneous with the Qur'anic concern for the less fortunate. Fazlur Rahman states:

> It is not at all surprising that *riba* is condemned in so early a revelation; rather the absence of such early condemnation could have not only been surprising but also contrary to the wisdom of the Qur'an. The Meccan verses of the Qur'an are replete with the denunciation of the economic injustice of contemporary Meccan society, the profiteering and stinginess of the rich, and their unethical commercial practices such as cheating in the weights and measurements, etc. How is it possible, then, that the Qur'an would have failed to condemn an economic evil such as *riba*?[6]

The second verse of the Qur'an to discuss *riba* appears to have been revealed in Medina immediately after the battle of Uhud (3/625), which was almost eleven years after the first condemnation of *riba* in Mecca. This verse states: "O Believers! Do not consume *riba*, doubling and redoubling, and fear God so that you may prosper."[7]

The context of this verse was the loss of the battle of Uhud, where a potential victory had become a grave defeat, resulting in the death of seventy Muslim men, who left behind orphans, widows, and aged parents who were in need of financial support and assistance.[8] This situation required that assistance be provided for those in need, and this had to be given on the basis of charity rather than *riba*. Immediately after declaring that Muslims should not engage in *riba* transactions, the Qur'an commands them to be God-conscious, to fear hell, to obey God and the Prophet, and to hasten for forgiveness from God. Notably, this God-consciousness is described as being manifested by those "who spend in prosperity and adversity"[9] to relieve the suffering of the needy.

The Qur'an unequivocally prohibits *riba* by saying: "Do not consume *riba*."[10] Tabari explains the meaning of the term as used in this verse:

> Do not consume *riba* after having professed Islam as you have been consuming it before Islam. The way pre-Islamic Arabs used to consume *riba* was that one of them would have a debt repayable on a specific date. When that date came the creditor would demand repayment from the debtor.

The latter would say, "Defer the repayment of my debt; I will add to your wealth." This is the *riba* which was doubled and redoubled.[11]

The doubling and redoubling of *riba* in the pre-Islamic period is further elaborated as follows:[12]

> *Riba* in the pre-Islamic period consisted of the doubling and redoubling [of money or commodities], and in the age [of the cattle]. At maturity, the creditor would say to the debtor, "Will you pay me, or increase [the debt]?" If the debtor had anything, he would pay. Otherwise, the age of the cattle [to be repaid] would be increased ... If the debt was money or a commodity, the debt would be doubled to be paid in one year, and even then, if the debtor could not pay, it would be doubled again: one hundred in one year would become two hundred. If that was not paid, the debt would increase to four hundred. Each year the debt would be doubled.[13]

This indicates that even if the initial debt is small, in some circumstances "it can consume all the wealth of the debtor"[14] through the "repeated increases"[15] that occur as a result of the inability of the debtor to repay as agreed.

These reports indicate that *riba*, as practised in the pre-Islamic period (referred to as *riba al-jāhiliyya*), involved adding an amount to the principal against an extension of the maturity of an existing debt due to the debtor's inability to repay on time. None of the reports quoted by Tabari (which constitute some of the earliest exegetical sources available at present) suggest that any increase was added at the time the debt was contracted. All available reports suggest that the increase in the debt occurred after the contract was concluded and at the maturity date and was due to the inability of the debtor to meet the obligation. These reports refer to debts but do not reveal whether they were the result of loans or deferred payment sales.

Further *riba*-related verses were revealed towards the end of the Prophet's mission. Reports available in Tabari's commentary on the Qur'an suggest a date of 8/630 or later. There is general agreement among commentators that Qur'an 2:275–78 were the last verses revealed in relation to the prohibition of *riba*.[16] These verses read:

> Those who devour *riba* shall not rise except as he arises, whom Satan has confounded by his touch. That is because they said, "Buying and selling is like *riba*." And yet God has made buying and selling lawful, and *riba* unlawful.[17]

The term *riba*, as used in these verses, does not differ from its earlier usages in the Qur'an.[18] Tabari, for instance, interprets *riba* in these verses with reference to the pre-Islamic period:

> God has forbidden *riba* which is the amount that was increased for the capital owner because of his extension of maturity for his debtor, and deferment of repayment of the debt.[19]

Muhammad Rashid Rida (d. 1935),[20] the well-known disciple of Muhammad Abduh (d. 1905), also comments on the meaning of *riba* in this verse:

> The particle "*al*" in the term *riba* [in this verse] indicates knowledge and familiarity, which means, "Do not consume the *riba* which was familiar to you and that you used to practise in the pre-Islamic period."[21]

Moral context of the Qur'anic prohibition of *riba*

From the earliest time of the Prophet Muhammad's mission, the Qur'an encouraged Meccans to help the poor, the needy, and the orphans. According to the Qur'an, those who did not perform prayer (*salāt*) and who did not feed the destitute would be punished in hell.[22] In other early verses, the Qur'an states that beggars and the destitute have a right to a share of the wealth of the affluent.[23] The Qur'an castigated the unbelievers on the basis that they did not encourage the provision of food and support to the destitute.[24] On many occasions, the Qur'an condemned the affluent in Meccan society,[25] using parables to demonstrate the unfortunate consequences of preventing the poor from having a share in the wealth of the rich.[26]

The Qur'an often reiterates the importance of "spending", that is, giving, to relieve suffering. This emphasis on the giving of money in the very early period of the Prophet's mission indicates its importance. The Qur'an concerns itself deeply with the weaker strata of the community[27] and insists on the social responsibility of the rich to the economically disadvantaged. Within the Qur'an there are many instances of the rich being commanded to care for the disadvantaged, and to provide financial support for relatives,[28] orphans,[29] debtors,[30] beggars, wayfarers,[31] migrants,[32] prisoners of war,[33] the divorced,[34] the deprived,[35] the destitute,[36] the poor,[37] and slaves.[38]

The Qur'an reminds the affluent that wealth is both a trust and a test[39] and asserts that the amassing of wealth without consideration for the socially and economically disadvantaged does not lead to salvation, either in this world or the hereafter, and that it has no intrinsic value in the eyes of God.[40] The Qur'an condemns arrogance and pride in wealth, with statements such as "God does not like the haughty and arrogant."[41] The Qur'an also notes that God has destroyed many rich people for their arrogance and their lack of concern and feeling for the poor and needy.[42] Likewise, it severely condemns greed,[43] and asserts that the rich must overcome selfishness and greed in order to attain salvation.[44]

The Qur'an makes spending obligatory by means of *zakāt* (obligatory giving, alms), and maintains that Muslims should give voluntarily and generously in any situation that demanded intervention to reduce the misery and suffering of a person or a group. This spending can occur in the form of a gift or donation, although where such a donation is difficult, a loan can be made instead, without imposing any extra charges or other burden on the needy person. This type of loan is referred to in the Qur'an as *qard hasan* (a benevolent loan)[45] as it is advanced for the sake of God to relieve the suffering of the disadvantaged, and not to exploit them. The contexts of all verses where the Qur'an uses the term *qard hasan* indicate that the recipients of such loans are generally the disadvantaged in the community.[46] According to the Qur'an, if on maturity of this loan the debtor is experiencing hardship and is unable to pay, no extra charges or any form of interest should be imposed. On the contrary, the debtor should be given sufficient time to repay the loan. The Qur'an asserts that the best course of action may be to forgo even the principal and so relieve the suffering of the debtor altogether, if the creditor can afford to do so: "It is better if you give [even the principal] as charity."[47]

The context of these verses affirms the moral emphasis the Qur'an places on the prohibition of *riba*. The fourteen verses that precede the last *riba*-related verses to be revealed[48] exhort Muslims to spend charitably (*infaq*), and the root of the term *infaq* is used many times. This spending is identified as being for the sake of God.[49] The Qur'an emphasises that the recipient's feelings should not be hurt by reminding him or her of the favours that have been granted.[50] A little further on, the Qur'an states:

> And give to the needy who, being wholly wrapped up in God's cause, are unable to go about the earth in search of livelihood. He who is unaware of their condition might think that they are wealthy, because they abstain from begging; but you can recognise them by their special mark: they do not beg of men with importunity. And whatever good you may spend on them, verily God knows it all.[51]

After these exhortations to provide money to relieve the suffering of the poor, and having declared the manifold reward for this spending, the Qur'an goes on to condemn those who consumed *riba* and who justified their actions by saying that "*riba* is like trade". The Qur'an rejects this justification, and outlines the permissibility of trade and the unlawfulness of *riba*.[52] Having contrasted *riba* with *sadaqa* (voluntary giving, charity), the Qur'an commands Muslims to waive the remaining *riba* charges and to receive only the principal advanced to the borrowers,[53] asserting that failure to do so will result in "war from God and the Prophet".[54] Finally, the Qur'an exhorts Muslims to give more time to the debtor who finds it difficult to repay.[55] For several early exegetical authorities, the term "debtor in difficulty" (*dhu 'usratin*) refers primarily to debtors who are poor and unable to pay their debts. Dahhak (d. 105/724) states: "The expression, 'If you give [the principal] as charity it is better for you,' refers to the debtor who is in serious difficulty and, therefore, unable to pay the debt."[56]

According to the Qur'anic scholar, Suddi (d. 127/745), "the principal as charity (*sadaqa*) should be given to the poor".[57] Although some early scholars suggest that the principal could be given as charity to both the rich and poor, Tabari seems to be of the view that the poor should receive this charity. His preferred interpretation of the verse is: "It is better for you to give even the principal as charity to the poor debtor who is unable to pay the debt."[58]

Rationale for prohibition of *riba*

Two important statements in the final *riba*-related verses perhaps shed some light on the nature of the *riba* as prohibited in the Qur'an. The first statement is "you are entitled to your principal" (*lakum ru'ūsu amwālikum*), which is immediately followed by the second phrase "you do not commit injustice and no injustice will be committed against you" (*la tazlimūna wa la tuzlamūn*).[59]

The two pieces of advice appear to be interdependent and one should not be evoked without the other. If they are taken separately and one of them is ignored, there is a danger that the intended message of the Qur'an could be distorted. However, traditional exegetical literature (*tafsīr*) emphasised only the first statement and almost completely ignored the second. This may reflect the methodology that was followed in almost all schools of Islamic law, wherein the constituent elements of each command or prohibition in the Qur'an were interpreted through an examination of the most immediate and literal meaning of the relevant text. Once a prohibition or a command was recognised, its literal meaning was emphasised, often at the expense of the underlying reason or rationale.

This methodology followed in various schools of law demanded that commands or prohibitions be followed irrespective of whether or not the rationale was known. In fact, any attempt to arrive at a rationale was usually dismissed as a fruitless exercise, although some scholars still attempted to do so. Since almost all commentators of the Qur'an belonged to various schools of law, and such rationales were generally ignored in these schools, the commentators did not seem to find it an attractive option to interpret the meaning of *riba* in the light of its rationale. This is particularly apparent in the context of the rationale that can be identified based on the reference to justice in the statement (*la tazlimūna wa la tuzlamūn*) in the verse. The attitude of the commentators towards this statement is exemplified in Razi's view of prohibition of *riba*:

> The prohibition of *riba* is proved by a clear text [*nass*]. It is not necessary for humankind to know the rationale of all duties. Therefore, the prohibition of *riba* must be regarded as definitely known even though we may not know the rationale for it.[60]

Razi here emphasises that searching for the rationale for the prohibition is not important. Rather, humankind simply has to comply.

In the modern period, Rida (d. 1935) states that, "*riba* is prohibited because it is an injustice",[61] and furthermore, that "*riba*, which was an exploitation of the need of their [that is, the Meccans' and Medinans'] brothers, was prohibited".[62] The Hanbali scholar Ibn Qayyim (d. 751/1350) outlines a similar perspective:

> In the pre-Islamic period, *riba* was practised by giving extra time to repay a debt and adding a charge against this extension [thus, increasing the amount of the debt] until one hundred became thousands. In most of the

cases, only a needy individual would keep doing so as he would have no choice but to defer the payment of the debt. The creditor agreed to defer his demand for repayment of the debt, and waited so that he might gain more profit on the principal. On the other hand, the debtor was forced to pay the increased amount to ward off the pressing demands of the creditor and the risk of the hardships of prison. Thus, as time passed and the loss of the debtor went on increasing, his troubles multiplied and his debt accumulated until all his possessions and belongings were lost to the creditor.[63]

Riba in hadith: A move away from the Qur'anic concerns?

The Qur'an uses the term *riba* in the context of debts. It does not, however, make any reference to the source of the debts: which could be either a loan or a deferred payment sale.[64] On the other hand, the hadith literature mainly uses the term *riba* in relation to certain types of sales in barter transactions, practised in the pre-Islamic period. Most of the hadith that refer to *riba* are related to specific forms of sale.

One such hadith came to be quite prominent in the discussion of *riba* and can be referred to as the "six commodities hadith". Although there are many versions of this hadith, one of the best-known versions is as follows:

> The Prophet said: Gold for gold, silver for silver, wheat for wheat, barley for barley, dates for dates, and salt for salt should be exchanged like for like, equal for equal and hand-to-hand [on the spot]. If the types of the exchanged commodities are different, then sell them as you wish, if they are exchanged on the basis of a hand-to-hand transaction.[65]

According to this hadith, Muslims were permitted to exchange these six commodities only if they followed these guidelines.

Juristic debate in virtually all Islamic schools of law tends to focus on the elaboration of what *riba* is and what kind of transactions should be considered *riba*, based primarily on the hadith that prohibit these types of sales. There is very little discussion in the Qur'anic commentaries or in the legal literature as to the rationale behind the Qur'anic prohibition of *riba*, as this is either considered to be obvious and therefore not requiring elaboration or as marginal to the debate. This omission occurs despite the fact that the Qur'an seems to suggest that *riba* is closely associated with unfairness and injustice (*zulm*).

Riba debate in the modern period

For almost a millennium the *riba* debate remained solely along the lines described above. In the modern period, however, the changed context and the dominance of new forms of finance and banking have led to a significant interest in developing further the interpretation of *riba*. Many modernist

Muslim scholars argue that the rationale for the prohibition of *riba* in the Qur'an was to protect the poor from exploitation, since borrowing in that society was undertaken primarily by the poor to meet basic needs. Modernist scholars like Fazlur Rahman (d. 1988) and Muhammad Asad (d. 1992) emphasise the moral aspect of the prohibition of *riba*, and relegate the "legal form" of *riba*, as interpreted in Islamic law, to a secondary position. They argue that the raison d'être for the prohibition is preventing injustice, as formulated in the Qur'anic statement, "Do not commit injustice and no injustice will be committed against you" (*lā tazlimūna wa lā tuzlamūn*).[66]

Modernists have also found some support for their views in the works of early scholars, like Razi, Ibn Qayyim, and Ibn Taymiyya. For example, Razi, in his enumeration of reasons for the prohibition of *riba*, states: "The fourth reason is that the lender mostly would be rich, and the borrower poor. Allowing the contract of *riba* involves enabling the rich to exact an extra amount from the disadvantaged poor."[67]

The Hanbali scholar, Ibn Qayyim, also links the prohibition to its moral aspects. Referring to pre-Islamic *riba*, he indicates that in most cases the debtor was destitute with no choice but to defer the payment of the debt.[68] This, according to the modernists, makes the prohibition morally sustainable in a changing socio-economic environment. According to Muhammad Asad, for example:

> Roughly speaking, the opprobrium of *riba* (in the sense in which this term is used in the Qur'an and in many sayings of the Prophet) attaches to profits obtained through interest-bearing loans involving an exploitation of the economically weak by the strong and resourceful ... With this definition in mind, we realise that the question as to what kinds of financial transactions fall within the category of *riba* is, in the last resort, a moral one, closely connected with the socio-economic motivation underlying the mutual relationship of borrower and lender.[69]

Another modern commentator, Abdullah Yusuf Ali, also attempts to define *riba* from this moral perspective:

> There can be no question about the prohibition [of *riba*] ... The definition I would accept would be: undue profit made, not in the way of legitimate trade, out of loans of gold and silver, and necessary articles of food such as wheat, barley, dates and salt ... My definition would include profiteering of all kinds, but exclude economic credit, the creature of modern banking and finance.[70]

Fazlur Rahman, remarks on the attitude of many Muslims towards interest:

> Many well-meaning Muslims with very virtuous consciences sincerely believe that the Qur'an has banned all bank interest for all times, in woeful disregard of what *riba* was historically, why the Qur'an denounced it as a

gross and cruel form of exploitation and banned it, and what the function of bank interest [is] today.[71]

For these scholars, the exploitation of the needy, that is, the type of lending that attempts to profit from the financial difficulties of others, is prohibited, rather than the concept of interest itself.

Lawful and unlawful interest

For the pre-modern Muslim scholars, generally speaking interest on loans would be considered *riba*. In the modern period, however, many thinkers of the modernist trend have attempted to differentiate between various forms of interest practised under the traditional banking system by advocating the lawfulness of some, while rejecting others.[72] Their criteria for rejection have generally been based on the perceived injustice of a particular form of interest. Abd al-Razzaq Sanhuri (d. 1971), the Egyptian authority on Islamic law, suggests that compound interest was first and foremost prohibited in Qur'an 3:130. As exegetical reports explaining pre-Islamic *riba* have testified[73] – and also by implication – simple interest perhaps would not be prohibited. Another Egyptian scholar of Islamic law, Ibrahim Zaki Badawi (d. 2006), argues that the strict prohibition of *riba* should apply only to the pre-Islamic form, which according to him could be described as "the increase in debt principal at the time of the accrual in order to receive a new loan".[74]

Sanhuri maintains that the prohibition of *riba* in all its forms should be the norm, although the level of prohibition would vary. For this reason, he argues, *riba* cannot be regarded as lawful except for necessity (*darūra*) or need (*hāja*). According to Sanhuri, pre-Islamic *riba* was the worst form of *riba*, and he argues that this is "similar to what we call compound interest today". Therefore, he is of the opinion that it should be prohibited without qualification. Sanhuri further states that even necessity does not accommodate permission in the case of the creditor.[75] In terms of interest on loans, Sanhuri comments:

> In a capitalist economic system, capital is owned by individuals, institutions and banks; it is not owned by the government. There is a general need for the entrepreneur to obtain capital for investment ... As long as there is a need for obtaining capital by means of a loan, and the capital is not owned by the government, interest on capital within the stated limits would be lawful, as an exception from the original prohibition. The individual owns capital, which he saved by his labour and effort; he has an obligation not to do injustice and a right not to have any injustice done unto him.[76]

Having regarded simple interest on capital as lawful in the instance of need (*hāja*), Sanhuri is quick to state that the law should specify limits to the interest rate, the method of payment, and the total interest to be paid so as to estimate what is required for each particular case.[77]

Some modernists, like the Syrian politician, Maarouf al-Doualibi (d. 2004), have differentiated between consumption loans and production loans: interest on production loans is deemed lawful, but charging interest on consumption loans is considered unlawful.[78] This approach is based on an understanding that Qur'anic verses relating to *riba* occur in the context of alleviating the misery of the poor, the needy, the weaker sections of the community, and those who, having got into debt, were then unable to discharge that debt. Since there is no direct evidence of the existence of loans for production purposes on a wide scale in the pre-Islamic period, credit for investment – according to this view – is a post-Qur'anic phenomenon, and therefore should be evaluated in terms of the rationale of prohibition, that is, injustice.[79]

Some scholars argue that the prohibition of *riba* only covers individuals, rather than companies, banks, or governments. Conversely, the view has been expressed that receipt of interest by an individual from such groups should not be prohibited, because an individual cannot exploit a larger organisation like a bank.[80] The Council of Islamic Ideology in Pakistan, in 1964, was hesitant to declare interest relating to institutional credit as *riba*:

> The Advisory Council of Islamic Ideology agrees that "*riba*" is forbidden but is in disagreement as to whether "interest in the form in which it appears in public transactions" which in the opinion of Council includes "institutional credit" as well, would also be covered by *riba* [as] specified in the Holy Qur'an.[81]

Another view is that Islam has prohibited "usury" rather than "interest". Based on Qur'an 3:130, the Egyptian scholar and Abdul Aziz Jawish (d. 1929), in the early part of the twentieth century, asserted that the *riba* that is prohibited, and on which there is consensus of opinion, can be considered to be interest when it equals the principal or more. According to this view, the claim that an amount of interest that is less than the principal is not lawful is debatable.[82] This is the position that was adopted in the Egyptian civil code, which states that a creditor is not permitted, under any circumstances, to receive interest that exceeds the amount of the principal.[83] It is no coincidence that some modern Qur'anic commentators in English, such as Muhammad Asad,[84] use the term "usury" for *riba*; whereas in his translation of Maududi's (d. 1979) commentary on the Qur'an, the translator Zafar Ishaq Ansari (a scholar associated with Maududi's Jamaat-i Islami of Pakistan) uses the term "interest".[85]

Fiqh literature has identified that the debt in a loan could be either a commodity or money. If it is a commodity, jurists have generally held the view that the debtor should repay with a similar commodity (a kilo of wheat in payment for a kilo of wheat, for example) insofar as such a commodity exists. Alternatively, the equivalent value would be sufficient, if this value has not changed since the loan contract was concluded. However, differences of opinion exist among scholars as to the correct response when the value of the commodity has changed.[86]

In terms of monetary debts, the Hanafi jurists in general and the famous Hanbali scholar Ibn Taymiyya in particular are of the view that the initial value should be repaid in circumstances where the value has changed.[87] However, there is no consensus on the issue of whether, in an inflationary or deflationary situation, equal units of currency should be paid in repayment of a loan. A Pakistani scholar, Qureshi, summarises the argument as follows:

> According to Islamic principles of finance, the like should be returned for the like and any excess over the loan amount would be defined as *"riba"*. In [the] case of physical capital or metal or [a] commodity such as gold, the repayment of [the] loan would strictly retain the original form, shape and substance of the borrowed capital. Translated in terms of paper currency and modern financial transactions, the condition of retaining the form, substance and shape may be satisfied by repaying the loan in terms of [the] undiluted purchasing power of the original amount of loan.[88]

The interpretations of modernists and the exceptions to the blanket *riba* prohibition they have advocated have been met by textualist critics with both economic and scriptural counter-arguments. A leading Islamic banking theorist, Siddiqi, summarises this situation:

> Efforts of some pseudo-jurists to distinguish between *riba* and bank interest and to legitimise the latter [have] met with almost universal rejection and contempt. Despite the fact that circumstances force many people to deal with interest-based financial institutions, the notion of its essential illegitimacy has always remained.[89]

The position of the modernists is further undermined by two factors: their inability to present a consistent theory of *riba* on the basis of the rationale of prohibition which is specified in the Qur'an, and the rise of Islamic banking institutions inspired by a more textualist view of *riba*, according to which "any interest is *riba*, and as such is prohibited".[90]

A number of scholars interpret *riba* in a way that does not allow any increase over and above the principal in a loan. Mawdudi, for example, defines *riba* as "the amount that a lender receives from a borrower at a fixed rate of interest".[91] A report from the Council of Islamic Ideology of Pakistan is more explicit: "There is complete unanimity among all schools of thought in Islam that the term *riba* stands for interest in all its types and forms."[92] Mohammad Uzair, an early Islamic banking theorist, asserts that interest in all its forms is synonymous with *riba*, and claims the existence of consensus on the issue:

> By this time, there is a complete consensus of all five schools of Fiqh ... and among Islamic economists, that interest in all forms, of all kinds, and for all purposes is completely prohibited in Islam. Gone are the days when people were apologetic about Islam, and contended that the interest for

commercial and business purposes, as presently charged by banks, was not prohibited by Islam.[93]

This interpretation has become the basis of current Islamic banking theory as well as practice.

Emphasis on the legal at the expense of the moral

Although there have been attempts in the modern period at understanding *riba* by returning to what appears to be the Qur'anic rationale for its prohibition, the dominant view remains the one that supports the idea that *riba* should be understood primarily from a legal perspective and that the form of the transaction should be given priority. Thus, any increase over and above the principal in a loan transaction (that is, interest) is understood to be *riba*. This view emphasises the form of *riba* as expressed in Islamic law, and requires that the words specified in the Qur'an be taken at their literal meaning, regardless of what was practised in the pre-Islamic period.[94] Although several leading figures, such as Mawdudi[95] and Qutb,[96] discuss the issue of injustice in relation to *riba*, they generally refrain from suggesting that redressing injustice was the intention of the prohibition. Mawdudi states: "The contention that *zulm* (injustice) is the reason why interest on loans has been disallowed and hence all such interest transactions as do not entail cruelty are permissible, remains yet to be substantiated."[97]

However, the Qur'an clearly related the prohibition of *riba* to the concept of voluntary spending (*sadaqa*), and argued that the economically vulnerable should be protected and assisted, rather than exploited. It was in this context that the Qur'an commanded Muslims not to impose any charge on debtors if they were unable to pay their debts on time, and to accept only the principal. When the Qur'an further stated that forgoing the principal may be preferable, it was perhaps indicating that forcing further debt on an already burdened poor debtor in such a difficult context is unethical, immoral, and against its humanitarian objectives. Modern interpretations could use awareness of this context and of the modern context to identify which types of interest have similar results to debtors, and to identify if other types of interest could benefit the disadvantaged within Muslim society.

The changed modern context, in terms of finance, requires revisiting the Qur'anic prohibition of *riba* to identify exactly what it was prohibiting, to determine the rationale for this prohibition, and to apply this to the modern period.

Concluding remarks

Pre-modern commentators generally interpret the Qur'anic texts on *riba* in a similar way, although many struggle to define it and identify what was actually prohibited by the Qur'an. Many other scholars moved away from a focus on the kinds of practices that existed in Mecca and Medina, to an emphasis on some of the hadith material that was available on the issue of *riba*, which focuses on the prohibition of the sale of certain commodities in certain transactions.

In the *tafsir* literature, there is little discussion about the nature of the *riba* that was prohibited in the Qur'an, with the exception of brief references to it. Much of the *tafsir* literature had to rely on the little that commentators like Tabari actually provided in their commentaries, and scholars found it difficult to obtain a sense of what was prohibited in the Qur'an from the pre-modern discussions on *riba*.

In the pre-modern discussions, the kind of *riba* that is prohibited by the Qur'an remained ill-defined. Scholars do not elaborate on this or develop a theory of *riba* as such. Jurists focused on certain transactions, mostly sales, and there is very little mention of debts or interest in such debates.

A number of Muslim scholars of the modern period argue that the *riba* that was prohibited in the Qur'an was concerned with protecting the poor from exploitation. For them, the Qur'an addressed itself to a society that lived in a subsistence economy, where meeting even day-to-day basic needs was a major problem. The institution of pre-Islamic *riba* had a propensity to lead the debtor into more debt, and the more calamitous the situation, the more the debtor plunged into debt. Unlike today, at least in some economies, relatively stable personal incomes associated with full-time or part-time employment were largely unknown in Mecca and Medina at that time, and debtors were unable to rely on such incomes in repaying their debts. In pre-Islamic Arab society there was little protection for debtors: for example, no legislation existed to prevent a creditor from forcing the debtor into bonded labour. Given the unpredictable economic and financial situation, entering into a loan agreement – however small the amount may be   would be an immense risk for any poverty-stricken person. Recognition of this fact may have induced the Prophet to discourage Muslims from borrowing. In many of his sayings, and even in several of his prayers, the Prophet reminded Muslims of the undesirability of borrowing unless absolutely necessary.

In the present context debt is not necessarily associated with poverty. This is particularly true of large-scale borrowing for the production of goods and services. Even when borrowing takes place for the purchase of consumer products, unlike borrowers who lived in the pre-Islamic period, modern debtors (at least in well-off contexts) depend often on predictable future incomes to repay their debts, either on the basis of employment or likely future income from business or other sources. Moreover, laws exist in many countries to protect borrowers, particularly small-scale borrowers, in case they cannot repay their debts on time. In general in the vast majority of contexts today, the debtor will not be forced into bonded labour, and would, at most, be deprived of their personal assets even where these do not cover the debt. In most cases the debtor has another opportunity to build a new life, free from debt obligations, after declaring bankruptcy, a practice that now exists in Islamic law also, and continuation of the debt from parents to children does not occur. The substantial difference in context between a modern debtor and a pre-Islamic debtor should not be ignored if meaningful discussion on the issue of *riba* is to take place.

Although a contextually relevant interpretation of *riba* is supported by many modernist, and by extension, "contextualist" Muslim thinkers, the textualist approach has continued to dominate this issue. This can be attributed to the development of Islamic banking and finance from the 1970s, based on the idea that any kind of increase (= interest) over and above the principal in a loan, accruing to the creditor must be considered *riba* and therefore must be prohibited. Even though Islamic banking and finance face enormous difficulties in putting into practice this traditional understanding of *riba* in the area of loans, many today would argue that Islamic finance has created a range of stratagems in order to keep their interpretation of *riba* alive in the modern context. Many contextualists would argue that rather than creating fixes, it is perhaps better for Muslims in the very different financial and economic context of today to revisit the Qur'anic prohibition and the debates on *riba* in the pre-modern period, and reconsider the available historical and contextual information, in order to develop a more contextually relevant interpretation that can be supported and followed.

Notes

1 This dating is based on the internal evidence of the Qur'an; see Fazlur Rahman, "Riba and Interest", *Islamic Studies*, March (1964), 1–43: 3.
2 Qur'an 30:39.
3 Qur'an 30:37.
4 Qur'an 30:38.
5 Qur'an 30:39.
6 Rahman, "Riba and Interest", 3.
7 Qur'an 3:130.
8 Ibn Hisham, *al-Sira al-Nabawiyya*, ed. Mustafa al-Saqqa *et al.* (Cairo: Mustafa al-Babi al-Halabi, 1955), 11, 122–29.
9 Qur'an 3:134.
10 Qur'an 3:130.
11 Tabari, *Jami' al-Bayan, tafsir* of Q. 3:130, www.altafsir.com.
12 Ibn Hajar, *Tahdhib al-Tahdhib* (Hyderabad, 1327 AH), III, 395.
13 Tabari, *Jami' al-Bayan, tafsir* of Q. 3:130.
14 Jar Allah al-Zamakhshari, *al-Kashshaf 'an Haqa'iq al-Tanzil, tafsir* of Q. 3:130.
15 Nasir al-Din Abu Sa'id Abd Allah b. Umar b. Muhammad al-Baydawi, *Tafsir al-Qur'an al-Karim* (Cairo: al-Matba'at al-Bahiyya, 1925), *tafsir* of Q. 3:130.
16 Imad al-Din Abu al-Fida' Ibn Kathir, *Tafsir, al-Qur'an al-Azim, tafsir* of Q. 2:275–77, www.altafsir.com.
17 Qur'an 2:275.
18 Ibn Kathir, *Tafsir, tafsir* of Q. 2:275–77.
19 Tabari, *Jami' al-Bayan, tafsir* of Q. 2:275–77.
20 Sayyid Muhamad Rashid Rid, *Tafsir al Manar*, second edition, *tafsir* of Q. 2:275–77 (Cairo: Dar al-Manar, 1367 AH).
21 Rida, *Manar, tafsir* of Q. 2:275–77.
22 Qur'an 74:41–44.
23 Qur'an 70:24–25.
24 Qur'an 69:34.
25 Qur'an 89:17–20.

26 Qur'an 68:17–33.
27 William Montgomery Watt, *Muhammad at Mecca*, 60–72.
28 Qur'an 8:41.
29 Qur'an 2:177, 220; 8:41; 76:8–9.
30 Qur'an 9:60.
31 Qur'an 2:177; 8:41; 9:60.
32 Qur'an 24:22.
33 Qur'an 76:8–9.
34 Qur'an 2:236.
35 Qur'an 51:19; 70:19–25.
36 Qur'an 8:41; 76:8–9.
37 Qur'an 2:271; 9:60.
38 Qur'an 2:177; 9:60; 58:3.
39 Qur'an 2:155; 3:186; 8:28.
40 Qur'an 34:37.
41 Qur'an 57:24.
42 Qur'an 17:16; 23:64; 28:58; 28:80–81.
43 Qur'an 57:24.
44 Qur'an 59:9; 64:15–16.
45 Qur'an 2:245.
46 Qur'an 2:245; 5:12; 57:11, 18; 64:17.
47 Qur'an 2:280.
48 Qur'an 2:275–80.
49 Qur'an 2:261, 262, 272.
50 Qur'an 2:262–64.
51 Qur'an 2:273.
52 Qur'an 2:275.
53 Qur'an 2:278.
54 Qur'an 2:279.
55 Sayyid Abul A'la Mawdudi, *Towards Understanding the Qur'an*, trans. Zafar Ishaq Ansari (Leicester: Islamic Foundation, 1988), 1, 31.
56 Tabari, *Jami' al-Bayan, tafsir* of Q. 2:275–77.
57 Tabari, *Jami' al-Bayan, tafsir* of Q. 2:275–77.
58 Tabari, *Jami' al-Bayan, tafsir* of Q. 2:275–77.
59 Qur'an 2:279.
60 al-Fakhr al-Razi, Mafatih al-Ghayb: al-Tafsir al-Kabir, *tafsir* of Q. 2:275, www.altafsir.com.
61 Razi, *Manar, tafsir* of Q. 2:275.
62 Rida, *Manar, tafsir* of Q. 2:275–77.
63 Ibn Qayyim al-Jawziyya. *A'lam al-Muwaqqi'in 'an Rabb al-'Alamin* (Dar al-Jil, n.d.), II, 154.
64 Tabari, *Jami' al-Bayan, tafsir* of Q. 2:275–77.
65 al-Naysaburi, *Sahih*, V, p.44.
66 Qur'an 2:279.
67 Razi, *Tafsir, tafsir* of Q. 2:275.
68 Ibn Qayyim, *A'lam al-Muwaqqi'in*, II, 157ff.
69 Muhammad Asad, *The Message of the Qur'an* (Gibraltar: Dar al-Andalus, 1984), 633.
70 A. Yusuf Ali, *The Holy Qur'an* (Lahore: Sheikh Muhammad Ashraf, 1975), lll.
71 Fazlur Rahman, "Islam: Challenges and Opportunities", in ed. Alford T. Welch and Pierre Cachia, *Islam: Past Influence and Present Challenge* (Edinburgh: Edinburgh University Press, 1979), 326.
72 Nabil A. Saleh, *Unlawful Gain and Legitimate Profit in Islamic Law* (Cambridge: Cambridge University Press, 1986), 29.
73 Abd al-Razzaq Sanhuri, *Masadir al-Haqq fi al-Fiqh al-Islami* (Beirut: al-Majma' al-Arabi al-Islami, 1967), III, 241–42.

74 Cited in Chibli Mallat, "The Debate on Riba and Interest in the Twentieth Century Jurisprudence", in ed. Chibli Mallat, *Islamic Law and Finance* (London: Graham and Trotman, 1988), 80.

75 Sanhuri, *Masadir al-Haqq*, III, 241–42.

76 Sanhuri, *Masadir al-Haqq*, III, 243–44.

77 Sanhuri, *Masadir al-Haqq*, III, 244.

78 Abu Zahra, *Buhuth fi al-Riba* (Kuwait: Dar al-Buhuth al-Ilmiyya), 52–57; Saleh, *Unlawful Gain*, 29.

79 N. A. Jafarey, "The Case for Ijtihad in Respect of Interest on Production Loans", *Journal of Islamic Banking and Finance*, Spring (1988), 15–19.

80 Abdul Jabbar Khan, "Divine Banking System", *Journal of Islamic Banking and Finance*, Winter (1984), 29–50: 30–32; D. M. Qureshi, "Islamisation of Financial Institutions in Pakistan: Assessment", *Journal of Islamic Banking and Finance*, Winter (1984), 58–71: 66–67.

81 This was in response to a question from the Ministry of Finance, Pakistan, and the decision was taken on 13 January 1964; Zaidi, "Islamic Banking in Pakistan", 21.

82 Muhammad Abd Allah Draz, *al-Riba fi Nazar al-Qanun al-Islami* (Cairo: IAIB, n.d.), 9.

83 Civil Law, Article 9.29; Asad, *The Message*, 61–62.

84 Asad, *The Message*, 61–62.

85 Mawdudi, *Towards Understanding the Qur'an*, I, 213–14, 217, 220, 286.

86 Shawqi Dunya, "Taqallubat al-Quwwat al-Shira'iyya li al-Nuqud", *al-Bunuk al-Islamiyya*, 43 (1985), 32–52: 39–45; Jaziri, Fiqh, II, 338–45; Ibn Qudama, *al-Mughni* (Riyadh: Maktabat al-Riyadh al-Haditha, 1981), IV, 352–53.

87 Dunya, "Taqallubat al-Quwwat al-Shira'iyya", 32–52.

88 D. M. Qureshi, "Instruments of Islamic Banking: An Evaluation." *Journal of Islamic Banking and Finance*, Spring (1984), 65–78: 73.

89 Muhammad Nejatullah Siddiqi, *Issues in Islamic Banking: Selected Papers* (Leicester: Islamic Foundation, 1983).

90 Siddiqi, *Issues in Islamic Banking*, 9.

91 Mawdudi, *Towards Understanding the Qur'an*, I, 213.

92 CII (Council of Islamic Ideology), *Consolidated Recommendations on the Islamic Economic System* (Islamabad: Council of Islamic Ideology, 1983), 7.

93 Mohammad Uzair, "Impact of Interest Free Banking", *Journal of Islamic Banking and Finance*, Autumn (1984): 39–50: 40.

94 See, for instance, Abu Zahra, *Buhuth fi al-Riba*; Mawdudi, *al-Riba*, trans. Muhammad Asim al-Haddad (Beirut: Dar al-Fikr, n.d.).

95 Mawdudi, *Riba*.

96 Sayyid Qutb, *Tafsir Ayat al-Riba* (Cairo: Dar al-Buhuth al-Ilmiyya, n.d.).

97 Mawdudi, "Prohibition of Interest in Islam", 7; for Razi's view on the rationale of the prohibition, see Razi, *Tafsir*, VII, 94.

Part IV

Concluding remarks

15 Epilogue

Throughout this book I have attempted to make a case for a contextualist approach to the interpretation of the Qur'an. In the process, a range of principles and issues that are of significant interest for such an approach were examined. Furthermore, a number of case studies explored both pre-modern and modern interpretations of Qur'anic texts. At this point, it is possible broadly to reflect upon the contextualist project as a whole.

A contextualist reading of the Qur'an is critical for contemporary Muslims for a number of reasons. A textualist reading of the relevant Qur'anic texts which does not sufficiently take into account the context does not do justice to the underlying objectives and spirit of the Qur'an. Such a reading results in those texts either being viewed as largely irrelevant to many of the vexing problems contemporary Muslim societies face or their being applied inappropriately, thereby distorting the underlying fundamental principles of Qur'anic teachings. For these reasons, without an approach similar to the one outlined in this book, a number of texts in the Qur'an will seem to be irrelevant and inappropriate to a contemporary context. Religious texts such as scriptures are supposed to offer guidance to the people who follow them, and appropriate interpretation of this guidance for any given context is therefore crucial.

The Qur'an has been identified as a text that was organically linked with the broader social, cultural, intellectual, economic, and political context of its immediate audience in seventh-century Mecca and Medina, and as one which therefore addressed a whole range of concerns and issues that were of particular relevance to people living there during that period. At the same time, however, the Qur'an clearly addresses more universal issues and concerns. That is to say, although the Qur'an was closely connected to the specificities of the society and culture at its origin, it has been – and continues to be – the fundamental guiding force for Muslims in innumerable contexts, stretching over a period of over 1,400 years. The Qur'an carries with it the potential to be relevant to the new and emerging needs of Muslims in the contemporary context and has the capacity to accommodate new and changing societal circumstances as it did in the past.

However, a central issue for interpretation is the way in which the Qur'an has been made relevant to various Muslim societies over the last 1,400 years.

Most of the texts of the Qur'an explores ethical, moral, theological, spiritual, and historical issues, and addresses the human being in a way that transcends specific contexts. In this sense, its teachings can be generalised to accommodate new situations and circumstances. The Qur'an often does not address issues in their particularities but at the level of general moral principles. This is exemplified in the Qur'an's references to how God constantly upholds the moral imperatives of fairness and justice, and its concern for the marginalised, the weak, and the vulnerable alongside issues of accountability and the afterlife, and the morally edifying value of historical narratives. These Qur'anic references are read and re-read, interpreted, understood and applied in a wide range of circumstances. In fact, even most of the ethico-legal teachings of the Qur'an are easily applicable to a wide range of circumstances, places, and times, including the contemporary context. There are a relatively small number of Qur'anic texts that pose difficulties in relation to interpretation and application today. The contextualist approach that has been considered throughout this book offers a response to these difficult texts and interpretations.

The number of Qur'anic texts that occupy the problematic position in modern debates nevertheless have a significant impact on society because an inappropriate reading based on a textualist approach can create harm to many people. For example, although the number of texts that are used in the unequal and disadvantageous construction of gender roles are few, these texts and their textualist interpretations are afforded the power to dictate the status of women and the ways in which men and women relate to each other, disadvantaging women who constitute one-half of the population, in many ways.

The interpretive emphases given to the problematic texts at present are likely to be different to those given at the time of revelation as well as in the generations that followed the first. Over the course of the first three centuries of Islam, the development of Islamic law and its concurrent interpretive methodologies worked to shape Qur'anic interpretation in particular ways. The contexts – be they political, social, or intellectual – in which Muslim commentators and jurists functioned were reflected in their interpretations. A small number of texts and their rather narrowly focused textualist interpretations were allowed to become the prime sources in determining social frameworks. This meant that the significance of some texts was inflated, and particular interpretations were valorised over others. That is to say, the thinking of the jurists and commentators focused on aspects of the Qur'an that were in line with their contexts. They overemphasised particular texts and insisted on particular interpretations at the expense of others.

As a result, there are a number of challenges for a contextualist reading of the Qur'an today. In the twenty-first century, a strong movement within Islam tries to curtail new kinds of thinking in relation to the methodology of interpretation or reform of Islamic law. This, as exemplified, for example, in the modern trends of Islam that strongly emphasise literalism, has a far-ranging influence. Contemporary Muslim thinkers and scholars who are engaged in intellectual debate surrounding Qur'anic interpretation, methodologies of

Islamic law, reform of Islamic law, or any rethinking of the classical juristic approaches are often branded as anti-Islamic to varying degrees. These trends are often anti-intellectual and are in opposition to the rationalistic tradition within Islamic thought, be it in theology or law. The trends emphasise a literalistic reading of the Qur'an and appear to be quite comfortable with the idea that the pre-modern Islamic tradition does not need to be questioned. Accordingly, Qur'anic interpretation is seen as a relatively straightforward matter: it should resemble the textualist readings of the Qur'an in the pre-modern period.

Such trends marginalise various tendencies within Islamic thought that have developed over the last 1,400 years, ranging from rational to mystical schools of thought. The textualist approach often constructs Islam in a way that is apologetic and reductionist. Such an approach often propagates the idea that any Muslim has the ability to read and interpret the Qur'an and Sunna simply by referring to more or less eclectically chosen texts from the Qur'an and the "canonical" hadith compendia without developing or following any systematic method of interpretation, and can easily interpret their messages and simply follow them. Following this logic, there is no need for interpretive methodologies or principles, and there is certainly no room for any philosophical or hermeneutical debates. Furthermore, it is based on the logic that there is no need to introduce alternative approaches and principles. The simplicity of this position is seldom debated or challenged, and is, in fact, popularly received by a very large number of Muslims.

The popularity of this textualist approach is facilitated by a number of factors. The textualist trend today relies very heavily on its appeal to the sanctity of Islam in relation to criticism from the West. By this I mean, the textualist viewpoint posits itself as defending the ideals of Islam in the face of Western imperialism. From this perspective, ideas that have arisen from the West – regardless of their content – are treated with suspicion, to put it mildly. Based on this view, any interpretation or discussion that addresses the hermeneutics of the Qur'an and is counter to the textualist tradition is rejected as being Western, and thus, necessarily, acting to subvert Islam. The idea that there are two distinct domains of "Islam" and the "West" that cannot – or should not – overlap, underpins the textualist trend. This idea is undoubtedly tied to the painful memory of colonialism and the post-colonial realities that many Muslim communities are facing in the contemporary context.

As is well known, throughout the twentieth century, many Muslim societies suffered under various dictatorships, which were supported by various Western powers. Although this was a political issue, the textualists have translated these conflicts into the arena of Islamic thought, and in particular into the area of Qur'anic interpretation. Here they argue that particular Islamic ideas must not be "diluted" or "contaminated" by "alien" thought, but rather strengthened in the face of such political threats. An example is that of the position attributed to women in society, with the idea that any opening up of interpretation in this area will lead to the destruction of the crucial cultural values tied to honour.

Overall, the textualist approach argues that the adoption of ideas from elsewhere will necessarily bring about the destruction of Muslim societies, thus interpretations other than textualist must be rejected as antithetical to Islam and Muslim values and norms. The interpretation of the Qur'an is seen, in this context, as the site of an ongoing and never-ending struggle between Islam and the West.

Another issue that provides a basis for the popularity of the textualist approach is tied to the fact that a very large number of Muslims are living in complex and fluid societies as a result of globalisation where communication is instant. Many Muslims are not attracted to approaches to their religious heritage, which are more complex and multifaceted in nature. Rather, they feel that a clear and simple approach will better suit their needs for "certainty". Such simplicity is often understood as holding the potential to reduce the burden of the contemporary world's complexity. The textualist approach offers a way to navigate the extreme complexity and fluidity of contemporary experience through a simple and straightforward framework of ideas. The skills needed for interpretation are Arabic linguistic skills: if you know the language then you understand the message. The strengthening of this hard textualist trend, typified by its literalism and simplicity, and its consequent attractiveness to a large number of Muslims around the world, is one of the most difficult challenges for Muslim intellectuals and thinkers today.

This book shows that the contextualist approach to the Qur'an is not anti-Islamic; in fact, the contextualist reading of the Qur'an is deeply rooted in the Islamic tradition. Muslims have always used ideas that require a contextualist reading of the Qur'an. As we have seen, even in the first century of Islam, in the first Muslim community, figures such as Umar b. al-Khattab interpreted a range of problematic texts found in the Qur'an with due regard to their context. His acts of interpretation were made immediately after the death of the Prophet in a way that many Muslims of today who are sympathetic to the textualist approach would consider highly problematic, if not blasphemous. Umar understood Qur'anic revelations in terms of their fundamental principles or objectives, why they came about, what they were responding to, and how Muslims should relate to and respond to the Qur'an's message given the change of context. Despite the fact that there are limited sources of knowledge for the time of Umar and his particular hermeneutic approach, by and large the available sources do suggest that his approach was contextualist in nature. Although Umar's views are peculiar they remain in the tradition. However, the full interpretative implication of Umar's thinking was not recognised in the tradition.

This book also demonstrates that Muslims have always engaged in thinking about interpretation of the Qur'an, and in practice many Muslims are already involved in this contextualist interpretation today. Examples of this are found in the work of many contemporary women scholars who are referred to in the book. In addition, contemporary engagement in the contextualist approach is occurring in relation to a wide range of issues related to areas of family law, human rights, inter-religious relations, and economics. In relation to these issues in particular, many Muslim thinkers and scholars are putting forward new ideas, principles, and methodological tools in the service of a contextualist approach.

Thus, this book is not making a set of new claims. Rather, it documents the development of a trend, and clarifies certain issues. At the same time, it brings together a number of concerns and dilemmas that are of relevance to the contextualist approach. Although the contextualist approach is under attack by "hard textualists" right now, my sense is that there will be an increased acceptance of this approach at both theoretical and practical levels by Muslims. This is already happening on the ground, which is to say, Muslims are reinterpreting, for example, Qur'anic verses that have been assumed to be disadvantaging women in today's context, and challenging the bias towards the use of some texts at the expense of others. In a number of Muslim majority countries, such as Morocco, Islamic family law reform has adopted a discourse more sympathetic to gender equality. Such reinterpretations usually follow a contextualist approach. This is a trend that is likely to grow. Although there are opposing forces at work, the majority of Muslim societies seem to be moving in a direction that is more or less in line with contemporary expectations of equality and human rights. Despite the challenges that exist, I believe that the contextualist interpretation of the Qur'an is here to stay and that many more Muslim scholars will adopt this particular approach. This book is a small contribution toward this critical and growing debate: a debate that will undoubtedly shape Muslim thought well into the future.

Bibliography

Abd al-Jabbar, Abu al-Hasan b. Ahmad. *al-Mughni fi Abwab al-Tawhid wa al-Adl*. Cairo: Wuzarat al-Thaqafa wa al-Irshad al-Qawmi, 1960–69.

Abdel Haleem, Muhammad. *The Qur'an: A Modern Translation*. Oxford: Oxford University Press, 2004.

Abduh, Muhammad. *Risalat al-Tawhid*. Cairo: Dar al-Hilal, 1980.

Abu Basir. *Hukm al-Islam fi al-Dimuqratiyya wal-Ta'adudiyya al-Hizbiyya*. Available online at www.tawhed.ws/r?i1/41478&c1/45306. Accessed 17 June 2012.

Abu Zahra. *Buhuth fi al-Riba*. Kuwait: Dar al-Buhuth al-Ilmiyya, 1970.

Abu Zayd, Nasr Hamid. *Mafhum al-Nass: Dirasa fi 'Ulum al-Qur'an*. Cairo: al-Hay'a al-Misriyya al-'Amma lil-Kitab, 1990.

——*al-Nass wa al-Sulta wa al-Haqiqa*. Dar al-Bayda: al-Markaz al-Thaqafi al-Arabi, 2000.

——*Rethinking the Qur'an: Towards a Humanistic Hermeneutics*. Amsterdam: Humanistics University Press, 2004.

——"The Nexus of Theory and Practice." In *The New Voices of Islam: Rethinking Politics and Modernity, A Reader*. Ed. Mehran Kamrava. Berkeley and Los Angeles: University of California Press, 2006.

Ahmed, Leila. *Women and Gender in Islam: Historical Roots of a Modern Debate*. New Haven, CT: Yale University Press, 1992.

Ali, A. Yusuf. *The Holy Qur'an*. Lahore: Sheikh Muhammad Ashraf, 1975.

Ali, Muhammad. *The Religion of Islam*. Lahore: Ahmadiyya Press, 1936.

Ali, Syed Ameer. *The Legal Position of Women in Islam*. London: Hodder & Stoughton, 1912.

Amin, Qasim, *Tahrir al-Mara'a*. Cairo: Dar al-Ma'arif, 1970, 89–91.

Anawati, Georges C. "Isā." In *Encyclopaedia of Islam*. Second edition. Ed. P. Bearman, Th. Bianquis, C. E. Bosworth, E. van Donzel, and W. P. Heinrichs. Leiden: E. J. Brill, 2011.

Arkoun, Mohammed. "The Notion of Revelation: From Ahl al-Kitab to the Societies of the Book." *Die Welt des Islams*, 28 (1988), 62–89.

Armajani, Jon M. "Islamic Thought in the West: Sacred Texts, Islamic History, and Visions of Islam in a Transnational Age." PhD dissertation, University of California, Santa Barbara, 1999. Published as *Dynamic Islam: Liberal Muslim Perspectives in a Transitional Age*. Lanham, MD: University Press of America, 2004.

Asad, Muhammad. *The Message of the Qur'an*. Gibraltar: Dar al-Andalus, 1984.

as-Suyuti, Jalal al-Din. *The History of Khalifahs who Took the Right Way*. London: Ta-Ha Publishers, 1995.

Ayoub, Muhammad. "The Story of the Passion." *The Muslim World*, 70 (1980), 91–121.

Azad, Mawlana Abul Kalam. *Tarjuman al-Qur'an*. New Delhi: Sahitya Academy, 1966.

Badran, Margot. "The Feminist Vision in the Writings of Three Turn-of-the-Century Egyptian Women." *British Society for Middle Eastern Studies*, 15 (1988), 11–20.

——*Feminists, Islam and Nation: Gender and the Making of Modern Egypt*. Princeton: Princeton University Press, 2001.

——*Feminism in Islam: Religious and Secular Convergences*. Oxford: Oneworld, 2009.

Baltaji, Muhammad. *Manhaj Umar bin al-Khattab fi al-Tashri'*. Cairo: Dar al-Salam, 2006, 151–52.

al-Baqillani, Abu Bakr Muhammad. *al-Taqrib wa al-Irshad*. Beirut: Mu'assasat al-Risala, 1998.

Barlas, Asma. "The Qur'an and Hermeneutics: Reading the Qur'an's Opposition to Patriarchy." *Journal of Qur'anic Studies*, 3, 2 (2001), 15–38.

——*"Believing Women" in Islam: Unreading Patriarchal Interpretations of the Qur'an*. Austin: University of Texas Press, 2002.

——"Globalizing Equality: Muslim Women, Theology, and Feminism." In *On Shifting Ground: Muslim Women in the Global Era*. Ed. Fereshteh Nouraie-Simone. New York: Feminist Press at the City University of New York, 2005.

al-Baydawi, Nasir al-Din Abu Sa'id Abd Allah b. Umar b. Muhammad. *Tafsir al-Qur'an al-Karim*. Cairo: al-Matba'at al-Bahiyya, 1925.

Bravmann, M. M. *The Spiritual Background of Early Islam: Studies in Ancient Arab Concepts*. Leiden: E. J. Brill, 1972.

Brown, Daniel. *Rethinking Tradition in Modern Islamic Thought*. Cambridge: Cambridge University Press, 1996.

al-Bukhari. *Sahih al-Bukhari*. Available online at www.usc.edu/org/cmje/religious-texts/hadith/bukhari/032-sbt.php. Accessed on 23 September 2013.

Burton, J. *The Collection of the Qur'an*. Cambridge: Cambridge University Press, 1997.

Campanini, Massimo. *The Qur'an: Modern Muslim Interpretations*. Trans. Caroline Higgitt. Abingdon and New York: Routledge, 2011.

——"The Mu'tazila in Islamic History and Thought." *Religion Compass*, 6, 1 (2012).

Chande, Abdin. "Symbolism and Allegory in the Qur'an: Muhammad Asad's Modernist Translation." *Islam and Christian–Muslim Relations*, 15, 1 (2004), 79–89.

CII (Council of Islamic Ideology). *Consolidated Recommendations on the Islamic Economic System*. Islamabad: Council of Islamic Ideology, 1983.

Cole, Juan Ricardo. "Feminism, Class, and Islam in Turn-of-the-Century Egypt." *International Journal of Middle East Studies*, 13, 4 (1981), 387–407.

Cook, Michael. "The Opponents of the Writing of Tradition in Early Islam." *Arabica* (1997), 437–530.

Dakroury, Aliaa Ibrahim. "Toward a Philosophical Approach of the Hermeneutics of the Qur'an." *The American Journal of Islamic Social Sciences*, 23, 1 (2006), 15–51.

Draz, Muhammad Abd Allah. *al-Riba fi Nazar al-Qanun al-Islami*. Cairo: IAIB, n.d.

Duderija, Adis. "The Evolution in the Canonical Sunni Hadith Body of Literature and the Concept of an Authentic Hadith During the Formative Period of Islamic Thought as Based on Recent Western Scholarship." *Arab Law Quarterly*, 23, 4 (2009), 1–27.

——*Constructing a Religiously Ideal "Believer" and "Woman" in Islam: Neo-Traditional Salafi and Progressive Muslims' Methods of Interpretation*. New York: Palgrave, 2011.

——"Evolution in the Concept of Sunnah During the First Four Generations of Muslims in Relation to the Development of the Concept of an Authentic Hadith as Based on Recent Western Scholarship." *Arab Law Quarterly*, 26 (2012), 393–437.

Dunya, Shawqi. "Taqallubat al-Quwwat al-Shira'iyya li al-Nuqud." *al-Bunuk al-Islamiyya*, 43 (1985), 32–52.

El Fadl, Khaled Abou. *Conference of the Books: The Search for Beauty in Islam*. Lanham, MD: University of America Press, 2001.

——*Speaking in God's Name*. Oxford: Oneworld, 2001.

——"Can Individual Rights and Popular Sovereignty Take Root in Faith?" In *Islam and the Challenge of Democracy*. Ed. Khaled Abou El Fadl, Joshua Cohen, and Deborah Chasman. Princeton: Princeton University Press, 2004.

Esack, Farid. *Qur'an, Liberation & Pluralism*. Oxford: Oneworld, 1997.

Esen, Muammer. "Early Debates on 'The Word of God'" (Kalāmullah/Qur'an). *Journal of Islamic Research*, 2, 2 (2009), 34–45.

Esposito, John L. *Islam: The Straight Path*. Oxford: Oxford University Press, 1988.

Fuller, Graham. *Future of Political Islam*. New York: Palgrave Macmillan, 2003.

al-Ghanuchi, Shaykh Rashid. "Self-Criticism and Reconsideration." *Palestine Times*, 94 (1999).

Gibb, H. A. R. and Krambers, J. H. *The Concise Encyclopaedia of Islam*. Leiden: Brill, 2001.

Goldziher, Ignaz. *Muslim Studies*. Volume II. Trans. C. R. Barber and S. M. Stern. London: Allen & Unwin, 1971.

——*Introduction to Islamic Theology & Law*. Princeton: Princeton University Press, 1981.

al-Gorshy, Salah Eldeen. "Deepening Democracy: A New Mission Ahead of Islamic Thought." *Al Arabi*, 456 (1997).

Hakim, Avraham. "Conflicting Images of Lawgivers: The Caliph and the Prophet: Sunnat 'Umar and Sunnat Muhammad." In *Method and Theory in the Study of Islamic Origins*. Ed. Herbert Berg. Leiden: Brill, 2003, 159–78

Hallaq, Wael b. *A History of Islamic Legal Theories: An Introduction to Sunni Usul al-Fiqh*. Cambridge: Cambridge University Press, 1997.

——*The Origins and Evolution of Islamic Law*. Cambridge: Cambridge University Press, 2005.

Hasan, Masud-ul-. *Hadrat Abu Bakr, Umar, Usman, Ali*. Lahore: Islamic Publications, 1982.

al-Hasani, Isma'il. *Nazariyyat al-Maqasid 'ind al-Imam Muhammad al-Tahir bin 'Ashur*. Virginia: IIIT, 1995.

al-Hibri, Azizah. "A Study of Islamic Herstory: Or, How Did We Ever Get into this Mess?" *Women's Studies International Forum*. Special Issue: *Women and Islam*, 5 (1982), 207–19.

——"Divine Justice and the Human Order: An Islamic Perspective." In *Humanity Before God: Contemporary Faces of Jewish, Christian, and Islamic Ethics*. Ed. William Schweiker, Michael A. Johnson, and Kevin Jung. Minneapolis: Fortress Press, 2006, 238–55.

Hidayatullah, Aysha. "Women Trustees of Allah: Methods, Limits, and Possibilities of 'Feminist Theology' in Islam." PhD dissertation, University of California, Santa Barbara, 2009.

Hoebink, Michel. "Thinking about Renewal in Islam: Towards a History of Islamic Ideas on Modernization and Secularization." *Arabica*, 46, 1 (1999), 29–62.

Ibn Hajar. *Tahdhib al-Tahdhib*. Hyderabad, 1327 AH.

Ibn Hanbal, al-Imam Ahmad. *Musnad al-Imam*. Beirut: Alam al-Kutub, 1998.

Ibn Hazm, Abu Muhammad Ali. *al-Ihkam fi Usul al-Ahkam*. Cairo: Matba'at al-Imam, n.d.

Ibn Hisham. *al-Sira al-Nabawiyya*. Ed. Mustafa al-Saqqa *et al.* Cairo: Mustafa al-Babi al-Halabi, 1955.

Ibn Kathir, Imad al-Din Abu al-Fida'. *Tafsir al-Qur'an al-Azim*. Available online at www.altafsir.com. Accessed 20 July 2013.

Ibn Qayyim al-Jawziyya. *A'lam al-Muwaqqi'in 'an Rabb al-'Alamin*. Dar al-Jil, n.d.

Ibn Qudama. *al-Mughni*. Riyadh: Maktabat al-Riyadh al-Haditha, 1981.

Ibn Sa'd. *al-Tabaqat al-Kubra*. Beirut: Dar Sader, 1968.

Ibn Shabba. *Tarikh al-Madina al-Munawwara*. Beirut: Dar al-Kutub al-Ilmiyya, 1417 AH.

Ibn al-Salah, *Muqaddimat Ibn al-Salah*, Ed. A'isha bint Abd al-Rahman. Cairo: Dar al-Ma'arifa, 1990.

al-Ikhwan al-Muslimin, Barnamij Hizb (The Party Program). Available online at www.islamo nline.net/arabic/Daawa/2007/08/ikhwan.pdf. Dated 25 August 2007.

Islahi, Amin Ahsan. *Fundamentals of Hadith Interpretation*. Lahore: Al Mawrid, 2013.

al-Jabri, Muhammed Abed. *Democracy, Human Rights and Law in Islamic Thought*. New York: I. B. Tauris, 2009.

Jackson, Sherman. "From Prophetic Actions to Constitutional Theory: A Novel Chapter in Medieval Muslim Jurisprudence." *International Journal of Middle Eastern Studies*, 25 (1993), 71–90.

——"Fiction and Formalism: Towards a Functional Analysis of Usul Al-Fiqh." In *Studies in Islamic Legal Theory*. Ed. B. Weiss. Leiden: Brill, 2002, 177–201.

Jafarey, N. A. "The Case for Ijtihad in Respect of Interest on Production Loans." *Journal of Islamic Banking and Finance*, Spring (1988), 15–19.

Jahanbakhsh, Forough. *Islam, Democracy and Religious Modernism in Iran (1953–1997)*. Leiden: Brill, 2001.

Jawad, Haifaa A. *The Rights of Women in Islam: An Authentic Approach*. Hampshire: Palgrave Macmillan, 1998.

Jaziri, Abd al-Rahman. *al-Fiqh 'ala al-Madhahib al-Arba'a*. Sixth edition. Cairo: al-Maktabat al-Tijariyya al-Kubra, n.d.

Jomier, Jacques. *Le Commentaire coranique du Manar: tendances modernes de l'exégèse coranique en Égypte*. Paris: G. P. Maisonneuve, 1954.

Juynboll, G. H. A. *Muslim Tradition: Studies in Chronology, Provenance and Authorship of Early Hadith*. Cambridge: Cambridge University Press, 1983.

Kahf, Moja. "Huda Sha'rawi's Mudhakkirati: The Memoirs of the First Lady of Arab Modernity." *Arab Studies Quarterly*, 20 (1998), 53–83.

Kamali, Mohammad Hashim. *Principles of Islamic Jurisprudence*. Chicago: Paul & Company Pub Consortium, 2003.

Kecia, Ali. *Marriage and Slavery in Early Islam*. Cambridge, MA: Harvard University Press, 2010.

Khalidi, Tarif. *Arabic Historical Thought in the Classical Period*. Cambridge: Cambridge University Press, 1994.

Khan, Abdul Jabbar. "Divine Banking System." *Journal of Islamic Banking and Finance*. Winter (1984), 29–50.

Khan, Muhammad Muhsin. *Summarized Sahih al-Bukhari*. Riyadh: Darussalam Publishers and Distributors, 1996.

Lawson, Todd. *The Crucifixion and the Qur'an: A Study in the History of Muslim Thought*. Oxford: Oneworld Publications, 2009.

Mallat, Chibli. "The Debate on Riba and Interest in the Twentieth Century Jurisprudence." In *Islamic Law and Finance*. Ed. Chibli Mallat. London: Graham and Trotman, 1988.

Maududi, Abul A'la. *Political Theory of Islam*. Trans. Khurshid Ahmad. Lahore: Islamic Publications, 1976.

Maududi, Sayyid Abul A'la. *Tafhim al-Qur'an: The Meaning of the Qur'an.* Available online at www. englishtafsir.com/Quran/4/index.html#sdfootnote194sym. Accessed 23 September 2013.

Mawdudi, Sayyid Abul A'la. "Prohibition of Interest in Islam." *al-Islam*, June (1986), 6–8.

——*Towards Understanding the Qur'an*, Trans. Zafar Ishaq Ansari, Leicester: Islamic Foundation, 1988.

——*al-Riba*. Trans. Muhammad Asim al-Haddad. Beirut: Dar al-Fikr, n.d.

Moosa, Ebrahim. "The Poetics and Politics of Law after Empire: Reading Women's Rights in the Contestations of Law." *UCLA Journal of Islamic & Near East Law*, 1 (2001–2): 1–46.

Moussalli, Ahmad S. "Hasan al-Turabi's Islamist Discourse on Democracy and Shura." *Middle Eastern Studies*, 30 (1994): 52–63.

Muslim Brotherhood. *The Role of Women in Islamic Society According to the Muslim Brotherhood*. London: International Islamic Forum, 1994.

"al-Mu'allafa Qulubuhum". *Encyclopaedia of Islam*. Second edition. Brill Online, 2012.

al-Naysaburi, Muslim b. Hajjaj. *Sahih Muslim*. Available online at www.usc.edu/org/cmje/ religious-texts/hadith/muslim/. Accessed 23 September 2013.

Numani, Shibli. *Umar*. London: I. B. Tauris, 2004.

Nyaze, Imran. *Theories of Islamic Law: The Methodology of Ijtihad*. Islamabad: International Research Institute, 2000.

Parray, Tauseef Ahmad. "Text, Tradition, and the Interpretations of the Shura: A Study of the Views of Modern Indo-Pak Mufassirun (Exegetes)." *Hamdard Islamicus*, 34 (2011), 7–22.

al-Qummi, Ali b. Ibrahim. *Tafsir al-Qummi*. Ed. al-Sayyid al-Tayyib al-Musawi al-Jaza'iri. Najaf: Matba'at al-Najaf, 1966/7.

Qureshi. D. M. "Instruments of Islamic Banking: An Evaluation." *Journal of Islamic Banking and Finance*, Spring (1984), 65–78.

—— "Islamisation of Financial Institutions in Pakistan: Assessment." *Journal of Islamic Banking and Finance*, Winter (1984), 58–71.

al-Qurtubi, Abu Abd Allah Muhammad. *al-Jami' li Ahkam al-Qur'an*. Available online at www.altafsir.com. Accessed 20 July 2013.

Qutb, Sayyid. *Fi Zilal al-Qur'an*. Cairo: Dar al-Shuruq, 1986.

——*In the Shade of the Quran*. Vol. III. Trans. Adil Salahi. Available online at http://islam-future.files.wordpress.com/2009/12/volume_3_surah_4.pdf.

——*Tafsir Ayat al-Riba*. Cairo: Dar al-Buhuth al-Ilmiyya, n.d.

Raccagni, Michelle. "The Origins of Feminism in Egypt and Tunisia." Unpublished PhD dissertation for New York University, 1983.

Rahbar, Muhammad Daud. "The Challenge of Muslim Ideas and Social Values to Muslim Society". *The Muslim World*, 48, 4 (1958), 274–85.

Rahman, Fazlur. *Islamic Methodology in History*. Islamabad: Islamic Research Institute, 1965.

——"Riba and Interest." *Islamic Studies*, March (1964), 1–43.

——*Islam*. Chicago: University of Chicago Press, 1966.

——"Islam: Challenges and Opportunities." In *Islam: Past Influence and Present Challenge*. Ed. Alford T. Welch and Pierre Cachia. Edinburgh: Edinburgh University Press, 1979.

——"A Survey of Modernization of Muslim Family Law." *International Journal of Middle East Studies*, 11 (1980), 451–65.

——*Major Themes of the Qur'an*. Chicago: Chicago University of Press, 2009.

——*Islam and Modernity: Transformation of an Intellectual Tradition*. Chicago: University of Chicago Press, 1982.

——"The Living Sunnah and al-Sunnah wa'l Jama'ah". In *Hadith and Sunnah: Ideals and Realities – Selected Essays*. Ed. P. K. Koya. Kuala Lumpur: Islamic Book Trust, 1996.

——*Revival and Reform in Islam*. Ed. Ebrahim Moosa. Oxford: Oneworld, 2000.

al-Razi, al-Fakhr. *Mafatih al-Ghayb: al-Tafsir al-Kabir*. Available online at www.altafsir.com. Accessed 20 July 2013.

Rida, Sayyid Muhamad Rashid. *Tafsir al-Manar*. Second edition. Cairo: Dar al-Manar, 1367 AH.

Riffat, Hassan. "An Islamic Perspective." In *Sexuality: A Reader*. Ed. Karen Lebacqz. Cleveland, OH: The Pilgrim Press, 1999, 337–73.

Sachedina, Abdulaziz. *Islam and the Challenge of Human Rights*. New York: Oxford University Press, 2009, 125–26.

Saeed, Abdullah. *Interpreting the Qur'an: Towards a Contemporary Approach*. Abingdon and New York: Routledge, 2006.

——*The Qur'an: An Introduction*. Abingdon and New York: Routledge, 2008.

Saleh, Nabil A. *Unlawful Gain and Legitimate Profit in Islamic Law*. Cambridge: Cambridge University Press, 1986.

Sanhuri, Abd al-Razzaq. *Masadir al-Haqq fi al-Fiqh al-Islami*. Beirut: al-Majma' al-Arabi al-Islami, 1967, III.

Schacht, J. "Umm al-Walad." *Encyclopaedia of Islam*. Second edition. Brill Online, 2012.

al-Shafi'i, Muhammad b. Idris. *Kitab al-Umm*. Cairo: Dar al-Sha'b, 1968.

Shahroor, Mohammed. "A Proposed Charter for Muslim Activists." August 1999. Available online at http://islam21.org/charter/.

Shahrur, Muhammad. *The Qur'an, Morality and Critical Reason: The Essential Muhammad Shahrur*. Trans. Andreas Christmann. Leiden: Brill, 2009.

Shariati, Ali. "Iqbal Muslih–i Qarni Akhir." In *Majmu'ah–i Athar*, Vol. 5. Teheran: Husayniyah-i Irshad, 1979.

Sharify-Funk, M. "From Dichotomies to Dialogues – Trends in Contemporary Islamic Hermeneutics." In *Contemporary Islam: Dynamic not Static*. Ed. A. Abdul Aziz, M. Abu-Nimer, and M. Sharify-Funk. London: Routledge, 2006, 64–80.

Shavit, Uriya. "Is *Shura* a Muslim Form of Democracy?" *Middle Eastern Studies*, 46, 3 (2010), 349–74.

al-Shawkani, Muhammad b. Ali. *Fath al-Qadir*. Available online at www.altafsir.com. Accessed 20 July 2013.

Shooman, M. *The Righteous Wife*. Trans. Abu Talhah Dawood. London: Al-Hidaayah Publishing and Distribution, 1996.

Siddiqi, Muhammad Nejatullah. *Issues in Islamic Banking: Selected Papers*. Leicester: Islamic Foundation, 1983.

Soroush, Abdolkarim. "The Expansion of Prophetic Experience." In *The Expansion of Prophetic Experience: Essays on Historicity, Contingency and Plurality in Religion*. Brill E-Books, 2013. DOI: 101163/ej.9789004171053.i-355.6.

Soroush, Abdolkarim, Sadri, Mahmoud and Sadri, Ahmad. *Reason, Freedom, and Democracy in Islam: Essential Writings of Abdolkarim Soroush*. New York: Oxford University Press, 2000.

Souaiaia, Ahmed "On the Sources of Islamic Law and Practices." *Journal of Law and Religion*, 20 (2005), 125–49.

Sukidi, M. "Nasr Hāmid Abū Zayd and the Quest for a Humanistic Hermeneutics of the Qur'ān." *Die Welt des Islams*, 49, 2 (2009), 181–211.

Sulaiman, Sadek J. "Democracy and Shura." In *Liberal Islam: A Sourcebook*. Ed. Charles Kurzman. New York: Oxford University Press, 1998.

al-Sulaymani, Abd-al-Salam. *al-Ijtihad fi al-fiqh al-Islami*. Rabat: Wizarat al-Awqaf, 1996.

al-Suyuti. *al-Durr al-Manthur*. Available online at www.altafsir.com. Accessed 20 July 2013.

al-Tabari. *Jami' al-Bayan*. Available online at www.altafsir.com. Accessed 20 July 2013.

Tabataba'i. Allama Sayyid Muhammad Husayn. *Shi'ite Islam*. New York: State University of New York Press, 1977.

al-Tabataba'i, al-Sayyid Muhammad Husain. *al-Mizan fi Tafsir al-Qur'an*. Beirut: Muassasat al-Alami, 1970.

Taizir, Aswita. "Muhammad 'Abduh and the Reformation of Islamic Law." Unpublished PhD dissertation for McGill University, 1994.

al-Tamawi, S. *Omar Ibn Al-Khattab and the Origin of Modern Politics and Administration*. Cairo: Dar al-Fikr al-Arabi, 1976.

Thomas, David Richard. *Syrian Christians under Islam: The First Thousand Years*. Leiden: E. J. Brill, 2001.

al-Turabi, Hasan. *Nazrat fi al-Fiqh al-Siyasi*. Um al-Fahim: Markaz al-Dirasat al-Mu'asira, 1997.

Uthmani, Mufti Shabbir Ahmad. *Qur'an Majeed*. New Delhi: Taj Company, n.d.

Uzair, Mohammad. "Impact of Interest Free Banking." *Journal of Islamic Banking and Finance*, Autumn (1984), 39–50.

Vishanoff, David. *The Formation of Islamic Hermeneutics: How Sunni Legal Theorists Imagined a Revealed Law*. New Haven, CT: American Oriental Society, 2011.

Von Denffer, Ahmad. *Ulum ul Qur'an*. Available online at http://web.youngmuslims.ca/online_library/books/ulum_al_quran/. Accessed 23 September 2013.

Wadud, Amina. "Towards a Qur'anic Hermeneutics of Social Justice: Race, Class and Gender." *Journal of Law and Religion*, 12, 1 (1995–96), 37–50.

——*Qur'an and Woman: Rereading the Sacred Text from a Woman's Perspective*. Second edition. Oxford: Oxford University Press, 1999.

——"Qur'an, Gender and Interpretive Possibilities." *HAWWA*, 2 (2004), 331.

——*Inside the Gender Jihad: Women's Reform in Islam*. Oxford: Oneworld, 2006.

Wahyudi, Yudian. "Hassan Hanafi on Salafism and Secularism". In *The Blackwell Companion to Contemporary Islamic Thought*. Ed. Ibrahim Abu Rabi'. Malden, MA: Blackwell Publishing, 2006, 257–70.

Walbridge, John. *God and Logic in Islam: The Caliphate of Reason*. Cambridge: Cambridge University Press, 2011.

Watt, William Montgomery. *The Formative Period of Islamic Thought*. Oxford: Oneworld, 1998.

——*Muhammad at Mecca*. Karachi: Oxford University Press, 2000.

Zafar, S. M. "Accountability, Parliament, and Ijtihad." In *Liberal Islam: A Sourcebook*. Ed. Charles Kurzman. New York: Oxford University Press, 1998.

al-Zamakhshari, Jar Allah. *al-Kashshaf 'an Haqa'iq al-Tanzil*. Available online at www.altafsir.com. Accessed 20 July 2013.

Index

construction of 97–98; contextual 88; in
a contextualist interpretive framework
86–87; as emerging from relationships
87–88; esoteric and exoteric 16–17;
fluidity of 89, 97; historical 88;
immediate 18–19; implied 18, 19;
linguistic 88; literal 3, 9, 15, 17, 18, 19,
20, 88, 180–81, 182; pronounced 18;
stability in 88
Mecca 23, 58, 69, 83, 97, 99, 161, 172,
179
Medina 23, 30, 58, 69, 83, 97, 130 161,
172, 179
Melkites 139
men: "authority" over women 10, 11, 41,
76, 111–28; role and status of 6–7, 9; *see
also* gender; patriarchy
Mernissi, Fatima 42–43
metaphorical reading 17, 18
miracles 21, 61–62, 129, 132, 137
modern concerns and emphases 21–22
modernisation 41–42
modernist Muslims 21–22
monotheism (*tawhīd*) 59, 83
Moosa, Ebrahim 18
moral consciousness (*taqwa*) 97
moral values 6, 20–21
morality 20; and *riba* 163–64, 167
morphological aspects 16, 18, 45, 86,
94, 101
Moses 6
Mother of the Book 53
Mu'awiya 78
Muhammad, Prophet *see* Prophet
Muhammad
murder 68
Murji'a 83
Musa, Nabawiyya 39
Muslim Brotherhood 121, 154
Muslim feminists 24, 39, 42–47
mutables 90, 106
Mu'tazilis 57, 79, 83–84, 142
Muttalib clan 32
mystically-driven approach 15

Nasif, Malak Hifni (Bbahithat al-Badiyah)
39
Nawfal clan 32
Nestorians 139
non-Muslims: antagonistic relationship
with 72; marriage to 33–34; status of 7;
see also Christians/Christianity; Jews
non-patriarchal readings 45, 46–47, 120–24
Nu'Mani, Shibli 32

obedience, to God and husband 113, 114–15
obligatory values 64, 65–66, 91
occasions of revelation literature 99
orphans 99, 102–4; women 99–100, 101

parables 62, 100
paradise 100
parallel texts 73–82, 101–5
patriarchy 24, 38, 40; *see also*
non-patriarchal readings
People of the Book (*ahl al-kitāb*) 14
permission 65, 91
Pharaoh 6
philology 14, 15, 16
Pickthall, Mohammed 131
pilgrimage (*hajj*) 65
political Islamists 24, 153–54
polygamy 39, 94, 98–99, 99–100, 101,
102, 103, 106
polytheism 99, 153
prayer 64, 65, 91; call to (*adhān*) 27;
communal 34–35; nightly (*tarāwīh*)
34–35
Preserved Tablet 53, 56, 84
prior texts 44
prohibition 65–66, 67, 91
pronounced meaning 18
Prophet Muhammad 6, 13, 14, 17,
27–28, 40, 83; family of, and war
booty 32; as legislator 80; and revelation
53–55, 56, 57, 63, 76; Sunna of 76–77,
79, 80, 92, 105
protectional values 64, 66–67, 91–92
punishments 67–68; for apostasy 93; for
blasphemy 92–93; for theft 32–33; for
unlawful sexual relations 67; for wine
consumption 33

Qadiyanis 141–42
al-Qummi, Ali b. Ibrahim 118
Qur'an: as communicative act 83, 86–87,
97; as God's speech 83–89, 97; as guide
for humankind 96; temporal aspect of
83, 84
Qureshi 170
al-Qurtubi 10; on men's "authority" over
women 112, 115–16; on *shūra* 149,
150–51, 153, 156
Qutb, Sayyid 10, 141; on *riba* 171; on *shūra*
151, 152, 153

Rahbar, Daud 23
Rahman, Fazlur 23, 24, 47, 80, 94, 96,
98–99, 102–4, 106; on men's authority

Introducing Islam
2nd Edition

By William E. Shepard

Series: *World Religions*

"*Introducing Islam* is a fine, balanced and approachable text for bringing a basic understanding of Islam to undergraduates."
- *Rocco Gangle, Endicott College, USA*

Just what is Islam and what does it mean to be a Muslim in the world today? Since the events of 9/11 and 7/7, Islam has become one of the most controversial and misunderstood religions in the world. *Introducing Islam* encourages students to put aside their preconceptions and explore this fascinating religion.

William Shepard traces the history of Islam from its origins in the life and career of Mohammed, through its classical expressions, to its interactions with the West in the modern world. A chapter is devoted to each major topic, including The Qur'an, Islamic law, Islamic theology, and the Sufi movement, as well as community rituals and Islamic art and culture. There is a survey of modern developments and four chapters are dedicated to individual countries, Turkey, Iran, Egypt and Indonesia.

Fully revised and updated, the second edition of this core textbook adds crucial material on contemporary issues such as women in Islam and democratization and human rights. Illustrated throughout, the book also includes learning objectives, a glossary of key Arabic terms, comprehensive further reading lists and critical thinking boxes, helping students to critically engage with the material in each chapter. Additional resources are provided via a companion website.

January 2014 | 368 Pages
PB: 978-0-415-53345-4 | HB: 978-0-415-53342-3
www.routledge.com/9780415533454

Available from all good bookshops

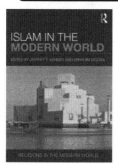

Printed and bound by PG in the USA

USA2018PGIL